RISING POWER AND CHANGING PEOPLE

THE AUSTRALIAN HIGH COMMISSION IN INDIA

RISING POWER AND CHANGING PEOPLE

THE AUSTRALIAN HIGH COMMISSION IN INDIA

EDITED BY DAVID LOWE
AND ERIC MEADOWS

Australian
National
University

ANU PRESS

Australian
National
University

ANU PRESS

Published by ANU Press
The Australian National University
Canberra ACT 2600, Australia
Email: anupress@anu.edu.au

Available to download for free at press.anu.edu.au

ISBN (print): 9781760465278
ISBN (online): 9781760465285

WorldCat (print): 1333172509
WorldCat (online): 1333161191

DOI: 10.22459/RPCP.2022

Cover design and layout by ANU Press. Cover photograph supplied by E Meadows, private collection.

This book is published under the aegis of the Social Sciences Editorial Board of ANU Press.

Contents

Abbreviations   vii

List of Figures   ix

Select Chronology   xi

Australia–India Relations: The View from New Delhi   1
David Lowe and Eric Meadows

1. Creating the Diplomatic Relationship   19
    Eric Meadows

2. Two Conferences on Asian Matters in New Delhi   39
    Julie Suares

3. New Delhi and Canberra in the 1950s   57
    Eric Meadows

4. The Ambassador Extraordinary and the Formidable Public
    Servant: Sir James Plimsoll and Sir Arthur Tange, 1963–69   75
    Peter Edwards

5. The Buildings and their Locally Engaged Staff   87
    David Lowe

6. The Bangladesh Crisis Seen from New Delhi   105
    Ric Smith

7. Mediating Middle Powers: Shaw, Grant, Curtis and Upton,
    1972–83   137
    David Lee

8. Arresting the Drift: The Graham Feakes Era   153
    Meg Gurry

9. Trade and Education: Australia–India, 1998–2008   169
    Michael Moignard and Quentin Stevenson-Perks

10. Building an Indo-Pacific Security Partnership   183
    Ian Hall

11. High Commissioners as Scholarly Observers: Crocker on
Nehru, and Grant on Indira Gandhi   201
David Lowe

Reflections on Australia–India Relations since the 1990s,
by Peter Varghese AO, October 2016   221
As reported by David Lowe

Australian High Commissioners to India   227

Select Bibliography   229

Notes on Contributors   239

Index   243

Abbreviations

AAERI	Association of Australian Education Representatives in India
AAP	Architectural Advisory Panel
AIIA	Australian Institute of International Affairs
AIPS	Australian Institute of Political Science
ALP	Australian Labor Party
ANZUS Treaty	Australia, New Zealand and United States Treaty
APEC	Asia-Pacific Economic Cooperation
ASEAN	Association of South-East Asian Nations
CECA	Comprehensive Economic Cooperation Agreement
CHOGM	Commonwealth Heads of Government Meeting
DEA	Department of External Affairs
DFA	Department of Foreign Affairs
DFAT	Department of Foreign Affairs and Trade
ESOS Act	*Education Services for Overseas Students Act 2000*
FTA	Free trade agreement
ICISS	International Convention on Intervention and State Sovereignty
ICWA	Indian Council of World Affairs
IIC	India International Centre
LES	Locally engaged staff
LNG	Liquefied natural gas

MoU	Memorandum of Understanding
NPT	Non-Proliferation Treaty
SEATO	Southeast Asia Treaty Organization
UNHCR	United Nations High Commission for Refugees

List of Figures

Figure 0.1. High commissioner's official residence, 1970.   8

Figure 4.1. High Commissioner James Plimsoll, after presenting his credentials, with Indian President Dr Radhakrishnan, 10 March 1963.   78

Figure 5.1. Stein's Australian Chancery, New Delhi, 1966.   95

Figure 5.2. Chancery building, 1970.   96

Figure 6.1. ABC correspondent Don Hook with Bengali refugees, Calcutta, 1971.   109

Figure 6.2. Dacca family fleeing the city with their staff and luggage piled on an oxcart on the way to the countryside, 29 March 1971.   112

Figure 6.3. Recognise Bangladesh Rally in Trafalgar Square, 8 August 1971.   118

Figure 6.4. 'Once we've worked out how to recognise them, let's try it out on China!' Stewart McCrae, *Courier Mail*, 1971.   123

Figure 6.5. Sheikh Mujibur Rahman pictured in Dacca, Bangladesh, 3 March 1971.   131

Figure 7.1. Photo of the welcome for Sir Patrick and Lady Shaw, Assam, March 1973.   139

Select Chronology

1940   Australia appoints a trade commissioner to India based in Calcutta.

1941   An Indian trade office is established in Sydney.

1943   Agreement to exchange high commissioners between India and Australia.

1944   Australia's first high commissioner, Sir Iven Mackay, arrives in New Delhi.

1947   Asian Relations Conference in New Delhi.

India gains independence from Britain and the subcontinent is partitioned.

First Indo–Pakistan war breaks out, in Kashmir.

1948   Assassination of Mahatma Gandhi.

1949   Asian Conference on Indonesia held in New Delhi.

Change of government in Australia. Robert Menzies becomes prime minister of a Liberal/Country Party coalition.

1950   India becomes a republic within the (British) Commonwealth.

The Colombo Plan for Cooperative Economic Development in South and South-East Asia signed.

Security Council appoints Sir Owen Dixon as 'mediator' in the Kashmir dispute. Dixon's plan to solve the crisis is rejected by Nehru.

Robert Menzies's first visit to India.

Korean War begins.

1951   Trade Agreement between India and Australia signed.

Australia, New Zealand and United States (ANZUS) Treaty signed.

1954   Southeast Asia Treaty Organization (SEATO) Treaty signed.

1955   Bandung Conference of Asian and African nations.

1956   Suez Crisis.

1961   Indian annexation of Goa and other Portuguese territories in India.

1962   Indo–Chinese war.

1964   Death of Nehru. Lal Bahadur Shastri becomes prime minister.

1965   Second Indo-Pakistan war. Death of Shastri at the Tashkent peace conference.

1966   Indira Gandhi, Nehru's daughter, becomes Indian prime minister.

        Opening of the Australian High Commission Chancery in New Delhi.

1967   The first 'Officials Talks' between the Indian and Australian external affairs ministries is held.

1968   Mrs Gandhi visits Australia, the first Indian prime minister to do so.

1971   Cultural Agreement between India and Australia comes into effect.

        Indo-Soviet Treaty of Peace, Friendship and Cooperation, signed.

        Third Indo-Pakistan war. Creation of Bangladesh.

1972   Election of the Australian Labor Party as the Government of Australia. Gough Whitlam both prime minister and foreign minister.

1973   Visit to India by Gough Whitlam.

1974   India conducts its first underground nuclear test.

1975   Visit to Nepal and India of Australia's governor-general, Sir John Kerr.

        Declaration of a State of Emergency in India.

        Dismissal of the Whitlam Government. The Liberal/National parties return to power with Malcolm Fraser as prime minister.

1976   Science and Technology Agreement between India and Australia comes into effect.

1977   Janata Party led by Morarji Desai, leads the first non-Congress Government of India.

1978   Sydney Hilton bombing aimed at Moraji Desai visiting Australia for the Commonwealth Heads of Government Meeting.

Malcolm Fraser pays an official visit to India.

1980   Mrs Gandhi, leading the Indian National Congress Party (I), wins a general election.

1983   The Australian Labor Party led by Bob Hawke wins the general election.

Hawke visits India.

1984   Mrs Gandhi is assassinated by her Sikh bodyguard. Her son, Rajiv Gandhi, takes her place as prime minister.

1989   India–Australia Joint Ministerial Commission created.

1991   Assassination of Rajiv Gandhi by a Tamil suicide bomber.

Indian National Congress led by P.V. Narasimha Rao wins the general election and begins a major reform of India's regulated economy.

1992   Australia–India Council created.

1996   The Bharatiya Janata Party led by Atal Bihari Vajpayee, wins its first general election.

The Liberal/National Party coalition wins government in Australia, led by John Howard.

1998   Indian nuclear tests at Pokhran; Pakistan also tests nuclear devices.

1999   Warfare breaks out between India and Pakistan in the Kargil region of Kashmir.

2000   John Howard visits India.

2004   Indian National Congress (I), wins the general election with Manmohan Singh as prime minister.

2006   Australia–India Strategic Research Fund announced during John Howard's visit to India.

2007   First Quadrilateral Security Dialogue (Quad) takes place between the United States, India, Japan and Australia.

The Australian Labor Party returns to office in Australia with Kevin Rudd as prime minister.

2009   Indian students in Australia are targets of attacks.

Joint Declaration on Security Co-operation made.

2010   Creation of the Australia–India Education Council.

2011   Negotiations on a free trade agreement between India and Australia start.

2013   Australia's Defence White Paper introduces the concept of the Indo-Pacific, thus highlighting the importance of India in Australian strategic thinking.

2014   Civil Nuclear Co-operation Agreement is signed.

Tony Abbott, while prime minister of Australia, visits India.

Narendra Modi (Bharatiya Janata Party), Indian prime minister, visits Australia and addresses a joint sitting of both houses of Parliament.

2017   Malcolm Turnbull visits India, as prime minister of Australia.

2018   India's president, Ram Nath Kovid, visits Australia.

2020   Mutual Logistics Support Agreement and Comprehensive Strategic Partnership established.

Australia–India Relations: The View from New Delhi

David Lowe and Eric Meadows

Australia's relationship with India is its oldest continuous formal diplomatic relationship with any Asian country. Diplomatic relations were established in time of war, 1943–44, and before Indian independence, and were accompanied by a mixture of optimism, confusion and mistaken assumptions on both sides. As the first chapter of this book shows, Australia's first high commissioner, Sir Iven Mackay, struggled to find the right language with which to describe an India on the path towards independence, but hoped that some form of kinship between Australia and India might underpin the re-emergence of the British Commonwealth as a force in world affairs.[1]

These early diplomatic exchanges between Australia and India have teased historians for their suggestions of potential unrealised, for opportunities missed, especially when compared with the very recent excitement about the future of Australia–India relations. One of the most eagerly awaited strategic documents mapping Australia's economic future with India illustrates this point. In mid-2018 Peter Varghese, recently retired secretary of Australia's Department of Foreign Affairs and Trade, and high commissioner to India before that, handed to government his 500-page report, *An India Economic Strategy to 2035*.[2] The executive summary points to the 700,000-strong Indian diaspora, the fastest growing diaspora in Australia, as a source of underappreciated people-to-people connections,

---

1   See Chapter One.
2   Peter Varghese, *An India Economic Strategy to 2035: A Report to the Australian Government by Peter N. Varghese AO* (Canberra: DFAT, 27 April 2018), www.dfat.gov.au/publications/trade-and-investment/india-economic-strategy/ies/index.html, accessed 27 January 2022.

creating network opportunities in India and also influence in Australia. The summary envisages dramatic increases in Australian exports to India, tripling in value from A$14.9 billion in 2017 to a projected A$45 billion by 2035; and investment rocketing from A$10.3 billion to more than A$100 billion.[3] The sense of untapped opportunity and complementarity between the two countries comes with a feeling that it is time to make up for missed chances.

It was not the case that these opportunities were present in the early days of official relations. As is told in more detail in this collection of essays, the hardening lines of the Cold War quickly began to circumscribe the nature of relations between Australia and India, and the outbreak of the Korean War in June 1950 dragged attention towards East Asia. But even a history of Australia and India from the inception of the Cold War to the early 1990s—which this volume is not—would still invite investigation of such aspects as trade, investment, education, tourism and cultural exchanges, and also the question of the extent to which Australian–Indian relations escaped the bipolarity of the Cold War.

Interpreting the breadth of official 'relations' between two countries such as Australia and India invites both well-known and alternative forms of historical interpretation. Adding a special focus on the Australian High Commission in New Delhi is also best served by diversity in interpretive approach. Histories of diplomatic representation have enjoyed a resurgence in recent years, spurred by cultural and social perspectives being brought to bear, including innovative methodologies borrowed from disciplines such as anthropology and geography. They have also benefited from a constructive tension between the necessarily state-based starting point for considering diplomacy and the trend towards decentring the state and enabling diplomats forms of agency and representation beyond the status of mere ciphers and reporters for their governments. The new journal, *Diplomatica*, launched in 2019, is a testament to the renewed historical energy around diplomacy. The journal's subtitle, 'A Journal of Diplomacy and Society', also reflects the high level of interest in the official world, gaining social and cultural lenses of interpretation, of the public meeting the private in the hands of historians.[4]

---

3   Ibid., 'Executive Summary and Overview', www.dfat.gov.au/publications/trade-and-investment/india-economic-strategy/ies/overview.html, accessed 27 January 2022.
4   *Diplomatica: A Journal of Diplomacy and Society*, vols 1–3, 2019 and 2021 to date. See also the special issue of *New Global Studies* 11, no. 2 (2017). For a recent perspective on women and Australian diplomacy see: Rachel Miller, *Wife and Baggage to Follow* (Canberra: Halstead Press, 2013).

How these methodological shifts might yield interpretive riches in the case of Australian diplomats overseas is a question that will continue to be answered in coming years. In the chapters that follow here, a concern with establishing missing parts of the story of Australian diplomatic representation in India, drawing primarily on government records, meets the 'new diplomatic history' in ways that are suggestive for future work. These essays derive, in part, from two conferences held in 2016 on the work of Australia's diplomatic representatives in New Delhi, one held at the high commission itself and another at Deakin University. As such, they include not only historians' views of aspects of the bilateral relationship, but also the perspectives of 'practitioners', those who served at the post in New Delhi, including locally engaged staff members.

The State and the Diplomat

Diplomats across the world enjoyed greater standing than in recent times in the period prior to the Second World War. Indeed, their reputation suffered afterwards for being unable to prevent it. Historians of diplomacy tend to see the war years as marking the rise of political leaders in diplomacy, aided by the growth of executive level summitry.[5] In establishing formal diplomatic relations and representation during 1943–44, during the rise of wartime summits, Australian and Indian governments acted at a time of some questions around the future of professional diplomats. But both nations attached considerable importance to a robust diplomatic service as they sought a stronger diplomatic presence in the postwar world. From an Indian perspective, the developments of 1943–44 constituted a pre-independence marker of state agency in international relations. The core argument of Srinath Rhagavan's study of India's Second World War is that the conflict spurred the institutional and practical foundations of the modern Indian nation-state more than the subsequent actions around independence.[6] Australian historians such as Stuart Macintyre and David

---

5   Gordon Craig and Felix Gilbert (eds), *The Diplomats: 1919–1939* (New York: Atheneum, 1963); and Gordon Craig and Francis Loewenheim (eds), *The Diplomats, 1939–1979* (Princeton: Princeton University Press, 1994). Also see: David Reynolds, *Summits: Six Meetings that Shaped the Twentieth Century* (London: Allen Lane, 2007); and David Stome, *War Summits: The Meetings that Shaped World War II and the Postwar World* (Washington DC: University of Nebraska Press, 2005).
6   Srinath Raghavan, *India's War: The Making of Modern South Asia, 1939–1945* (Milton Keynes: Allen Lane, Penguin, 2016).

Lee have similarly pointed to the crucial role of the war in the centralising of Canberra's power with respect to citizenry and the powers of the states and territories.[7]

When Indian independence was declared in August 1947, the new government embarked on the rapid building of a diplomatic service consistent with Prime Minister Jawaharlal Nehru's vision of a strong international identity. This growth of the Indian foreign service unfolded roughly in parallel with the professionalisation and expansion of the young Australian diplomatic service. Indeed, the management of relations between the two countries demonstrates the development of Australian diplomacy, from amateur appointments much influenced by British styles[8] to strong appointments of some of the most senior officers of the Australian service. If developing in parallel, it is harder to make the case that there was equal weight in how the two diplomatic services regarded each other. Simply put, for long stretches of time, the governments of the two countries proved unwilling or unable to elevate the relationship beyond second billing status.

The high quality of Australian appointments to New Delhi reflected a recurrent wish by Canberra for greater substance between the two countries, but underlying differences made this difficult. Until recent years, the relationship went through bouts of enthusiasm followed by long periods when there was little substance in each country's dealings with the other.[9] In the early years of the relationship, under the Chifley Labor Government in Australia, there were expectations that substance would be found in a common internationalism. These hopes proved overblown, partly because Australia's white-only immigration policy presented an affront to Indian opinion.[10] Trade relations, having grown selectively

---

7   Stuart Macintryre, *Australia's Boldest Experiment: War and Reconstruction in the 1940s* (Sydney: NewSouth Publishing, 2015); David Lee, 'Politics and Government', in Joan Beaumont (ed.), *Australia's War, 1939–45* (Sydney: Allen & Unwin, 1996), 82–106, doi.org/10.4324/9781003115007-4.

8   Even as late as 1973, the Australian high commissioner to India possessed a British diplomatic uniform with a plumed hat, gold braided jerkin and an accompanying sword. He did not, however, use this in New Delhi where there were no opportunities for such imperial grandeur. Instead it was used in Kathmandu at the annual levee held by the King. (Author's personal knowledge.)

9   See: Alan Watt, *The Evolution of Australian Foreign Policy, 1938–1965* (London: Cambridge University Press, 1968), 220–36. Also see: Meg Gurry, *Australia and India: Mapping the Journey 1944–2014* (Carlton: Melbourne University Press, 2015).

10   See: Eric Meadows, '"He No Doubt Felt Insulted": The White Australia Policy and Australia's Relations with India, 1944–1964', in Joan Beaumont and Matthew Jordan (eds), *Australia and the World: A Festschrift for Neville Meaney* (Sydney: Sydney University Press, 2013), 81–98, doi.org/10.2307/j.ctv1rm259b.9.

with British India, then stuttered under the strictures of India's planned economy from the 1950s onwards. Above all, the two governments had fundamentally different views of the world. Australia was aligned with the United States, formally through the ANZUS Treaty (Australia, New Zealand and United States) from 1951. India, by contrast, was famously non-aligned, pursuing an independent foreign policy in the context of the Cold War. The sense of divergence took other forms, too. From 1974 onwards, when India tested its first thermonuclear device in the Thar Desert, the two countries had radically different views on nuclear disarmament.

Nonetheless, as the essays here show, there were regular attempts by Australia to add substance to the relationship. For instance, Iven Mackay suggested a student exchange. Under his successor, Roy Gollan, Australia participated in an important conference in New Delhi on Indonesia's struggle for independence. An Australian, Sir Owen Dixon, was appointed by the United Nations to mediate in the Kashmir dispute; his attempts to find a solution failed. Prime Minister Robert Menzies remained interested in Kashmir and tried to use the Commonwealth of Nations connection to bring the parties together, again without success. During the 1950s, High Commissioner Walter Crocker argued the case—unsuccessfully—for ameliorating the ill will generated in Asia by the White Australia policy through introducing a quota for Indian immigrants. The India–China War in 1962 brought hope that India would become more sympathetic to the West's anti-communism. The Australian Government was supportive of India's position in the Bangladesh crisis of 1971, and Australian aid and early recognition of Bangladesh brought much goodwill in India. And Rajiv Gandhi and Bob Hawke established a genuine rapport, but were unable to turn this into breakthroughs on economic or political cooperation.

The creation of the Australia–India Business Council in 1985 was the start of a renewed emphasis on providing alternative forums for interaction. The gradual economic liberalisation of India from 1991 under then finance minister Manmohan Singh made it possible for trade to grow. Above all, it was the end of the Cold War and India's engagement with Asia to its east, the area of Australian strategic interest, that allowed both countries to find common ground. The end of the stand-off between the two on the Nuclear Non-Proliferation Treaty was critical. When the Gillard Government agreed to supply India with uranium, this removed a block to dialogue. In addition, the age of terrorism has provided opportunities for intelligence sharing to mutual benefit. Major Indian immigration to Australia has, moreover, provided the bedrock for the people-to-people dimension to the relationship that continues to grow stronger.[11]

The People of the High Commission

What makes a good high commissioner to India? Beyond tact and managing personal relationships, the more generic qualities hoped for in senior diplomatic representatives were summarised by Joan Beaumont in her analysis of Australian diplomats serving overseas up to 1969 as:

> integrity, intelligence, negotiating skills. The ability to win the trust of foreign governments and leaders in the wider community, sociability, cultural sensitivity, a willingness to acquire an understanding of the political and historical background of other countries, and of course, diplomacy itself.[12]

Whether one might profitably search for an 'Australian style' in distinctive diplomatic behaviour will always be contentious. In their 2003 study of the making of Australian foreign policy, Allan Gyngell and Michael Wesley concluded that, for all the advances in communications, the performance of Australian diplomats overseas still turned on their skills relating to information gathering, reporting and advocacy. Gyngell and Wesley attempted, through surveys, to dig a little deeper and found that Australian diplomats liked to claim an Australian style of diplomacy. This, they argued, was characterised by behaviour that was direct, energetic, imaginative, informal and well prepared.[13]

Alan Renouf, former secretary of the Department of Foreign Affairs (1974–76), argued in his memoirs that Australia rarely obtained the best value from its diplomats posted abroad.[14] The diplomat abroad was not encouraged to make 'a personal and intellectual contribution to foreign policy'. The creation of Australian foreign policy has largely been the

---

11   See Chapter Twelve. Also see: Robin Jeffrey, 'Australia–India: Reimagining the Relationship', *Inside Story*, 15 February 2010.

12   Joan Beaumont et al., *Ministers, Mandarins and Diplomats: Australian Foreign Policy Making, 1941–1969* (Melbourne: Melbourne University Press, 2003), 162.

13   Allan Gyngell and Michael Wesley, *Making Australian Foreign Policy* (Cambridge: Cambridge University Press, 2003), 126–31, doi.org/10.1017/CBO9780511755873.

14   Alan Renouf, *The Champagne Trail: Experiences of a Diplomat* (Melbourne: Sun Books, 1980), 134.

preserve of prime ministers.[15] A forceful foreign minister such as Percy Spender or Gareth Evans could overturn this maxim, but heads of mission overseas, until very recently, have had little influence on key parts of policy towards their country of posting. Indeed, Crocker thought he had been naïve to think he could shape policy.[16]

Elsewhere, the characteristics of the 'ideal' Australian ambassador were considered in a recent history of Australia's representation in the United States. Some of those commenting included former ambassadors who pointed to qualities such as the need to be able to manage a large, multi-focused staff, a capacity to weather a high flow of important visitors and a whirl of diplomatic–social events, and enough energy to ensure that they saw different parts of the big country and spoke to key stakeholders in their geographic homes.[17] Given the size and diversity of India, perhaps the qualities of coping with scale, being prepared to travel beyond the capital, and maintaining different relationships have the strongest resonance with a posting to New Delhi.

In the case of the High Commission in New Delhi, one high commissioner who stands out is Walter Crocker. His two postings to New Delhi, 1952–55 and 1958–62, gave him a ringside seat and high standing in Prime Minister Jawaharlal Nehru's India. Even his posting in between these two tenures seemed to shed light on India. Crocker spent the mid-1950s in Indonesia, arriving there in time for the famous Bandung conference of 1955, where Afro-Asian solidarity and non-alignment took shape, partly through the efforts of Nehru. An intellectual and avid note-taker and diarist, Crocker published a much-admired essay on Nehru that has stood the test of time. In addition, his journals, diaries and memorabilia open the door to different perspectives of the Australian high commission, enabling us glimpses of the Crockers' lives among others of the diplomatic set. Walter Crocker appears prominently in two of the following chapters.[18]

---

15   Peter Edwards, *Prime Ministers and Diplomats: The Making of Australian Foreign Policy 1901–1949* (Melbourne: Oxford University Press in association with The Australian Institute of International Affairs, 1983); and also 'The Role of the Executive, Especially the Prime Minister and the Foreign Minister, in the Making of Australian Foreign Policy 1945–1992', *Former Secretaries Meeting: The Making of Australian Foreign Policy 1945–1992* (Griffith University, Centre for the Study of Australia-Asia Relations, 1992).

16   Walter Crocker, *Travelling Back: The Memoirs of Sir Walter Crocker* (South Melbourne: Macmillan, 1981), 178.

17   David Lowe, David Lee and Carl Bridge, 'The Australian Embassy in Washington', in David Lowe, David Lee and Carl Bridge (eds), *Australia Goes to Washington: 75 Years of Australian Representation in the United States* (Canberra: ANU Press, 2016), 2–6, doi.org/10.22459/AGTW.12.2016.01.

18   See Chapters Three and Eleven.

Figure 0.1. High commissioner's official residence, 1970.
Source: National Archives of Australia: A1200, L89520.

For the most part, this volume considers the work of high commissioners thematically and chronologically rather than allocating discrete chapters to each commissioner. The exceptions, in addition to the attention owed to Crocker, are James Plimsoll and Arthur Tange, as a case study chapter of two of the best known of Australia's public servant mandarins in India; and the tenure of Graham Feakes who, in serving a double term of six years from 1984, was the longest continuously serving high commissioner.

The high commission was always more than its resident high commissioner. The Australian high commission buildings warrant attention for the symbolic significance of their architecture, for their local geography and for the social dimensions of diplomacy they enabled. Picking up on some of the themes made more visible through Crocker's copious writings, we offer thoughts on the significance of the buildings comprising of the Chancery and High Commissioner's Residence. This focus has two aims. The first is to gain an understanding of the symbolic significance of the Joseph Stein–designed buildings in the context of postcolonial India and the making of 'official' New Delhi. The site has a distinctive provenance and standing among other posts that has endured over time, even though one of the two Stein buildings was destroyed. The second and related aim is to widen the lens from high commissioners and senior advisers to consider the locally engaged, mostly Indian, staff who have worked with them. A good number of the locally engaged staff have worked at the high commission for many years, in contrast to Australian-based staff appointed for around three years. This makes the locally engaged staff the more enduring human components in the high commission's work.

Structure of This Book

The chapters that follow are organised chronologically in the main, allowing also for thematic dives where needed. Chapter One, by Eric Meadows, discusses the surprising beginnings to the relationship, before India's independence and at the initiative of the British Government. Mackay's job was to set up the mission and 'make Australia known' in India. Neither task proved easy in the midst of war and with the political uncertainties that led to Partition. He had almost no diplomatic colleagues with whom to discuss issues; the relationship with Australia was India's first at ambassadorial level. That, of course, was an issue that had to be sorted out during Mackay's time: what was the status of a 'high commissioner' and to which Indian ministry should he be accredited?

Some of Australia's most significant early diplomatic activity in New Delhi unfolded in exploratory ways, with blurred lines between official and unofficial, between public and private, as Julie Suares demonstrates in Chapter Two. New Delhi was the location for two major international conferences; the first on Asian relations in 1947; and the second on Indonesia in1949. Australian attendance at the first was unofficial—the Australian Institute of International Affairs and the Australian Institute of Political Science sent representatives. But the high commission provided valuable support. At the second, official Australian representatives tested how the 'old' Commonwealth could work with the 'new' Asian members, and moved between official settings and the home of Indian Prime Minister Jawaharlal Nehru in their negotiations. As Suares shows, these two conferences were important sources of information about decolonisation in Asia more generally, and they highlighted issues that Australian governments wrestled with throughout the fifties and sixties: sensitivity to Australia's domestic population policy and how it would be read in Asia; and the balance between Australia's Western alliance, geographic location and wish to have sustainable relations with an emerging Asia.

While Mackay's appointment was successful within the limitations of the times, his successor Roy Gollan was less suited to the circumstances of post-independence New Delhi and to Australia's need for a close analysis of India's developing foreign policy. Walter Crocker, on the other hand, as Eric Meadows discusses in Chapter Three, was unusually well-matched for his tasks. Chief among these was to observe and report on Nehru, something Crocker did in detail and with great insight. Crocker was fortunate to share an Oxbridge educational background with key members of the Indian bureaucracy, which facilitated access to a group of decision-makers that was still small enough, in the 1950s, for intimacy. But while Crocker personally could represent the best of an intelligent Australian view of current issues, his time in office showed the limitations of a diplomat's role when a home government had a world view different from that of the host. Meadows finds that while Crocker was forceful in arguing for reforms such as modifications to Australia's restrictive immigration policy and Australian participation in the Bandung conference in 1955, he enjoyed little support in Canberra. While Prime Minister Robert Menzies and External Affairs Minister Richard Casey thought differently from each other about India, neither prioritised it ahead of Cold War alliance diplomacy.

In Chapter Four, Peter Edwards considers the period 1963–69, during which two of Australia's senior diplomat mandarins, Sir James Plimsoll and Sir Arthur Tange, served in New Delhi. Both were consummate professionals looking to add greater substance to the Australia–India relationship. Edwards finds that, for a short time in the wake of Plimsoll's arrival in 1963, it looked as if conditions were more favourable for the relationship, with the Indian Government reeling from its bloodied nose in the border war with China. But this moment passed, and the Australian Government's attention shifted rapidly to escalating crises in Indonesia and Vietnam. Thereafter, Tange in particular observed firsthand what he had long argued: that the White Australia policy was having a disproportionate impact on Australian relations with countries such as India. Tange was, nevertheless, able to instigate greater high commission reporting on Indian politics in the Lok Sabha and take some early steps towards defence cooperation.

Chapter Five, by David Lowe, focuses on the staff of Australia's high commission and the building they inhabited. The first section of his chapter explores the symbolic significance of the Australian Chancery and Residence buildings by American-born architect Joseph Allen Stein, which opened in 1966 while Tange was high commissioner. Lowe shows that as Stein became famous for his many public buildings in post-independence New Delhi, the Australian site became part of a revered architectural history wherein the environment, modernism and internationalism mixed with local style. The site would remain a talking point, including when the chancery was pulled down in 2004 to make way for a bigger building. Drawing on interviews, the second part of the chapter explores the experiences of locally engaged staff, a large part of embassy communities that are often overlooked. Lowe finds that locally engaged staff can be important bridges between Australian 'national interests', which they tend to at least partly absorb, and the Indian political and business worlds. They offer insights into how boundaries are drawn between Australian-based and local staff, and the circumstances in which these boundaries can be relaxed.

In Chapter Six, Ric Smith, a junior diplomat in New Delhi from 1970 to 1973 working under the direction of High Commissioner Patrick Shaw, recalls the difficult birth of Bangladesh in 1971. This account of the crisis is written from observation, memories and conversations with others, as well as archival documents. Smith exposes the different positions taken by Shaw in New Delhi and Australia's High Commissioner in Islamabad, Francis Stuart. During the crisis, the Australian Government acted out of step with its traditional allies, in particular the United States. It took a different view of the causes of the crisis and, moreover, was openly sympathetic to India's difficulties in coping with a vast influx of refugees. Smith finds that Australia's early recognition of Bangladesh earned it much goodwill in New Delhi.

David Lee explores a period during which both Australia and India aspired to a new middle power status. He shows that the route each government took to thinking of itself in middle power terms was different. Lee's Chapter Seven covers the terms of four high commissioners in this 'middle power phase' between 1972 and 1983—Patrick Shaw, Bruce Grant, Peter Curtis and Gordon Upton. He finds serious attempts and some incremental gains, during both the Whitlam and Fraser prime ministerships, towards something that might be described as closer relations between Australia and India. But such initiatives could easily be derailed. Australia's negative reaction to India's testing of a nuclear device in 1974 did not help create closer relations. At the end of the decade, the Soviet invasion of Afghanistan prompted a tough response from Fraser that did not align well with Indian foreign policy.

Writing for Australian Foreign Minister Bill Hayden in 1984, Graham Feakes in the Department of Foreign Affairs identified a sense of 'drift' in Australian–Indian relations. Thereafter, Feakes spent two terms in New Delhi from 1984 to 1990 trying to arrest the drift. Meg Gurry examines the Feakes years in Chapter Eight, uncovering rich detail about his dedication to bettering relations. During the Feakes period, a warm relationship sprung up between prime ministers Bob Hawke and Rajiv Gandhi, and a joint Australia–India coal mining venture in Bihar augured well. As had happened previously, however, residual scepticism inside the public service bureaucracies of both countries did not match the enthusiasm of India's and Australia's leaders. Then a contretemps, this time the sale of Australian fighter jets to Pakistan, quashed Feakes's hopes for a new dawn in the Australia–India relationship.

The creation of Bangladesh out of the former East Pakistan had shifted the balance of power on the subcontinent very clearly in India's favour. It also prompted Canberra to discard the previous policy of treating Pakistan and India as of equal importance. But very little was done afterwards to give practical weight to India's importance. Up to the end of the 1980s, the Department of Foreign Affairs did not have a senior advocate for relations with India nor did it have a section solely focused on India. Trade was in the 'too hard' basket. It was easier for Australian exporters to look elsewhere. Chapter Nine, the second in this book written by practitioners involved at the time, shows how this began to change with educational exports after India began to open its economy in 1991. Michael Moignard and Quentin Stevenson-Perks recall how the student flows met a huge unmet demand for information about Australia in India.[19] Their chapter concentrates on the period from 1998 onwards when the two-way trade began to increase markedly. Large numbers of Indian students studying in Australia led to greatly increased tourism and immigration. More than this, two-way trade in commodities also grew. Moignard and Stevenson-Perks take this story of growing engagement further, showing how greater trade and migration brought mutual benefits and provided an underpinning to a relationship that had not been present before. Political and strategic collaboration would wait until after 9/11 and the rise of terrorism.

---

19   See: Eric Meadows, 'India: A Problematic Relationship', in Dorothy Davis and Bruce Mackintosh (eds), *Making a Difference: Australian International Education* (Sydney: UNSW Press, 2011), 294–301.

One of the most significant developments in the twenty-first century has been the rise of defence and strategic cooperation in the Australia–India relationship. Ian Hall analyses this in Chapter Ten, noting the importance of Australian Prime Minister John Howard's visit to New Delhi in 2006, and the eventual easing of tensions through Howard's resuming the sale of uranium to India. At the same time, Australian educators and business leaders increasingly beat a path to India where economic growth signalled greater opportunities. As Hall shows, the burgeoning defence ties survived some wobbling by the government of Kevin Rudd on the Quadrilateral Security Dialogues (Japan, Australian, India, United States), and re-emerged most strongly in the 'Indo-Pacific' language of two Australian White Papers in 2012–13, and in joint defence exercises in 2018–19. Concern for the rise of China played a powerful role in driving some of these developments but, as Hall argues, differences between the two governments' respective policies towards China has also made them wary of each other.

Two Australian high commissioners wrote of their times in India in ways that gave them enduring standing as commentators of influence. Crocker wrote several books about his distinguished service as a head of mission, but none is better than his study of Nehru, which David Lowe discusses, alongside Bruce Grant's depiction of Indira Gandhi, in Chapter Eleven. Crocker's book on Nehru is still regarded as an insightful account of Nehru as prime minister and was reprinted in 2008. Crocker saw himself as a scholar diplomat, a persona that some of his colleagues derided.[20] His reputation as a deep contemporary thinker on international relations persists, and his work on Nehru is seen in this context. Bruce Grant, on the other hand, was a distinguished journalist and novelist before his one appointment as a head of mission—New Delhi, 1973–76. His account of his time in India remains arguably the best Australian diplomatic memoir, and thus forms the second part of Chapter Seven. His focus was on India itself and Indira Gandhi as leader. Grant brought to his dispatches and to his memoir, *Gods and Politicians*,[21] a novelist's gift for language and an

---

20   For instance, the British view was that Crocker was a 'bit of an academic' whose disillusion with India would have been more tempered if he had wider regional contacts. 'He wants to warn his compatriots not to take Indian pretensions at face value. This lesson is not needed by Menzies.' Letter, Gore-Booth to Garner, 19 February 1962, The National Archives of the United Kingdom (TNA): DO 196/211.
21   Bruce Grant, *Gods and Politicians: Politics as Culture—an Australian View of India* (Sydney: Allen Lane Australia, 1982).

eye for exotic Asian backdrops. Both he and Crocker, in different ways, brought India to life for Australians through compelling pen portraits of Nehru and his daughter Indira.

The book ends with some broad-ranging reflections from Peter Varghese. As high commissioner from August 2009 to December 2012, and then secretary of the Department of Foreign Affairs until his retirement in July 2016, he is uniquely qualified for this task. In his reflections he notes key changes by Indian and Australian governments that have enabled their relations to strengthen and become more multidimensional. These include the opening up of the Indian economy from the 1990s, the increasing focus of Australian governments on the story of Asia's growth, and the rising numbers of the Indian diaspora in Australia. In a point that goes to the heart of this book, Varghese recalled how he sought to have the high commission drive the burgeoning relationship with India. In doing so, he was conscious of the limited 'bandwidth' available in a Canberra department experiencing significant resource pressures.

High Commissioners to India: 1990–2020

There have been, to date, 22 Australian high commissioners to India (not including the acting role of Charles Kevin in 1948). The availability of government archives enables us to cover those serving up to 1990 in some detail in this book. Other, later, holders of the office are not considered in the same depth, but it is important to recognise them briefly here. David Evans who had been ambassador to Russia and then high commissioner in Malaysia served in New Delhi from 1990 to 1993, in a time of considerable political and economic instability in India with two short-term administrations. The Janata Dal (Socialist) administration of Chandra Shekhar could not pass its budget and was replaced by the reforming administration of P.V. Narasimha Rao from March 1991 until 1996. After the growing chaos of the late 1980s and at the insistence of the International Monetary Fund, Rao with his finance minister began a period of major economic liberalisation. Evans's time in India coincided with the 'Look East' policy, under which India consciously began to develop its much neglected relations with South-East Asia. The Australia–India Council was established in 1992 to foster cultural connections between the two countries.

Against this background of India opening to freer trade and showing interest in Australia's prime area of strategic interest, the appointment of the first high commissioner from the Trade side of the portfolio was significant. Darren Gribble had been ambassador in South Korea before his appointment to India and had presided over an expansion of trade with that country. Gribble served in New Delhi from 1994 to 1997. He emphasised the importance of public diplomacy to increase awareness of Australia in India. The New Horizons program from 1996 showcased Australia as an exporter of services.[22] The Department of Foreign Affairs and Trade (DFAT) had published its important report, *India's Economy at the Midnight Hour*, which flagged to business how important India's economic future was to the Australian Government.

Rob Laurie's term as high commissioner (1997–2001) was overshadowed by the Pokhran nuclear tests in 1998. Australia's reaction to this put a severe dampener on the relationship. Laurie had served in India as deputy high commissioner from 1969 to 1971 including several months as acting high commissioner. He had been high commissioner to New Zealand and to Canada among other posts. During his tenure, the visit of President Clinton to India led to a thaw in relations between India and the United States.

Penny Wensley, who followed Rob Laurie, was the first woman to head the high commission, serving from 2001 to 2004. She came to the post from her role as Australian permanent representative to the United Nations in New York, senior roles in DFAT in Canberra and a posting as ambassador for the environment. Her period in India coincided with increased communal violence including the massacre of Muslims in Gujarat State, which was led at the time by Narendra Modi.

Two of Australia's most senior diplomats then followed. John McCarthy was high commissioner from 2004 to 2009, having been head of mission in six other posts, including the United States, Indonesia and, most immediately, Japan. He assisted Prime Minister Howard during his three-day visit to India in 2006. McCarthy encouraged Howard towards flexibility on the issue of the ban on uranium exports to India, which had become a major sticking point in relations. McCarthy recalled long conversations with Howard on the issue, with the prime minister reasoning that if the Australian public accepted the sale of uranium to

---

22 See Chapter Nine.

China, then they should be able to contemplate its sale to India.[23] The uranium ban was lifted soon afterwards, and other Australian exports such as coal, gold and iron ore increased during this period. By this time, the size of the Indian diaspora in Australia was also becoming a subject of considerable importance in Canberra and New Delhi. McCarthy managed the aftermath of the terrorist attacks in Mumbai in November 2008 that killed two Australians.

One of the biggest developments of this period was the increased flow of Indian students to Australia, as is described in Chapter Nine. While this was generally welcomed, McCarthy grew nervous about the nexus between education and permanent residency applications, and about differences in regulatory standards for education providers in the different Australian states. The latter part of his term coincided with the crisis in relations sparked by violence against Indian students in Australia in May 2009.[24] His successor, Peter Varghese, continued to manage the situation with various forms of public diplomacy. Varghese had previously been senior adviser to the prime minister, high commissioner to Malaysia and most recently director-general of the Office of National Assessments, 2004–09. His term in New Delhi, from August 2009 to December 2012, was marked by increased delegation visits by Australian politicians and university and business leaders. Prime Minister Kevin Rudd visited in November 2009 to sign a Joint Declaration on Security Cooperation with India; and his successor Julia Gillard visited in October 2012, at which time the two governments agreed to hold annual prime ministerial meetings.

Patrick Suckling followed Varghese in New Delhi from 2012 to the start of 2016. Suckling had previously headed the International Division of the Department of Prime Minister and Cabinet and served in New Delhi in the late 1990s. Prior to his appointment he had been head of DFAT's Consular, Public Diplomacy and Parliamentary Affairs Division. Prime Minister Tony Abbott was the first foreign head of government to travel to India to meet India's new prime minister, Narendra Modi. Abbott's visit came in September 2014, four months after Modi's electoral victory. There followed further negotiations towards a Comprehensive Economic Cooperation Agreement and the strengthening of defence and anti-terrorist cooperation.

---

23 John McCarthy interviewed by David Lowe, 8 May 2017, National Library of Australia (NLA): ORAL TRC 6870/1.
24 Ibid.

From the beginning of 2016 to early 2020 Harinder Sidhu was high commissioner. Born in Singapore to Indian parents, she brought linguistic capability (Hindi and Punjabi being two of her seven languages other than English) and policymaking experience acquired from time spent in the departments of Prime Minister and Cabinet and Climate Change, and in the Office of National Assessments. Prior to serving in New Delhi, she was head of DFAT's Multilateral Policy Division. Sidhu was involved in encouraging India's signing up to the Regional Comprehensive Economic Partnership, a goal that proved elusive. But during her time, a new consulate-general was opened in Kolkata and the commissioned report by Peter Varghese, *An India Economic Strategy to 2035*,[25] published in mid-2018, reflected the Australian Government's determination to further strengthen the relationship through initiatives in business, investment, education, resources, agribusiness, tourism, energy, health, infrastructure and science sectors.[26] Sidhu departed in the wake of India's general election that saw Narendra Modi's Bharatiya Janata Party returned with an increased majority.

The most recently appointed high commissioner, Barry O'Farrell, has been in situ since May 2020, a year in which the COVID-19 pandemic has retarded significant developments in the relationship. While the pandemic was an unforeseen disaster of global impact, it was hardly the first setback in Australia–India relations. Indeed, the ease with which relations have been set back after promising starts has been a recurring theme since the 1940s when official diplomatic relations began. An Australian parliamentary standing committee heard in 2009 of the need for Australia to work hard to gain India's attention, to keep Australia 'on India's "radar screen"'.[27] Since 2009, shared Australian–Indian anxiety about the rise of China might have aided in keeping Australia on India's radar screen; and Prime Minister Modi, visiting Australia in 2015, spoke of Australia as a partner in helping to secure India's progress and prosperity.[28] The important *India Economic Strategy to 2035* report begins with the

---

25 Varghese, *An India Economic Strategy to 2035*.
26 'Government Response to an India Economic Strategy to 2035: Factsheet', Department of Foreign Affairs and Trade (2019), www.dfat.gov.au/sites/default/files/government-response-to-an-india-economic-strategy-to-2035.pdf, accessed 2 November 2021.
27 Joint Standing Committee on Foreign Affairs, Defence and Trade, *Australia's Relationship with India as an Emerging World Power* (Canberra: The Committee, 2009), 5.
28 'Prime Minister's Address to the Joint Session of the Australian Parliament', Ministry of External Affairs, Government of India, 18 November 2014, www.mea.gov.in/Speeches-Statements.htm?dtl/24269/Prime_Ministers_Address_to_the_Joint_Session_of_the_Australian_Parliament_18_November_2014, accessed 29 October 2021.

comment: 'Timing has always been a challenge in Australia's relationship with India'.[29] As the Australian Government works to implement some of the ambitious recommendations in the report, this book adds to our understanding of why timing has been a challenge, and how those at the coalface of the relationship have grappled with it.

29   Varghese, *An India Economic Strategy to 2035*.

1

Creating the Diplomatic Relationship

Eric Meadows

The creation of the formal relationship between India and Australia in 1944 broke new ground for both countries. India was not yet independent and was learning how to construct its foreign relations. The role of a high commissioner in inter-dominion relations was changing. For Australia, India was the first country in Asia with which it exchanged full 'ambassadorial' level representation. But there were no clear expectations of what each high commission would do other than increase knowledge of their respective countries. India was interested in the operation of the White Australia policy; and Kama Maclean's recent study shows how, up to this point, race constantly informed and complicated the triangular Britain–India–Australia relationship.[1] Australia expected a close relationship to develop but had few ideas at first as to how that might happen.

Establishment

Australia and colonial India had a long informal relationship throughout the nineteenth and early twentieth century.[2] The formal relationship began in 1939 when trade commissioners were exchanged in Sydney and

---

1   Kama Maclean, *British India, White Australia: Overseas Indians, Intercolonial Relations and the Empire* (Sydney: UNSW Press, 2020).
2   See: ibid.; Joyce Westrip and Peggy Holroyde, *Colonial Cousins: A Surprising History of Connection between India and Australia* (Kent Town: Wakefield Press, 2010).

Calcutta. The initiative for full diplomatic relations came in 1942 from the Viceroy of India, Lord Linlithgow, who thought that India should establish relations with the other dominions. Having a direct relationship, rather than through Great Britain, was to be a sign to Indians of the coming of dominion status. The British secretary of state for India, Leo Amery, personally raised the matter with 'Doc' Evatt, Australian's minister for external affairs, and thought he was eager for an exchange of high commissioners.[3] Yet it took over a year for Cabinet in Australia to approve the exchange and to appoint Lieutenant General Sir Iven Mackay.[4] Mackay had had a distinguished career as a soldier in both world wars and as an educator between the wars.

The instruction caused great confusion and much political jockeying in New Delhi. Australia was the first country with which India had established full diplomatic relations and this caused something of a flap.[5] There was a tussle for influence between the Department of Overseas Indians and the Commerce Department through which the trading relationship had been conducted. The Department of Overseas Indians won this turf war. It mainly concerned itself with Indians in South Africa and its head, Dr Khare, had already noted that establishing relations with Australia would mean dealing with a country that discriminated against Indians. (Mackay was later to note that Khare was never particularly interested in Australia 'nor in Indian relations with members of the British Commonwealth other than South Africa'.[6]) Eventually, with a nod to Australia's susceptibilities, a Department of Commonwealth Relations was created out of the Overseas Indians Department, with Khare as its head.

There was confusion in Canberra too, with the Department of External Affairs wanting accreditation to take place through the Indian Department of External Affairs. This department looked after India's relations with neighbouring countries such as Tibet and was still controlled by British Indian Civil Service officers, but Canberra seemed not to understand this. The exact diplomatic status of a 'high commissioner' was still indeterminate, although it is clear that Khare regarded it as equivalent to an ambassador. Australia itself had only two full high commissioners other

---

3   Letter, Amery to Linlithgow, 29 May 1942, British Library (BL): IOR L/PJ/8/190.
4   Mackay was appointed on 20 October 1943, along with the positions of minister to the Soviet Union and high commissioner to New Zealand. See: National Archives of Australia (NAA): A2703, 70.
5   For a full account of these events, see: NB Khare, *My Political Memoirs of Autobiography* (Nagpur: J.R. Joshi, 1959).
6   Despatch 33/46, 8 July 1946, NAA: A4231, 1946/New Delhi.

than London, the first established in Ottawa in 1938, and the second in Wellington, which had just been created in early 1944. Relations between India and Canada were not formalised for two years after the relationship with Australia was created.

In 1944 India was on a war footing and accommodation in Delhi was difficult to find. The Viceroy, Field Marshall Lord Wavell,[7] had the Mackays stay at the Viceroy's House until a ramshackle house was found in Old Delhi[8] to house both the residence and the office of the high commission. The staff consisted of the high commissioner and his wife, the official secretary, Colin Moodie, an aide-de-camp to the high commissioner, and Mackay's daughter, who acted as his private secretary. They all worked in their bedrooms or in the dressing rooms. The mission moved several times in Old Delhi,[9] gradually improving its accommodation until a move was made to New Delhi, closer to the offices of the government. The Residence was established at 34 Ferozshah Road and offices were found in Connaught Place.

Mackay had discussions with the Government of India about the creation of a city diplomatic zone as early as 1946 and was urging Canberra that six or seven acres would be needed to house the Australian Residence, the chancery and accommodation for staff. He called on one of the pre-independence generation of British architects resident in New Delhi, Charles George Blomfield who worked closely with the more famous Edward Lutyens, to draw up some plans, and then sent these to Canberra. He wanted the buildings to have a 'distinctive Australian character' using Australian materials.[10] It was not until 1951 that Canberra approved the purchase of the 12-acre block on which the high commission now stands.[11]

Mackay arrived in India with few instructions from Evatt, except to keep him informed about the military situation. There was some criticism in parliament that such an able general should be sidelined into diplomacy, but the government brushed it off.[12] For the remainder of the war, Mackay wore his military uniform.

---

7   Wavell had known Mackay during the North African campaign.
8   Nabha House, 34 Alipore Road.
9   In July 1944, a separate office was found at 7 Metcalfe Road and then in September the Residence moved to Gwalior House, 37 Rajpur Road, both in Old Delhi.
10   Despatch 38/46, 23 August 1946, NAA: A4231, 1946/New Delhi.
11   Despatch 13/1952, NAA: A4231, 1946/New Delhi.
12   Commonwealth, *Parliamentary Debates*, Senate, 10 February 1944, 58–59, 'Adjournment' (HS Foll).

But what else was he to do? Wavell told Amery that Mackay would not have a great deal to do in India.[13] British officials thought the bulk of his work would be commercial.[14] Publicity and trade were the two tasks mentioned in the Australian press. Not much about Australia was known in India. In contrast, Mackay commented in a talk on the Australian Broadcasting Commission that his desire was 'to bring the two countries into closer friendship and understanding'. This would 'be brought about not merely by making Australia better known in India, but by finding out what India thinks, how she feels, how she looks at others'.[15] In some notes he wrote for an interview with General Blamey, Mackay said he thought the job would be to 'gather helpful information about trends of thought and opinion and perhaps influence good relations between these two sisters in the Empire'. He thought his military connections would be useful too, as India would soon become the 'centre of important events'.[16]

Trade and Education

In his press release at the start of his posting, Mackay noted that:

> trade is still the driving force (of relations between countries) and we hope to see a renewal and extension of general trade between Australia and India on the cessation of hostilities.[17]

Australia had offered to send wheat to India to help with the growing famine in Bengal and other parts of the country, and this had been well received in India. Wheat was to be a major part of the trading relationship for the next 20 years, despite the fact that in 1944 Australia was mostly known as an exporter of tinned fruit. At the start of the Second World War, trade had been running heavily in India's favour, exporting goods worth A£5.8 million and importing from Australia A£1.9 million in goods. While trade had been an important element in the relationship in the early part of the century—the Indian Army used horses bred in Australia called 'Whalers'—the Depression had caused a marked drop

---

13   Wavell to Amery, 18 April 1944, BL: IOR L/PJ/8/190.
14   Political Secretary to Secretary of External Department, 20 October 1944, BL: IOR L/PJ/8/190.
15   Reported in *The Daily Telegraph*, 22 November 1943.
16   Note by Mackay, 9 November 1943, Australian War Memorial: 92, 6850/183.
17   Statement by Lieutenant-General Sir Iven Mackay, 27 March 1944, BL: IOR L/PJ/8/190.

in Australian exports. The Second World War saw trade begin to flicker back to life, although Australia did not take full advantage of all the opportunities the situation presented.

In 1940 the British had set up a central provision office in New Delhi, the Eastern Group Supply Council, to purchase, hold stocks and act as a clearinghouse for essential procurement, both civil and military. Its region was the Middle East, Africa, India and the Far East. It thus had vast power potentiality. This power was largely unrealised by Australia. It had signed contracts for supply of munitions and other goods but did not live up to its commitments.[18] A delegation from the council in early 1944 pointed out Australia's failures and the urgent need of India for goods from Australia including railway parts. The delegation reported that India was the only source of supply for Australia of jute, mica, linseed, shellac and strychnine. The Australian Government noted the embarrassment caused in official and business circles in India by the failure to meet orders and the loss of prestige involved. The irony of this failure was that Australia's first representative on the council had been Sir Bertram Stevens, a former premier of NSW who went on to write the first major book calling for closer relations with India.[19] Stevens contended that India, with some assistance from the West, would become one of the world's great industrial powers; that the war had stimulated industrialisation; and that Australia's own future was inextricably linked with the extent to which it encouraged trade, especially with India, but also with other Asian countries. Australia's terms of trade had deteriorated and if its standard of living was to improve, it needed to seek fresh markets and India promised huge opportunities. There was a potential for Australia to export capital goods to a rapidly industrialising country as well as consumables and technical skill.[20]

One of Mackay's abiding concerns during his posting was the importance of Australia developing an educational and cultural relationship with India. This was exactly what Nehru wanted, Mackay reported.[21] Such linkages would give depth to the relationship and provide a stimulus for greater engagement. Early in his posting he argued for the exchange of teachers and research students between the two countries. Later, in 1946, India

18   Paul Hasluck, *Government and the People, 1942–1945* (Canberra: Australian War Memorial, 1970), 441.
19   Bertram Stevens, *New Horizons: A Study of Australian–Indian Relationships* (Sydney: Peter Huston, under the auspices of the Australian Institute of International Affairs, New South Wales Branch, 1946).
20   Ibid.
21   For example, see: Despatch 41/46, 6 September 1946, NAA: A4231, 1946/New Delhi.

proposed exchanging educational missions to explore facilities for research in each country with a view to cooperation. Moreover, the Government of India, Mackay reported, was interested in sending research students to study in Australia, for which it would pay. It saw such a link as a means of establishing cultural ties and good relations with Australia, not just the provision of a few places for students.[22] No response from Australia was made to Mackay's repeated requests and he was clearly frustrated by the lack of action. He understood that there was no administrative machinery in Australia to coordinate a response to such a request, but he asked that some government authority 'give these matters full consideration as part of an integrated foreign and commercial policy'.[23] Mackay began directly appealing to universities in an attempt to achieve some progress on this front without government help. This proved to be a mildly successful endeavour. In 1946 Melbourne University received 14 students to study geology and in June of that year, the first Indian student was enrolled at Duntroon with a view to a commission in the Indian Army.

Defence Links

Evatt had met Nehru in London in 1938, and was impressed with him. Both were socialists and had met at Stafford Cripps's home along with British leaders, Attlee, Bevan and Morrison. Brilliant but erratic as minister, Evatt expected that Australia's future security would be tied to a 'close friendship with India'.[24] He believed India and Australia should work together to watch over and guard the 'interests of countries in the Pacific and Indian Oceans and in South East Asia generally'. The Curtin Government even proposed a formal defence link with India in 1944, similar to the one it had signed with New Zealand. The Government of India in its reply noted that there was 'great scope for closer relations between Australia and India, especially for security and defence and in industrial and agricultural matters, in scientific research, and in the expansion of commerce'.[25] However, any agreement would have to wait until India's constitutional arrangements were settled.

---

22   Despatch 20/46, 24 April 1946, ibid.
23   Despatch 22/46, 29 April 1946, ibid.
24   Evatt to Chifley, 24 October 1948, in Pamela Andre (ed.), *Documents on Australian Foreign Policy (DAFP) 1937–49*, vol. 14, *The Commonwealth, Asia and the Pacific, 1948–1949* (Canberra: Department of Foreign Affairs and Trade, 1998), 147.
25   Khare to Mackay in WJ Hudson (ed.), *DAFP 1937–49*, vol. 7, *1944* (Canberra: Australian Government Publishing Service, 1988), 617–18.

A discussion about linking the armed forces was to continue for some years. In 1948, Evatt suggested that India should be represented 'on the Australian defence machinery' and vice versa. The Indian foreign secretary, KPS Menon, agreed in principle, but added the rider that India was still preoccupied with its domestic affairs and could not respond to the Australian offer. The suggestion seems to have lapsed at this point.[26]

The theme of a closer regional tie or alliance with India was to continue until the end of the Labor Government's tenure in December 1949, and was even mooted in 1951. Evatt's view was that Australia's 'security in the future will go hand in hand with close friendship with India'.[27] Although it went against Evatt's legal instincts that allegiance to the Crown was the test for membership of the Commonwealth, Chifley felt differently. Nevertheless, the former's position eventually prevailed and Australia ultimately agreed to the formulation, which allowed India to stay as a republic.[28] Much of the motivation for this was related to defence and the need to ensure that India could be relied on as a strategic partner in any major war with the Soviet Union. At one point Chifley noted that 'Australian–Indian close association was vital to peace in South East Asia'[29] and that India and Australia had a mutual interest in regional security in the Indian Ocean.[30] Mountbatten, who followed Wavell as viceroy, was influential in the negotiations, which developed the formula of the king as head of the Commonwealth. It is significant that one of the major reasons why he was so determined to be governor-general of both dominions following the transfer of power was to ensure that Britain remained influential in defence planning. Commonwealth unity was the basis of defence, just as it had been during the Second World War. Evatt persisted with this line well into 1949, urging the development of a regional pact within the Commonwealth to restore peace in South-East Asia.

Another strand in the determination to keep India in the Commonwealth at all costs was to ensure that the perception of Britain's power was retained. A unified Commonwealth was seen as a warning to potential aggressors.

---

26   Despatch 49/48, 20 August 1948, NAA: A4231, 1948/New Delhi.
27   Evatt to Chifley, 24 October 1948, in Andre, *DAFP*, vol. 14, 147.
28   See: Frank Bongiorno, 'Commonwealthmen and Republicans: Dr. H. V. Evatt, the Monarchy and India', *Australian Journal of Politics and History* 46, no. 1 (2000): 33–50, doi.org/10.1111/1467-8497.00084.
29   High Commission in London to Holloway and Dedman, 22 April 1949, in Andre, *DAFP*, vol. 14, 119.
30   Chifley to Evatt, 13 October 1948, in ibid., 187.

Evatt saw the Commonwealth as the 'Third Force'; its contribution to the victory over the Axis had been of the same order as that of the Soviet Union and the United States. But, even in early 1947 the Joint Intelligence Committee was warning that India would be susceptible to Russian influence.[31] Russia would calculate the importance of India for any move it might make in the Middle East and, at this time, the next major war was expected to be in that region. Worryingly, Indian neutrality was canvassed as a possibility that would facilitate Soviet policy in the event of war.

Immigration and the Asian Relations Conference

Immigration was a pressing issue, as it was to be for the next 30 years. The Australian high commission asked Canberra, in what became a regular request, to institute a quota for Indian migration to Australia. In a well-argued and moderately toned dispatch in 1946, Mackay commented that Australia's immigration policy was based on racial as well as economic and social grounds. There was no other way to explain why Australia would refuse to take a small number of Indian Westernised professional people, which Australia needed for its economic expansion. He noted the goodwill the United States had achieved by its quota of 100 Indians. Australia's stocks stood high in India apart from the White Australia policy. His main argument was, however, that this act of goodwill would be in Australia's strategic self-interest given the likely importance of independent India, and it would make no appreciable difference to the social make-up of Australia.[32] Nothing, however, happened. This was a policy that would take many years to dismantle.

Mackay's dispatch had an eye to the then forthcoming Asian Relations Conference at which Australia was to be represented.[33] Nehru was its driving force. His aim was to map out a path for Asian solidarity, led by India, 'the pivot and fulcrum',[34] as colonised countries became

---

31   Joint Intelligence Committee Appreciation 1/47, 27 March 1947, in WJ Hudson and Wendy Way (eds), *DAFP 1937–49*, vol. 12, *1947* (Canberra: Australian Government Publishing Service, 1995), 282.

32   Dispatch 52/46, 22 December 1946, in WJ Hudson and Wendy Way (eds), *DAFP 1937–49*, vol. 10, *July–December 1946* (Canberra: Australian Government Publishing Service, 1993), 534.

33   A full account of the conference can be found in Chapter Two.

34   Despatch 19/46, 12 April 1946, NAA: A4231, 1946/New Delhi.

independent. The national movement for freedom in Asia was the first item on the conference's agenda. In his opening address, Nehru commented that 'the countries of Asia can no longer be used as pawns by others; they are bound to have their own policies in world affairs'.[35] What came to be called 'non-alignment' was fairly clearly stated in his speeches during the proceedings.

> For too long we of Asia have been petitioners in western courts and chancelleries. … We propose to stand on our own feet and to co-operate with all others who are prepared to co-operate with us. We do not intend to be the playthings of others.[36]

Nehru specifically welcomed Australians at the conference, 'because we have many problems in common, especially in Pacific and South-East regions, and we have to co-operate together to find a solution'.[37] Moodie, who was one of the Australian representatives, noted in his report of the conference that although there were discussions on migration, nothing emerged detrimental to Australia's interests. Moodie's report highlighted the divisions in Asia over migration and internal discrimination. These provided a means for Australia to avoid challenge on this matter. The right of countries to institute quota systems for migration was recognised. Nonetheless, Moodie added:

> While principles on which Australian migration policy is based must remain, it may be possible to make our rules somewhat more flexible and less apparently exclusionist. Certain cultured and deserving types of Asiatics who do not fit into present categories might usefully be admitted and in such cases, the necessity for renewing their permits annually might be waived.[38]

Mackay was later to say that during his four and a half years in office in India, the White Australia policy was scarcely mentioned and never raised as an issue.[39] This is somewhat disingenuous, given the amount of press coverage on the matter and his knowledge of Khare's interest in

---

35   Quoted in Alan Watt, *The Evolution of Australian Foreign Policy 1938–1965* (London: Cambridge University Press, 1967), 226.
36   Nehru's inaugural address, 23 March 1947, BL: IOR L/I/1/152.
37   Burton to Kuskie, 2 April 1947, in Hudson and Way (eds), *DAFP,* vol. 12, 799.
38   Report on the Asian Relations Conference in ibid., 802.
39   Speech to the Australian Institute of International Affairs, 22 December 1949, NAA: A1838, 169/10/1 PART 1.

the question. As the Australian high commission's reports highlighted, the consciousness of racial slight implied in the policy was acute, and it remained one of the few things Indians knew about Australia.

From Mackay to Gollan

Mackay's appointment was a success. He was an unlikely diplomat but an intelligent observer who learnt how to report and advance his country's interests, however limited they might have been. Mackay's reporting was thorough and gave the Department of External Affairs a comprehensive overview of developments in India. A great deal of it was based on press clippings, but this was a time when the best newspapers were journals of record and journalists were experts in what they wrote. Mackay had good enough access to the Government of India to see key people when he needed to, and his reports were authoritative. But most of his time in India was during the transition period from colony to independence. As such, he was accredited to a government preoccupied with itself and its future, with only visionary rather than practical ideas about what external policy it would pursue once independence came. The personnel making those decisions would change and the bureaucracy to develop ideas was in flux. He had few key officials with whom to develop a dialogue about international issues who might challenge his own thinking about the relationship. His mission was isolated in New Delhi. There are almost no references to the views of other diplomats in his reporting and no sense of any community of observers with which he could exchange ideas. The Australian high commission was, for the most part, the only full mission in New Delhi for much of his time. Notably, however, Mackay was independent in his thinking and not captured by British views, a considerable achievement given his isolation. He and Moodie were in Simla during the conference on the future of India in 1945 and reported accurately on the shifts as India moved towards independence; Mackay argued that a firm date should be set to concentrate the minds of the negotiators. He developed a low opinion of Muslim League leader and future governor-general of Pakistan, Muhummad Ali Jinnah, and a high opinion of Nehru; he saw Jinnah as obdurate during the Simla talks. Mackay was able to see Nehru when it was needed after the latter joined the interim government on his release from prison in 1946. Evatt sent him to see Nehru, for instance, to urge keeping independent India within the Commonwealth. Officials in New Delhi in the middle part of 1947 were overwhelmed with the consequences of Partition, and even among the Indian members of the bureaucracy there was instability as people moved to Pakistan.[40] Commendably, Mackay spent much of that period using his considerable organisational skills to ensure the Australian community and his own Muslim servants remained safe.

Mackay was fortunate in that Evatt was interested in India. Evatt's thinking on the relationship was exploratory: how could it be otherwise when the nature of the independent country to be was inchoate for most of Mackay's time there? He proceeded by presenting ideas, in particular his views on a regional pact with India, and seeing what the reaction might be. Nehru's interest in Australia, first seen at the Inter Asian Regional Conference, was based on the indications given by Evatt that Australian thinking was independent and was creatively trying to think through how it might relate to Asia. Australia had started talking in terms of being a part of the wider Asia-Pacific region. In addition, the socialism of the Curtin/Chifley governments attracted Nehru. India was to take the path of a mixed economy, just as Britain was doing at the time. So Evatt and Chifley, in Nehru's mind, were part of the wider network of progressively thinking socialist leaders, the kind of people he felt most at home with. The auguries for the relationship, at the end of Mackay's posting, were strong.

H. Roy Gollan was announced as the next Australian high commissioner in 1948 and took up his post in January 1949. Gollan had been in India since 1937[41] and, given the acute shortage of senior people who could undertake senior overseas appointments, it was logical to move him into the role of high commissioner. It was not to be a brilliant appointment. He had a tense relationship with Mackay, who thought his patronising attitudes, among other issues, had hampered the development of bilateral trade.[42] Gollan carried no weight in Canberra and his grasp of the arts of diplomatic reporting was inadequate. He was fortunate in that his two deputies as official secretary were, in turn, Charles Kevin and Francis Stuart, both of whom were career officers of the Department of External Affairs and went on to head of mission positions. Kevin was not happy about the appointment. Having been acting high commissioner he was

40   See: Nayantara Pothen, *Glittering Decades: New Delhi in Love and War* (New Delhi: Penguin, 2012).

41   Gollan was posted to Bombay as representative of the Australian National Travel Association in 1937 and to Calcutta as trade commissioner in 1940, based first in Simla and then in Bombay.

42   Ivan Chapman, *Iven G. Mackay: Citizen and Soldier* (Melbourne: Melway Publishing, 1975), 296.

anxious that the practical solution of appointing Gollan from Bombay would be seen as a slight to him.[43] Secretary of the Department of External Affairs John Burton wrote to Gollan noting that his new position would solve the problems that had arisen in the high commission 'as regards jurisdiction of the High Commissioner over Trade Commissioners' and that he expected there would be amicable relations with all staff and in particular with Kevin.[44]

Burton's instructions to Gollan listed four areas on which detailed reporting was required. Two of these showed the extent to which the department was still thinking through how Australia might work with India in developing sound cooperation in South-East Asia. The first area related to India's desire for leadership in Asia and the undercurrent of rivalry with China in the area. The second concentrated on the fact that while India might accept that Australia had an interest in the region and in the Indian Ocean in particular, what would it take to develop a coherent policy? Third, Gollan was asked to report on the activities of other powers in the region, and fourth on the attitude of India towards membership of the Commonwealth.[45] In the event, Gollan was active in representing and in advancing Australia's commercial interests in a period when there was every expectation that the bilateral relationship would flourish. Australia's 'stocks' were on the rise, a combination of wheat exports, activity over Indonesia and various expert exchanges as well as work in international conferences.[46]

As is detailed in the following chapter, the first important international conference in independent India was on the developing crisis in Indonesia in 1949.[47] In Canberra a tussle developed as to who should represent Australia. Evatt wanted either Gollan, who was in the process of returning to India after briefing, or more junior officials to attend, but Burton had already lined up his attendance with Chifley. Moodie was to accompany him. Burton thought that Gollan or the others Evatt preferred would only

---

43   Cable 405, Australian High Commission: New Delhi to Department of External Affairs, 28 September 1948, NAA: A1838, 169/10/6 PART 1.

44   Burton to Gollan, 7 October 1948, NAA: A1838, 169/10/6 PART 1. A tussle in Canberra between the Department of External Affairs and Department of Commerce, which ran the Trade Commissioner Service, led to routine trade matters being sent to Commerce but through the External Affairs network. Matters of commercial policy were to be referred to the high commissioner. This set a pattern but never entirely eliminated tension between the two services.

45   Burton to Gollan, 12 October 1948, NAA: A1838, 169/10/6 PART 1.

46   Kevin to Burton, 24 March 1948, NAA: A1838, 169/10/6 PART 1.

47   See Chapter Two for a full account of the 1949 Indian Conference on Indonesia.

'lead us into trouble or on the other hand be too negative'.[48] He had been deeply involved in the Indonesian crisis, and with Evatt so much out of the country with his responsibilities in the United Nations, Burton had formed a good working relationship with Chifley.

By the time the conference began in late January, Gollan had arrived in New Delhi but was not in any sense part of the conference or its reporting. Burton and Moodie handled it all. Burton only wrote to Gollan to give him direction about what to say as he made his initial calls. He was to use it to facilitate his interviews and to emphasise the importance of Indo-Australian cooperation bearing in mind that Australia expressly wished to avoid any impression that it was 'ganging up' with Asia against the Western powers.[49]

The Change of Government in Australia

Gollan had not been a participant in any meaningful way in the two most important developments in the bilateral relationship in his time as high commissioner in 1949—the cooperation with India over Indonesia and the incorporation of India into the Commonwealth. He was, however, active in touring India, and his reporting on trade and economic issues was solid.[50] He used his past experience in trade to negotiate the first Australian trade 'arrangement' with India, which was signed in October 1951. In 1949 India introduced the first plank in what was to be colloquially called the 'permit raj' when it brought in the Indian Open General Licence system. This was an attempt to conserve foreign exchange by restricting imports. In addition, the growth of centralised planning led to long delays in the procurement, for instance, of jute goods and textiles for Australia. The Australian trade commissioner in Bombay, David Shubart, caused a flap in Indian Government circles when he suggested, while on home leave, that Australia had little prospect of increasing trade and that India was nearly bankrupt.[51] On the contrary, trade had in fact been increasing. In 1949–50 Australian exports to India were valued at A£37 million while imports were worth A£28 million. That was an increase of A£11 million

---

48   Burton to Evatt, 7 January 1949, NAA: A1838, 169/10/6 PART 1.
49   Ibid.
50   See, for instance, Gollan's last dispatch on the state of the Indian economy: Despatch 17, 14 March 1952, NAA: A4231, 1952/New Delhi.
51   Reported in *The Age*, 25 October 1950.

over 1947–48 and a thirteenfold increase since before the war. Australian imports were static but even they had increased from A£3 million in 1938–39.[52] The Trade Agreement negotiated by Gollan, the first signed with India, covered Australian imports of jute, edible oils and cotton and piece goods, while exports covered were wheat and other grains, metals such as lead and zinc, and some heavy machinery. It helped speed up the two-way trade. The permit raj was, however, to continue to be major impediment to the development of trade between the two countries.

The change of government in Australia in December 1949 coincided with preparations for the Colombo Conference of Commonwealth Foreign Ministers held in January 1950. The Colombo Plan, which came from this meeting and from the subsequent meetings in Sydney and London during 1950, in recent years has been covered in a glow of nostalgia, but this has at least rescued it from being a footnote in Australia's postwar history. Percy Spender, minister for external affairs in the Menzies Government, claimed credit for the Colombo Plan. Yet so did Ceylon's Minister for Finance J.R. Jayewardene and the United Kingdom's Foreign Secretary Ernest Bevin, and historian Sarvepalli Gopal claims some of it for Nehru.[53] Who first proposed it hardly matters, but the need for economic cooperation in the region was in active discussion in Australia in late 1949 before the change of government. There was agreement in Canberra among government departments that a program of 'political and economic action in South-East Asia' was needed as a response to the changes occurring in the region. In particular, the new Liberal minister for defence, Eric Harrison, thought that this program of action should be directed to 'arrest the spread of, and ultimately eliminate, Communism' and that Australia and the Western powers should work with the countries of the region to do this. India was thought to be especially important. This discussion acknowledged that this was a 'substantial re-orienting of Australian thought and practice'. South-East Asia should be a buffer region between Australia and the Asian mainland from where threat to Australia's

---

52 Statement issued by HR Gollan, 2 February 1949, NAA: A1838, 169/10/6 PART 1; Briefing for RG Casey, undated [late 1951], NAA: A1838, 169/10/11/3.

53 See: David Lowe, 'Canberra's Colombo Plan: Public Images of Australia's Relations with Post-Colonial South and Southeast Asia in the 1950s', *South Asia: Journal of South Asian Studies*, n.s., 25, no. 2 (2002): 183–204, doi.org/10.1080/00856400208723481. See also: Sarvepalli Gopal, *Jawaharlal Nehru*, vol. 2, *1947–56* (London: Johnathan Cape, 1980), 65.

security was likely to come.[54] Thinking was, however, concentrated on Indonesia, in particular, and on providing aid to the programs run by the United Nations. When the brief for the Colombo Conference was produced in December 1949, it debated the issue of what was causing the changes in the region—the growth of nationalism or the force of international communism? It noted that Australia's interests lay in the emergence of stable, moderate and friendly governments in the region, and that Australia must act to prevent communism from subverting these new states. It added that fostering the economic development of the region would be likely to assist Australia's political influence in the region. But, again, Indonesia, rather than India, was the focus.[55] Importantly, despite what Spender later claimed,[56] it was clear that the ideas and the brief that he took to Colombo had been developed under the previous government and, in particular, by Burton with the assistance of McIntyre and Tange who both went with him to the conference.[57] As was the case with the 1949 Indian Conference on Indonesia, there was again little significant contribution from the high commissioner.

The Kashmir Question

Despite Nehru's international reputation and his activity for world peace, India's strained relations with Pakistan continued. Most of the issues arising from Partition had been resolved[58] but the unsettled status of the princely state of Kashmir remained a source of bitter tension. Kashmir had a Hindu ruler but a Muslim majority population. The ruler decided to accede to India only under the duress of an invasion by tribesmen from Pakistan and with the connivance of the new Pakistan Army. India and Pakistan then fought a war, which left the state divided along a line of control. India had referred the dispute to the Security Council, which set up an investigatory commission. When this failed to find a solution,

---

54 'Australia and South-East Asia', Paper by the Department of External Affairs, 13 November 1949, cited in David Lowe and Daniel Oakman, *Australia and the Colombo Plan: 1949–1957* (Barton: Department of Foreign Affairs and Trade, 2004), 4.

55 'Brief for Cabinet for Commonwealth Conference, Colombo', December 1949, cited in Lowe and Oakman, *Australia and the Colombo Plan*, 22.

56 Percy Spender, *Exercises in Diplomacy: The ANZUS Treaty and the Colombo Plan* (Sydney: Sydney University Press, 1969).

57 Laurence 'Jim' McIntyre was head of the Pacific Division and Arthur Tange was head of the United Nations and Economic Relations Division.

58 In particular, sharing the waters of the Indus basin and settling property claims of refugees.

the council appointed a 'Representative' who, in effect, was to act as a mediator. That onerous task was given to the Australian High Court judge, Sir Owen Dixon.[59]

The department was not in favour of any Australian or even Commonwealth mediation if, as the department thought, it would fail. Australia would be likely to 'incur the odium of failure' and strained relations with one or both parties and Commonwealth relations would be damaged. But this opinion wavered as the atmosphere between India and Pakistan improved or sank during the early part of 1950. If a solution looked likely then Australia would reap the benefit of a successful outcome.[60]

Evatt had been active in 1948 while the warfare continued, urging India to accept his services as a mediator. Nehru politely turned him down. This was the start of regular Australian interest in solving the Kashmir dispute. The motivation for involvement was the same as that which animated the negotiations on Commonwealth membership: to ensure that both countries would be available to Western defence should war with the Soviet Union break out. A state of war on the subcontinent was inherently destabilising and left the region open to communist meddling.[61] While Dixon did not act as an Australian mediator as such, his participation fitted Menzies's strategic preoccupations with a coming war. It was impossible to imagine in 1950 how, in the event of war in the Middle East as a result of a Soviet invasion, the West could do without the 20 million Indian troops that had been so vital in the war just finished.[62] Menzies was to offer his services in mediation at the Commonwealth Prime Ministers Conference in London in January 1951 and, again in June 1951 when Indian troop movements appeared threatening.

Dixon's mission meant travelling between Karachi and New Delhi, putting proposals to both leaders and arranging a conference between them.[63] He kept in touch to some extent with both Australian high

---

59   United Nations Security Council Resolution 80, 14 March 1950, UN Doc S/Res/80(1950) [see also: S/1469].

60   Note for the Secretary from United Nations Division, 27 March 1950, NAA: A1838, 169/11/148/6.

61   See: HW Brands, 'India and Pakistan in American Strategic Planning, 1947–54: The Commonwealth as Collaborator', *The Journal of Commonwealth and Imperial History* 15, no. 1 (1986): 41–54, doi.org/10.1080/03086538608582728.

62   For example, see: Draft cable to the Australian Embassy in Washington, 24 January 1951, NAA: TS169/11/148/12, Part 1.

63   A full account of the Dixon mission can be found in William Reid, 'Sir Owen Dixon's Mediation of the Kashmir Dispute, 1950' (BA (Hons) thesis, Deakin University, 2000).

commissions seeking to determine just how far both countries could move on the essential issues.[64] Despite exhausting work, Dixon's mission failed. He is regarded, nonetheless, as having come closer than anyone to securing a lasting solution.[65] Dixon's mission report makes it clear that the responsibility for failure lay with India. In personal conversation, it was apparent he was furious with Nehru in particular. He distrusted Nehru: 'I wish a sense of honour existed here [in India]. I can hardly imagine a people with such crooked and dishonourable minds and natures as the Hindus possess'.[66] His last interview with Nehru was 'all lies as usual'.[67] Secretary of the Department of External Affairs Alan Watt noted on a file in early August, before the breakdown of the mission, that he had discussed Kashmir with Spender who thought 'the Indian attitude unreasonable' but agreed that pressure on India from Australia was of doubtful utility.[68]

The damage to Australia's view of India from the mission was considerable. As soon as he arrived home Dixon briefed Menzies personally in Melbourne. Dixon also briefed Watt and continued to be a sounding board for him in the development of foreign policy, especially on the large themes of the day, such as whether priority should be given to the Middle East or to Asian concerns.[69] Later, in 1952, the then minister for external affairs, Richard Casey, tried to persuade Dixon to revisit the subcontinent. He was, Casey said, the only person in whom Nehru would have confidence. Dixon, however, refused. He would only return if the American secretary of state, Dean Acheson, or someone of equal status asked him. Casey, Dixon thought, had no understanding of Kashmir.[70]

The distinct turn to Pakistan in Australian policy can be attributed to Dixon's experience of this mediation. If, as Dixon said some years later to Crocker, the plebiscite idea was one of Nehru's major mistakes,[71] it was also true that by taking the dispute to the United Nations Nehru

---

64 Cable 230, Australian High Commission to Department of External Affairs, 31 July 1950, NAA: TS169/11/148/12, Part 1.

65 For example, see: Dennis Kux, *India and the United States: Estranged Democracies* (Honolulu: University Press of the Pacific, 2002), 63; and AG Noorani, 'The Dixon Plan', *Frontline*, 25 October 2002.

66 Dixon to his wife, 21 August 1950 cited in Philip Ayres, *Owen Dixon: A Biography* (Carlton: Miegunyah Press, 2003), 214.

67 Francis Stuart, *Towards Coming of Age: A Foreign Service Odyssey* (Nathan: Griffith University, Centre for the Study of Australian-Asian Relations, 1989), 157.

68 File note by Watt, 5 August 1950, NAA: A1838, 169/11/148/6.

69 Ayres, *Owen Dixon*, 228.

70 Ibid., 228–9.

71 Despatch 57, 18 September 1952, NAA: A4231 1952/New Delhi.

had internationalised a problem that might have stayed internal and been resolved by the two countries working together.[72] In 1950 and for some years later, Pakistan was regarded as the key to maintaining Western influence in the northern part of the Middle East. The United States wanted an Asian partner once China failed and, disappointed with India's policies, Pakistan was the inevitable choice.

Francis Stuart[73] thought that the major diplomatic preoccupation for the high commission in the 1950s was 'watching the Kashmir crisis unfold'.[74] Menzies himself attempted mediation after his visit to India and Pakistan in December 1950.[75] There was an informal discussion of Kashmir at the Commonwealth Prime Ministers meeting in London in January 1951 in which Menzies took a lead, even suggesting a Commonwealth force to supervise a plebiscite of the state, but nothing came of this.[76] Menzies wrote to Acheson that after this discussion he formed the view that Nehru did not want to settle the Kashmir dispute, but prolong it in order to increase the prospects of the state acceding to India. He found Liaquat, Pakistan's prime minister, cooperative and was sympathetic to his situation.[77] Later that year Menzies had another tilt at this windmill by again offering his services to both prime ministers. Nehru's reply, while polite, was verging on the irritable.[78] The high commission's comment was that the ultimate responsibility for the deadlock over Kashmir remained with India, but there did not appear to be any Indian policy in place to meet the consequences of an inevitable future breakdown in the truce.[79]

---

72   Nehru admitted as much himself in a letter to his sister. See: Nehru to Vijaya Lakshmi, 13 February 1957, Nehru Memorial Museum and Library (NMML): Vijaya Lakshmi Pandit Papers, subject file, No. 50.

73   Stuart was official secretary to the High Commission in New Delhi at the time of the Dixon mission.

74   Stuart, *Towards Coming of Age*, 157.

75   Menzies observed in a cable to Sid Holland, prime minister of New Zealand, on 28 December 1950: 'This Kashmir business dominates all political thinking in Pakistan and a good deal of it in India. Unless it is settled, we … will be grievously weakened in the Middle East in the event of a great war'. NAA: A1838, 169/11/148/1.

76   Krishna Menon read out Nehru's account of this meeting in the Security Council debate on Kashmir in 1957. See: United Nations, Security Council Official Records, 764th Meeting, 24 January 1957, UN Doc S/PV.764. Further details can be found in Gopal, *Jawaharlal Nehru*, vol. 2, 113.

77   Menzies to Acheson, 24 January 1951, NAA: A1838, 169/11/148/1, cited in Meg Gurry, 'Leadership and Bilateral Relations: Menzies and Nehru, Australia and India, 1949–1964', *Pacific Affairs* 65, no. 4 (1992): 517, doi.org/10.2307/2760317.

78   Nehru to Menzies, 20 June 1951, NAA: TS169/11/148/12, Part 1.

79   Cable 213, Australian High Commission: New Delhi to Department of External Affairs, 19 July 1951, NAA: TS169/11/148/12, Part 1.

Conclusion

Gollan's appointment had begun in the last months of the Chifley Government. Evatt had been active in moving Australia to greater involvement with India and with regional issues, and both he and Chifley, however reluctantly, had played a major role in the negotiations to bring India into the Commonwealth as a republic. These negotiations had made Nehru question the extent to which Australia was locked into patterns of thinking dominated by colonial attitudes, just as the critical attitude of the Australian press towards the Indonesian conference in New Delhi had made him initially suspicious of Australia. Had Labor been returned in the 1949 election, developing a 'close friendship with India' would not have been straightforward.

By the time of Gollan's recall in 1952, India's non-alignment had been challenged by the progress of the Korean War. Nehru was disliked by all sides in the conflict and not trusted by the Chinese. His refusal to sign the Japanese Peace Treaty in 1951 on the grounds that an Asian country was still occupied by foreign powers had irritated the Americans who saw it as an attempt to dislodge Japan from the Western alliance.[80] Further, India's attitude to the Kashmir dispute had annoyed the Western powers that saw this potential flashpoint as a problem in securing southern Asia against communist advances.

The attitude of the Menzies Government towards India was coloured by the failure of the Dixon mission and by an impetus to line up with United States policies in the Cold War. Similarly, Indian views of Australia began to deteriorate. It became focused on its pan-Asian and global roles, and became more assertive in its non-alignment policy, leaving little room for a friendship with Australia to blossom. The sympathy that had existed between the two countries during Mackay's tenure and at the start of Gollan's term steadily dissipated during the early 1950s, leaving the relationship in unstable terrain.

---

80   Gopal, *Jawaharlal Nehru*, vol. 2, 137–38.

2

Two Conferences on Asian Matters in New Delhi

Julie Suares

This chapter examines Australia's diplomatic representation in India with a focus on two conferences on Asian matters—the 1947 Asian Relations Conference in New Delhi and the 1949 New Delhi Conference on Indonesia. These were two defining moments in Australia's early engagement with India that reveal a growing awareness by the Chifley Government of Australia's regional identity and the need to understand and accommodate 'Asian nationalism, non-alignment and incipient trends towards regionalism'.[1] Australia's attendance at these conferences was significant; an indication that the government understood that momentous change was occurring in the postwar world and that the old colonial order was ending in Asia. It was evident that by the end of the war the Labor Government's approach to foreign policy had undergone a fundamental change. As E.J. Williams, the United Kingdom's high commissioner in Canberra remarked in a 1946 report on Australian foreign policy, in the past:

> Australia was prepared to follow the lead of the United Kingdom
> on all major issues of foreign policy and to accept in principle that
> … the initiative in foreign affairs should come from London.[2]

---

1   David Lee, 'Indonesia's Independence', in David Goldsworthy (ed.), *Facing North, a Century of Australian Engagement with Asia,* vol. 1, *1901 to the 1970s* (Carlton South: Melbourne University Press, 2001), 134.
2   Cited in Christopher Waters, 'Australia, the British Empire and the Second World War', *War & Society* 19, no. 1 (2001): 100, doi.org/10.1179/072924701791201620.

In contrast, the Chifley Government and Dr Herbert Vere Evatt, as minister for external affairs, were determined to 'create a more activist and forceful style of foreign policy for Australia' in its own region.[3] The idea of closer engagement with Asia at a governmental level was 'barely on the agenda before World War II'.[4] However, the dismantling of the European colonial world order meant that Australia needed to 'engage with its region to all intents and purposes for the first time'.[5] There was an urgent need for intelligence about Australia's Asian neighbours and, in particular, on developments in Indonesia where a nationalist independence movement had developed. On 17 August 1945, two days after Japan surrendered, Sukarno and Mohammed Hatta proclaimed an independent Indonesian Republic. The Netherlands, with a national income reliant on the wealth obtained from the 'economic exploitation' of the Indies, refused to accept its loss of sovereignty.[6] Chifley was highly critical of Dutch colonialism in Indonesia. As he told journalists in October 1945, Dutch policy evidently was to let others 'do the reconquest and then step in and resume possession' of their former colony.[7]

Needing more information about its region, political scientist, academic, journalist and author, William Macmahon Ball, was appointed Australia's political representative to the commander of the Allied Forces in the Netherlands East Indies.[8] Ball had been a radio broadcaster with the Australian Broadcasting Commission since 1934.[9] He became a popular authority on Asia and international affairs and Prime Minister J.B. Chifley was one of his 'keenest listeners'.[10] Ball travelled to Batavia in early November 1945. His role was to gain firsthand intelligence on the situation in Indonesia. He was to determine 'how far the Republic was a genuine nationalist movement and to assess the calibre of the Republican leaders'.[11] In his reports from Batavia, Ball dismissed British

---

3   Christopher Waters, 'War, Decolonisation and Postwar Security', in Goldsworthy, *Facing North*, 108.

4   David Goldsworthy, 'Introduction,' in Goldsworthy, *Facing North*, 9.

5   Joost Cote, 'Review: Redefining the History of Australia's Asianness', *Asian Ethnology* 67, no. 1 (2008): 142.

6   Lee, 'Indonesia's Independence', 135–36.

7   Harold Cox Reports, 12 October 1945, National Library of Australia (NLA): MS 4554.

8   Philip Dorling (ed.), *Documents on Australian Foreign Policy (DAFP) 1937–49, Diplomasi: Australia & Indonesia's Independence*, vol. 1, *Documents 1947* (Canberra: Australian Government Publishing Service, 1994), xiii.

9   Ai Kobayashi, *W. Macmahon Ball: Politics for the People* (North Melbourne: Australian Scholarly Publishing, 2013), 46.

10   'In Canberra Today', *Cairns Post*, 31 May 1948, 5.

11   Dorling, *Diplomasi*, vol. 1, xiii.

intelligence because it was reliant on Dutch information, which was mere 'propaganda'.[12] He believed that if the Dutch returned to reoccupy Java under the protection of the British military, 'unlimited trouble' would result. Indonesian nationalist opposition to Dutch reoccupation was extensive.[13] Intelligence obtained from Ball's mission to Batavia, plus subsequent information gathered at the Asian Relations Conference, together with reports of the situation on the ground by Australian diplomats stationed in Indonesia, meant that Australia, together with India, would mobilise the United Nations in support of the Indonesian Republic.[14]

Chifley believed that India would be the 'leader of the Asian peoples' in the postwar world.[15] In 1947, the Australian Government supported independence for India and Chifley would play an important role at the 1949 Commonwealth Prime Ministers' Conference in facilitating the process whereby the Commonwealth was able to accommodate a republican India.[16] In addition, Chifley and Indian Prime Minister Jawaharlal Nehru agreed on the best ways to counter the spread of communism in Asia, believing that political reform and improved living standards, rather than a military response, was required.[17]

The Australian Government's support for the Indonesian Republic in its struggle for independence demonstrated its ability to respond positively to the decolonisation of Asia. But the international conferences of the decolonising peoples of Asia were a significant challenge to the government. These meetings raised the question of whether Australia should attend, and in what capacity—as observers or participants. In 1947, Australia's representation at the Asian Relations Conference in New Delhi was unofficial. An early example of public diplomacy, the representatives

---

12 Ball to Burton, 17 November 1945, in WJ Hudson and Wendy Way (eds), *DAFP 1937–49*, vol. 8, *1945* (Canberra: Australian Government Publishing Service, 1989), 620.

13 Ball to Burton, 22 November 1945, in Hudson and Way, *DAFP* vol. 8, 628–29.

14 Philip Dorling and David Lee (eds), *Documents on Australian Foreign Policy (DAFP) 1937–49, Diplomasi: Australia & Indonesia's Independence*, vol. 2, *Australia and Indonesia's Independence: The Renville Agreement: Documents 1948* (Canberra: AGPS, 1996), ix.

15 LF Crisp, *Ben Chifley: A Biography* (London: Longmans, 1963), 285. For an illustration of Chifley's longstanding interest in India, see: Ivan Chapman, *Iven G. Mackay: Citizen and Soldier* (Melbourne: Melway Publishing, 1975), 301.

16 Frank Bongiorno, 'British to the Bootstraps? H.V. Evatt, J.B. Chifley and Australian Policy on Indian Membership of the Commonwealth, 1947–49' *Australian Historical Studies* 36, no. 125 (2005): 38–39, doi.org/10.1080/10314610508682909.

17 Crisp, *Ben Chifley*, 292.

were appointed by non-government organisations. These observers were, however, given significant support behind the scenes by the Australian High Commission in New Delhi. In 1949, career diplomats represented the Australian Government at the New Delhi Conference on Indonesia.

The Asian Relations Conference, New Delhi: 23 March – 2 April 1947

The 1947 Asian Relations Conference was a major event in Asia. It was—as Nehru stated—a landmark occasion, in which 'Asia, after a long period of quiescence, has suddenly become important again in world affairs'.[18] An 'initiative' of Nehru, the conference was convened in 1947 by the Indian Council of World Affairs (ICWA).[19] Its purpose was to consider the economic, social and cultural problems common to all postwar Asian countries.[20] The most important issue was how to end the foreign domination of Asia, both politically and economically.[21] At first, it was thought the conference should be restricted to South-East Asian countries, but, eventually, it was decided that all Asian countries be invited to send delegates from cultural institutions, individual scholars and government observers.[22] The following countries sent delegations: Afghanistan, Armenia, Azerbaijan, Bhutan, Burma, Cambodia (including Cochin-China and Laos), Ceylon, China, Egypt, Georgia, India, Indonesia, Iran, Kazakhstan, Kirghizia, Korea, Malaya, Mongolia, Nepal, Hebrew University–Palestine, the Philippines, Siam, Tajikistan, Tibet, Turkey, Turkmenistan, Uzbekistan and Viet Nam.

Observers from the Arab League and the United Nations organisation were also invited.[23] In addition, a number of 'non-Asian countries including Australia, New Zealand, Britain, the U.S.A. and the Soviet Union' were invited to send representatives from cultural organisations.[24]

---

18 *Asian Relations: Being Report of the Proceedings and Documentation of the First Asian Relations Conference, New Delhi, March–April, 1947* (New Delhi: Asian Relations Organization, 1948), 21.
19 G Packer and JA McCallum, 'Australian Observers' Report on Asian Relations Conference, New Delhi - March 1947', National Archives of Australia (NAA): A1068, M47/9/6/15 PART 3, p. 1.
20 *Asian Relations*, 3.
21 Ibid., 1.
22 Ibid., 4–6.
23 Ibid., 8.
24 Ibid., 5

They were given the 'status of observers'.[25] The New Zealand Institute of International Affairs also received an invitation, but decided against sending an observer to the conference.[26]

On 2 January 1947, the Department of External Affairs (DEA) informed Dr Evatt that the Australian Institute of International Affairs (AIIA) and the Australian Institute of Political Science (AIPS) intended to accept the ICWA's invitation to attend the Asian Relations Conference and had requested financial support from the Australian Government to cover costs. The department thought it 'very desirable that these Australian organisations should be represented by observers', because, firstly, the conference, although unofficial, was 'undoubtedly regarded as important by the Indian Government', and secondly, the 'Conference should provide considerable information regarding the prevailing political trends in Asia'. The observers would be required to provide full reports on the conference 'which would be of great value to the Department'. The DEA emphasised that financial assistance from the Commonwealth did not change the status of the observers, who would be representatives of their respective organisations and not the Australian Government.[27]

The DEA's anxiety about the status of observers arose from its fear that Australia would be targeted because of its White Australia policy. Canberra wanted to 'avoid the risk of a government official being stood against the wall on the White Australia policy or something of that kind'.[28] At the same time, the department wanted to ensure that the observers were provided with all the support they required. The secretary of the DEA emphasised that the Commonwealth Government wanted to assist the observers in every way and would ask the Australian high commissioner in New Delhi, former soldier and university lecturer, Sir Iven Mackay, to provide this support.[29] Colin Moodie, secretary to the high commissioner, was informed that the 'Minister himself is most anxious that your office should keep the closest watch on the Conference and report precisely on it'. Moodie should probably have regarded it as close to a full-time job because of the quality of reporting expected. He was asked to 'protect' and

25   Ibid., 6.
26   Cable 5, Australian High Commissioner in Wellington to Department of External Affairs (DEA), 'Inter-Asian Conference', 9 January 1947, NAA: A1068, M47/9/6/15 PART 1.
27   DEA for the Minister, 2 January 1947, ibid.
28   DEA to CT Moodie, 4 February 1947, ibid.
29   Secretary of the DEA to Chair of the AIIA and to FR Barraclough (two letters), 8 January 1947, ibid.

'assist' the observers and a full report was expected from him.[30] Moodie would be detached from his other duties to allow him to review the conference, as 'its proceedings are bound to be very important'.[31]

AIPS chose John McCallum to represent it at the conference.[32] 'Kindly, quiet and scholarly', McCallum was a history lecturer and former schoolteacher. He was also a well-known international affairs commentator and frequent contributor to the AIPS journal, *The Australian Quarterly*.[33] Previously a leading figure in the Australian Labor Party—a man of 'high intellectual attainments', according to Chifley[34]—he had changed his political allegiance to become a founding member of the Liberal Party in 1944.[35] The AIIA chose as their representative Gerald Packer, former army and air force officer, businessman and adviser to the government. Packer was vice-president of the AIIA in 1946 and served as associate editor on the institute's journal, *Australian Outlook*.[36] He was also a member of the Round Table group,[37] as was McCallum.[38] Packer thought the assignment promised to be a 'sticky one'.[39]

The conference opened on Sunday, 23 March 1947, in 'spectacular fashion in a huge pandal [marquee] within the walls of the Purana Qila (Old Fort), New Delhi'. There were 230 delegates and 10,000 visitors at the first plenary session.[40] According to the Australian observers, Nehru delivered a very 'impressive' speech, the most 'significant part' of the opening ceremony.[41] The conference combined a 'mass appeal' to Asian nationalism, together with 'expert' deliberation in discussion groups on problems of common concern.[42] A number of practical suggestions from the discussion group on 'Cultural Problems' were noted to be of interest and worthy of consideration by Australian institutions, including

---

30 DEA to Moodie, 4 February 1947, ibid.
31 Cable 70, DEA to Australian High Commissioner in New Delhi, 5 March 1947, ibid.
32 FR Barraclough to Secretary of the DEA, 21 January 1947, ibid.
33 Michael Easson, 'McCallum, John Archibald (1892–1973)', *Australian Dictionary of Biography*, vol 15, *1940–1980* (Carlton South: Melbourne University Press, 2000), 164–65.
34 'Australian Labor – What It Stands for – the Martin Campaign Opened by Mr. J. B. Chifley', *National Advocate*, 30 June 1934, 1.
35 Easson, 'McCallum, John Archibald (1892–1973)', 164–65.
36 CD Coulthard-Clark, 'Packer, Gerald (1900–1962)', *Australian Dictionary of Biography*, vol. 15, 556–57.
37 Ibid., 557.
38 Easson, 'McCallum, John Archibald (1892–1973)', 164.
39 Gerald Packer to Peter Heydon, 7 February 1947, NAA: A1068, M47/9/6/15, PART 1.
40 Packer and McCallum, 'Australian Observers' Report', 6.
41 Ibid., 7.
42 Ibid., 2.

the appointment of teachers of Asian languages and the establishment of scholarships for foreign students.[43] The 'lines of cleavage' between South-East Asian countries and the emergent powers, India and China, were also very evident in the discussion group on 'Racial Problems and Inter-Asian Migration'.[44] Delegates were urged by the chair to avoid politeness when discussing issues such as the situation of Indian immigrants in Burma and Ceylon and Chinese immigrants in Malaya, Burma and Indonesia. It was very clear that there was resistance to Chinese and Indian immigration in South-East Asia.[45]

Hostile criticism of the White Australia policy was also expected at the conference by both the Australian Government and the Australian press.[46] The government had been warned repeatedly by diplomats and departmental officers of the resentment incurred by the policy,[47] but, according to the observers' report, Australian immigration policy was mentioned only once and was not contested. The report noted that the right of all countries to 'determine the future composition of their population was freely admitted and emphasized', and a quota system was advocated by some delegates. It was stressed, however, that any total exclusion of peoples of an Asian country would create ill feeling.[48] Although Australia escaped criticism at the conference, McCallum warned that it was a mistake to assume that the White Australia policy did not cause great offence.[49]

Significance of the 1947 Asian Relations Conference

The Asian Relations Conference generated a massive amount of information that had previously not been available in Australia. In his report to the DEA, Colin Moodie wrote that a 'steady bombardment of cables, Rapporteurs' Reports and newspaper articles' was sent from the

---

43   Ibid., 13.
44   Cable 138, Australian High Commissioner to unknown [Letter incomplete, probably to Min & DEA], 'Asian Relations Conference', 26 March 1947, NAA: A1068, M47/9/6/15 PART 1.
45   JA McCallum, 'The Asian Relations Conference', *The Australian Quarterly* 19, no. 2 (1947): 16–17, doi.org/10.2307/20631455.
46   Memorandum, McMillan per Secretary of the DEA to Secretary of the Department of Immigration, 19 December 1946, NAA: A433, 1950/2/1570; 'Inter-Asian Conference', *The Argus,* 15 February 1947, NAA: A1068, M47/9/6/15, PART 1.
47   Including Sir Iven Mackay, who was 'known to favour a quota system'. See Chapman, *Iven G. Mackay,* 296.
48   Packer and McCallum, 'Australian Observers' Report', 13–15.
49   McCallum, 'The Asian Relations Conference', 17.

office of the Australian high commissioner in New Delhi to the DEA.[50] Each discussion group had a 'highly qualified' expert or rapporteur who presented their report to a plenary session on that topic, summing up the discussion and the conclusions reached by the group.[51] These reports provided a representative section of 'Asian informed opinion upon Asian problems'.[52] The conference also presented opportunities for the Australian observers to meet and observe significant and influential Asian nationalist leaders. McCallum wrote that he had many opportunities to observe Nehru, the 'author, architect and presiding genius of the Conference'.[53]

> He spoke with great dignity, clarity and force without the slightest suggestion of artificiality. His oratory was that kind of elevated conversation which holds and convinces, and charms like Kreisler's playing. His manner in public and private is that of a great gentleman—an aristocrat and yet the kind of man we call Nature's gentleman—a polished diamond yet with the merits we imply when we call a man a 'rough diamond'.[54]

In addition, special attention was paid to the views of the Indonesian delegation.[55] According to Packer and McCallum, Indonesian Prime Minister Sutan Sjahrir gave a 'very statesmanlike' address[56] that 'indicated a sagacious outlook on foreign affairs'.[57]

Although patronising and caustic at times, the Australian observers' report provided important information about conditions in Asia. On reading this report, and, in particular, the accompanying rapporteurs' reports on the discussion groups, the great diversity in the 'political, social and economic development of the various Asian countries' was very evident.[58] Conference delegations were, however, united in their condemnation of 'political and economic imperialism' and their demand for the total withdrawal of the old European colonial powers from Asia.[59] Yet, while

---

50 Iven Mackay to Evatt, 16 April 1947, Moodie – 'Report on Asian Relations Conference, 23 March–2 April, 1947', NAA: A1068, M47/9/6/15 PART 2, p. 1.
51 Packer and McCallum, 'Australian Observers' Report', 2.
52 Gerald Packer, 'The Asian Relations Conference: The Group Discussions', *Australian Outlook* 1, no. 2 (1947): 4, doi.org/10.1080/00049914708565300.
53 McCallum, 'The Asian Relations Conference', 13.
54 JA McCallum 'Personalities at the Asian Relations Conference', *The Australian Quarterly* 19, no. 3 (1947): 43.
55 Iven Mackay to Evatt, 16 April 1947, Moodie – 'Report on Asian Relations Conference', 2.
56 Packer and McCallum, 'Australian Observers' Report', 4.
57 Ibid., 10.
58 Ibid., 25–26.
59 Ibid., 17.

the discussion group on 'National Movements for Freedom' generated a 'strong emotional reaction' that was 'anti-European, anti-American and possibly anti-Russian',[60] differences between South-East Asian countries and India and China were also apparent. It was feared that India and China would supplant the Western imperialists to become the new 'Imperialist powers exploiting Southeast Asia'.[61]

Throughout the conference, the Australian observers had also detected an 'undercurrent of distrust of Russia',[62] which, together with the United States, was one of the 'nascent Imperialisms' to be avoided.[63] This distrust challenged the view that Russian influence and communist agitation were the driving forces behind Asian nationalist movements. This intelligence informed and supported Chifley's belief that nationalist aspirations throughout Asia were real and deep-seated, and could not be ignored.[64] Further, it provided supporting evidence for the Australian Government's decision to back the Indonesian Republic in its struggle against the Netherlands, after the Dutch launched their first 'police action' or military offensive at midnight on 20 July 1947.[65]

On 30 July 1947, Australia, together with India, referred the Indonesian conflict to the United Nations Security Council. Australia's submission was given priority because it was stronger, in that it alleged that the peace had been breached.[66] The Chifley Government requested council intervention under Article 39 of the United Nations Charter, the first instance that the article had been used and the 'first ever ceasefire resolution adopted by the Security Council'.[67] This was the start of a combined effort 'by two smaller powers, Australia and India', to mobilise the United Nations 'to protect the beleaguered Indonesian Republic'.[68] The Chifley Government's actions were opposed, however, by the British Government, which supported the Netherlands, a 'fellow colonial power'.[69] The Australian Government

---

60   Ibid., 25.
61   Ibid., 17.
62   Ibid., 26.
63   Ibid., 11.
64   Commonwealth, *Parliamentary Debates*, House of Representatives, 2 September 1948, 66, 'Governor-General's Speech' (B Chifley MP).
65   Lee, 'Indonesia's Independence', 154.
66   Dorling and Lee, *Diplomasi*, vol. 2, x.
67   David Lee, 'Australia and the Security Council', in James Cotton and David Lee (eds), *Australia and the United Nations* (Canberra: Department of Foreign Affairs and Trade, 2012), 70.
68   Lee, 'Indonesia's Independence', 154.
69   Lee, 'Australia and the Security Council', 70.

justified its action because of the 'very great importance of accepting [the] challenge put forward by Asiatic peoples' and because 'Australia's geographical position must always be kept in mind'.[70]

The situation in Indonesia became increasingly volatile as negotiations dragged on. Economically, the naval blockade imposed by the Dutch was having a devastating impact on Indonesia.[71] In November 1948, Chifley informed Evatt that the government had received reports from Java that the Dutch were preparing to launch a second military offensive against the Republic. An irate and exasperated Chifley wrote that if the United Kingdom and the United States had been more forceful earlier on in pressuring the Dutch, a settlement might well have been reached. However, they had 'held off because of the position of the Netherlands in Western Union'.[72] The Australian Government's intelligence proved to be accurate, with the Dutch unleashing a second brutal military offensive against the Indonesian Republic on 18 December 1948.[73] Chifley acted swiftly, issuing a press statement that condemned the Dutch action[74] and Australia charged the Netherlands with carrying out the first outright violation of the United Nations Charter, the consequence of which, if the Security Council deemed it so, would be expulsion from the United Nations.[75] However, the Security Council's response was weak and ineffectual. This led Nehru to propose a conference be held in New Delhi, at ministerial level, in January 1949. The Indian Government hoped that the Chifley Government would 'respond favourably' to this proposal.[76]

Chifley, who was acting minister for external affairs, thought it 'only logical and reasonable' for Australia to accept the invitation to join such a conference, but believed there were certain 'political considerations' to weigh.[77] These included concerns that Australia would be perceived as 'ganging up' against Britain, America, the Netherlands and other western European powers, with Asian countries pursuing extremist agendas. In addition, the government was apprehensive that the conference would seek to override the Security Council when its longstanding position

70   Cable 194, Australian Government to Addison, 25 July 1947, in Dorling, *Diplomasi*, vol. 1, 154.
71   Cable 38, DEA to Officer, 20 May 1948, in Dorling and Lee, *Diplomasi*, vol. 2, 164.
72   Cable E.90, Chifley to Evatt, 3 November 1948, in ibid., 347–48.
73   Lee, 'Indonesia's Independence', 164.
74   Press Statement by Chifley, 21 December 1948, in Dorling and Lee, *Diplomasi*, vol. 2, 461.
75   Cable 281, Hodgson to DEA, 23 December 1948, in ibid., 495.
76   Cable 1, Kevin to DEA, 1 January 1949, in David Lee (ed.), *DAFP 1937–49*, vol. 15, *Indonesia, 1949* (Canberra: Department of Foreign Affairs and Trade, 1998), 1.
77   Cable E128, DEA to Evatt, 31 December 1948, in Dorling and Lee, *Diplomasi*, vol. 2, 553.

was that all disputes should be settled within the framework of the United Nations.[78] However, Chifley was 'characteristically definite' that Australia should attend the conference and would not be budged from this decision.[79]

On 1 January 1949, Australia was invited to attend the New Delhi Conference on Indonesia. Nehru was convinced that the Dutch would continue their military aggression against the Republic. The Indonesian cause would be assisted, however, if 'interested governments in the region' considered what steps they could take to assist the Security Council to deal with Dutch intransigence and refusal to adhere to United Nations proposals to settle the Indonesian dispute in a just manner. The conference was in no way designed to supplant the authority of the Security Council; its aim was to assist the council through the special understanding of the region possessed by those countries attending the conference.[80] Nehru 'desired particularly' to emphasise that 'communists cannot be permitted to be [the] sole protagonist of the Indonesian case'.[81] Twenty countries were invited, including 'Australia, New Zealand, Afghanistan, Persia, Egypt, Burma, Nepal, Pakistan, the Philippines, Ceylon, Saudi Arabia, Iraq, Syria, Lebanon, the Yemen, Ethiopia, Transjordan, China, Siam, and Turkey'. Only Turkey declined the invitation.[82] Britain was not invited, because the Soviet Union would then have to be issued an invitation as well.[83]

On 5 January 1949, the Australian Government announced that two senior officers of the DEA would attend the New Delhi conference. These officers were the secretary of the DEA, Dr John Burton, and career diplomat, Colin Moodie, both of whom would report the views of the conference to the Australian Government.[84] The status of the Australian representatives would depend on the situation at the time of the conference.[85] The office of the Australian high commissioner in New Delhi was also asked to convey a message from Chifley to Nehru that,

78   Cable 2, Burton to Gollan, 7 January 1949, in Lee, *DAFP 1937–49*, vol. 15, 32–33.
79   Cable E8, Burton to Evatt, 9 January 1949, in ibid., 47–48.
80   Cable 1, Kevin to DEA, 1 January 1949, in ibid., 1.
81   Cable 10, Kevin to DEA, 6 January 1949, in ibid., 30.
82   'Full Powers at Delhi – Australia's Position', *The Sydney Morning Herald*, 19 January 1949, NAA: A1838, 383/1/2/5.
83   Cable 27, Australian High Commission in New Delhi to DEA, 11 January 1949, in Lee, *DAFP 1937–49*, vol. 15, 61.
84   Press Release, 'Proposed Asian Conference', 5 January 1949, NAA: A1838, 401/3/1/1 PART 6.
85   Letter, Burton to Bedi, 4 January 1949, in Lee, *DAFP 1937–49*, vol. 15, 9.

although the government was not able to send a minister of Cabinet rank, the prime minister would be 'following developments at the Conference with the closest attention and interest'.[86] Sir Girja Shankar Bajpai was secretary-general of India's Ministry of External Affairs. Nehru valued Bajpai's candour and his expertise, and referred to him as his 'tower of strength'.[87] Bajpai had wanted Evatt to attend the conference, possibly as a 'draw-card'. He was satisfied, however, when it was pointed out that the Australian representatives' positions were as senior as his own.[88] There had been some concern in Canberra that Australia had been 'singled out as the only white nation invited to the Conference'. This was incorrect. Bajpai assured the government that 'racialism' did not play any part in India's selection of countries to attend the conference. India was 'primarily influenced by geography', which is why Australia and New Zealand had been invited.[89]

In contrast to the Australian Government, which avoided the use of 'observer', instead emphasising the 'official status' of Burton and Moodie,[90] the New Zealand Government stressed that their representative would attend the conference strictly as an observer.[91] This question of status, whether the Australian representatives were 'observers' or 'participants', took on considerable importance in both India and in Australia. In New Delhi, the effectiveness of Australia's contribution to the conference hinged on this issue. Although Nehru 'greatly appreciated' the Australian Government's decision to send representatives, he was concerned that criticism of his motives in Australia had been reported in the Indian press.[92] Thus, Burton and Moodie were initially received 'on trial and with the greatest reserve' by Nehru. According to Burton, this was due to extensive coverage in the Indian media of domestic criticism in the Australian press concerning Australia's presence and status at the conference and harsh comments by the Menzies Opposition 'regarding Asiatics as being Communist inspired'.[93]

---

86   Cable 3, DEA to Kevin, 5 January 1949, in ibid., 20.
87   Srinath Raghavan, *War and Peace in Modern India* (Basingstoke: Palgrave Macmillan, 2010), 21, doi.org/10.1057/9780230277519.
88   Cable 16, Kevin to Burton, 7 January 1949, in Lee, *DAFP 1937–49*, vol. 15, 36.
89   Cable 14, Australian High Commission in New Delhi to DEA, 7 January 1949, NAA: A1838, 383/1/2/5.
90   Cable 46, Burton to Evatt, 18 January 1949, in Lee, *DAFP 1937–49*, vol. 15, 102–3.
91   Cable 26, McIntosh to Burton, 19 January 1949, in ibid., 104.
92   Cable 10, Kevin to DEA, 6 January 1949, in ibid., 30.
93   Burton to Evatt, Memorandum for the Minister, 'Asian Conference on Indonesia', 26 January 1949, in ibid., 155.

The New Delhi Conference on Indonesia, 20–23 January 1949

Australia was one of 15 countries with full powers attending the conference, while four nations, New Zealand, Siam, Nepal and China, sent observers.[94] In an informal meeting at Prime Minister Nehru's home, the evening before the conference began,[95] the heads of delegations, together with observers, met to discuss conference procedures.[96] The Australians put forward their proposals and, in the absence of any other suggestions, these were accepted.[97] The Indian high commissioner in Canberra, Lieutenant-Colonel D.S. Bedi, had earlier asked the DEA for advice on conference procedure. The department had suggested that a 'precise programme' be adopted, based on British Commonwealth conference procedures, which also sought to discover the views of all participants and avoid any vote. A 'composite statement' would then be drafted and sent to the Security Council as a unanimous proposal. The DEA advised that the council and Western countries might be watching for any signs of discord or delay to discredit 'effective Asian regional consultation in the future'. Therefore, a 'positive' approach was needed, rather than a 'vindictive' one. A unanimous statement reached after a meeting of two or three days using British Commonwealth conference procedures would 'cut the ground' from any criticism of the conference.[98]

At the opening plenary session on 20 January, Australia and New Zealand received a special welcome from Nehru, countries 'whose interest in tranquillity and content in Indonesia' was as great as any country present at the conference. Burton informed Chifley and Evatt that Nehru's speech established the 'tone for temperate discussion'. Nehru declared that the conference should focus on Indonesia and not be diverted to other situations. It was agreed that the conflict had to be settled by the Security Council or, if it refused to act, through discussions with those countries who were involved in the dispute. Burton wrote that Nehru wanted

---

94   'Full Powers at Delhi – Australia's Position', *The Sydney Morning Herald*, 19 January 1949, NAA: A1838, 383/1/2/5.

95   Burton to Evatt, Memorandum for the Minister, 'Asian Conference on Indonesia', in Lee, *DAFP 1937–49*, vol. 15, 155.

96   Cable 53, Burton to Prime Minister and Minister and DEA, 19 January 1949, in ibid., 107.

97   Burton to Evatt, Memorandum for the Minister, 'Asian Conference on Indonesia', in ibid., 155.

98   Cable 13, DEA to Australian High Commission in New Delhi, 10 January 1949, in ibid., 53–54.

'concrete results' and there was little emotional outpouring or anti-Dutch rhetoric.[99] After observing that other delegates were participating, Burton decided it was appropriate for him to contribute to the discussion.[100] He declared that the Australian Government would take the earliest opportunity to consider the reports it received at the conclusion of the conference. There was little he could add to Prime Minister Nehru's opening address, which was very much in harmony with the sentiments of the Australian Government.

Burton argued that the conference could make a real contribution to solving the Indonesian dispute. Wisdom did not rest solely with those countries with 'great economic and military power'. The countries gathered together in New Delhi had a 'special knowledge' of the region and therefore had a duty to advise the United Nations. He added that Australia had, from the start, attempted to find a solution to the Indonesian conflict. Burton declared: 'We will not rest content until peace is restored'.[101] The Australian high commissioner in New Delhi, Roy Gollan, reported there had been a very favourable response to Burton's speech; the reaction from foreign and local sources and from journalists, suggested a 'good impression has been created by Australia'.[102] By the time the private session was held that night, Burton wrote that it was obvious that the Australian representatives were 'fully accepted'.[103] This meeting was the 'most remarkable attempt to deal with the subject matter objectively and on [the] basis of facts'. Nehru showed extensive knowledge of the situation and a common-sense approach to the issue was very evident.[104]

In a significant move, Australia, India, Pakistan and Ceylon—all members of the Commonwealth—were appointed to a Drafting Committee to draw up recommendations for the Security Council to aid in finding an early settlement of the Indonesian conflict.[105] The committee's three resolutions were agreed to at a private meeting on 22 January and presented at the

99 Cable 58, Burton to Prime Minister, Minister and DEA, 20 January 1949, in ibid., 126–27.
100 Burton to Evatt, Memorandum for the Minister, 'Asian Conference on Indonesia', in ibid., 155.
101 Speech by Burton at New Delhi Conference, '"Grave Mistakes" In Indonesia', 20 January 1949, in ibid., 112–13.
102 Cable 56, Australian High Commission in New Delhi to Prime Minister, Minister & DEA, 20 January 1949, in ibid., 125.
103 Burton to Evatt, Memorandum for the Minister, 'Asian Conference on Indonesia', in ibid., 155.
104 Cable 61, Burton to Prime Minister, Minister and DEA, 'Asian Conference', 21 January 1949, in ibid., 129–30.
105 'Key Role for Australia—Indonesian Talks', *The Sydney Morning Herald,* 22 January 1949, NAA: A1838, 383/1/2/5.

plenary session the following day.[106] All delegates regarded their approval of the resolutions as 'ad referendum' to be forwarded to the Security Council and to their representative governments for approval.[107] On 25 and 27 January 1949, Australia, India and the Indonesian Republic urged the Security Council to include the first resolution from the New Delhi conference in a draft resolution that had been put forward by the United States, China, Cuba and Norway. An amended resolution was subsequently put to the Security Council.[108] On 28 January 1949, the United States was able to gain majority support in the Security Council for a joint resolution. The main recommendations called for elections for a Constituent Assembly of Indonesia to be held by 1 October 1949 and the full transfer of sovereignty to the United States of Indonesia by 1 July 1950.[109]

Significance of the 1949 New Delhi Conference

The 'display of Asian unity' and the 'world-wide media attention' that the conference received[110] exerted pressure on the United States, which previously had been much more concerned to keep its European allies on side and saw Asia not on its own terms, but through the Cold War filter of American–Soviet relations. Because of popular support for the republicans, American policy became more supportive of the Indonesians.[111] And just over four years after the declaration of the Republic, Indonesia would win its independence.[112] Although a small to medium power with little influence on the world stage, Australia's presence at the conference and the work of diplomats such as Burton and Moodie was recognised. *The New York Times* noted the 'moderating influence of Prime Minister, Nehru,

---

106 Cable 73, Burton to Minister and DEA, 'Asian Conference', 22 January 1949, in Lee, *DAFP 1937–49*, vol. 15, 138–39.

107 Cable 75, Burton to Prime Minister, Minister and DEA, 23 January 1949, in ibid., 143.

108 Margaret George, *Australia and the Indonesian Revolution* (Carlton: Melbourne University Press, 1980), 132.

109 Lee, *DAFP 1937–49*, vol. 15, xiv.

110 Julie Suares, 'Engaging with Asia: The Chifley Government and the New Delhi Conferences of 1947 and 1949', *Australian Journal of Politics and History* 57, no. 4 (2011): 507, doi.org/10.1111/j.1467-8497.2011.01610.x.

111 TK Critchley, 'View from the Good Offices Committee', in John Legge (ed.), *New Directions in Australian Foreign Policy: Australia and Indonesia 1945–50* (Clayton: Monash Asia Institute, 1997), 71.

112 Lee, 'Indonesia's Independence', 169.

of India and the Australian delegate, J. W. Burton'.[113] For Burton, the conference itself was even more important than the Indonesian problem it was considering. It showed that Australia could work with this group of countries; they were eager and keen to work with Australia and would do so in accordance with the United Nations Charter. Burton wrote that no questions of 'national prestige or political ideology' were brought to bear on discussions, which were based on facts and careful deliberation. In future, he thought Australia should be represented at a ministerial level if the government wished to influence this group of nations.[114]

Burton's sentiments were echoed by Roy Gollan and Colin Moodie. Gollan noted that India's request for Australian participation at the conference derived from the close consultation between the two countries regarding initiatives on the Indonesian–Dutch conflict. In addition, Australia's reputation for 'brisk and frank treatment of international issues' was recognised by the Indian Government. Australia's presence was essential in order to prevent the conference from appearing as 'purely an Asian conference', and to avoid any perception of East–West polarity. The high commissioner noted the 'political vacuum' left with the absence of European, and especially British, power in South-East Asia. He suggested this vacuum could be filled by an association of India and Australia.[115] Colin Moodie wrote that the fact that the Australians did not limit their participation to an 'observer status' was proven wise in hindsight. He also commented on the 'moderateness of all delegates', which was attributed to the effectiveness of India's work 'behind the scenes'. According to Moodie, the success of the conference was due to the work of Nehru as chair and Bajpai as the primary adviser. Moodie wrote that 'John Burton made an extremely good impression on Nehru and the other Indians he met'. Their attitudes changed from 'suspicion and caution in the first place' to 'smiles and friendliness at the end'.[116] Burton had also impressed Bajpai, who wrote that he enjoyed meeting Burton and hoped they could work together again in the future.[117]

---

113 Cable 65, Australian Embassy in Washington to Evatt and DEA, 25 January 1949, NAA: A1838, 383/1/2/5.
114 Burton to Evatt, Memorandum for the Minister, 'Asian Conference on Indonesia', in Lee, *DAFP 1937–49*, vol. 15, 157.
115 Gollan to Burton, 'Some Reflections on the Asian Conference', 3 February 1949, in ibid., 185.
116 Letter, Moodie to McIntyre, 17 February 1949, in ibid., 232–35.
117 GS Bajpai, Ministry of External Affairs and Commonwealth Relations, New Delhi, to Burton, 10 February 1949, NAA: A1838, 383/1/2/5.

Conclusion

Representation at the 1947 Asian Relations Conference by unofficial observers from the AIIA and the AIPS meant that the DEA received expert Asian opinion on Asian affairs. An 'intelligence gathering exercise', the conference generated a great deal of information that had previously not been available in Australia. It also provided opportunities for the Australian observers to meet, and convey to the government, their impressions of important Asian nationalist leaders, such as Nehru and Sjahrir. This information no doubt further 'informed and supported Chifley in his resolve to back the Indonesian nationalists in their struggle against the Dutch'.[118] The support provided to the Australian observers in 1947 by Mackay and Moodie pointed to the pivotal role that the Chifley government hoped that Nehru and India would play in ensuring the economic and political security of the region.

Australia, together with India, was excluded from 'effective participation in international relations' because of the power politics deployed by the great powers.[119] The 1949 New Delhi conference provided a forum through which pressure could be applied to the United Nations and the voices of small to medium powers could be heard. Furthermore, the relationships established at the conference promised new possibilities for Australian foreign policy in Asia; in particular, a sound foundation had been laid for a close working relationship with India in the future.[120] Through diplomatic representation at the 1949 New Delhi conference, Australia, together with India and other Asian countries, conveyed to the United Nations Security Council, their 'special knowledge' of the Indo-Pacific region. Thus, Australia, in collaboration with India, contributed to one of the Security Council's 'earliest and most emphatic successes'. Instead of many years of ongoing warfare—as occurred in Indochina—Indonesia achieved independence in December 1949.[121]

---

118 Suares, 'Engaging with Asia', 509.
119 Christopher Waters, *The Empire Fractures: Anglo-Australian Conflict in the 1940s* (Melbourne: Australian Scholarly Publishing, 1995), 166.
120 Meg Gurry, *Australia and India: Mapping the Journey 1944–2014* (Carlton: Melbourne University Press, 2015), 34.
121 Lee, 'Australia and the Security Council', 72; Lee, 'Indonesia's Independence', 169.

3

New Delhi and Canberra in the 1950s

Eric Meadows

By the time of Walter Crocker's appointment as Australian high commissioner to India in 1952, a widening gap was discernible on almost all issues that mattered in New Delhi and in Canberra. India might have been thought of as 'the most important power in Asia'[1] but both countries had fundamentally different views of international communism and its relationship to the nationalist movements in Asia. Any similarity on these matters that might have existed in the heady days following independence in 1947 had entirely gone. By 1952, with a different government in Canberra, attitudes in both India and Australia had hardened and, as Indian foreign policy spokesman Krishna Menon put it, they had 'somewhat drifted apart'.[2] They were to drift further apart with their different views of the utility of military alliances, and as non-alignment developed into an international movement. In addition, Australia's immigration policy became an issue of public controversy during Crocker's posting and the limits of his influence on policy became clear in this matter, as well as on the larger issue of Australia's relations with non-aligned Asia. This chapter explores these points of difference and the dynamic between the high commission under Crocker's leadership and foreign policymakers in Canberra.

---

1   Despatch No. 33, 6 July 1950, National Archives of Australia (NAA): A4231, 1950/New Delhi.
2   Krishna Menon quoted by the India Information Service, welcoming Crocker's appointment, 21 June 1952, NAA: A1838, 169/10/1 PART 2.

Policy towards India

A useful note by the Department of External Affairs in August 1952 succinctly summarised Australian policy in Asia. On India, its intent was blunt:

> To ensure that India does not become aligned with the U.S.S.R. but continues to adopt an independent policy (short range) and is attracted towards active alignment with the Western world (long range).[3]

It added that, to be successful in this objective, there would have to be a settlement of the Kashmir dispute and an improvement in India's relations with Pakistan. Although Pakistan was more ready to cooperate with the West, in the long run India was the more important power, and it was thus important not to cause Indian hostility or to isolate it in the United Nations. While economic assistance should be given in the Colombo Plan, the main effort to keep India on side had to be political.[4]

The Menzies Government was in no doubt that South-East Asia and Australia were in danger from penetration by 'Communist imperialism'.[5] External Affairs Minister Percy Spender, in his important speech in the House of Representatives of 9 March 1950, noted that the objective of the Soviet Union was to achieve world communism by infiltration in all democratic governments. Australia was opposed to any attempt by one country to impose its will on another. As the 'hydraulic' Cold War language of the time put it, the success of the Western democracies in holding a firm front in Europe against communism was partly responsible for the flow of interest shown by the Soviet Union in fostering the spread of communism in Asia. The victory of communism in China had played into the hands of the Soviets and, although it was uncertain how the Sino–Soviet Treaty of Friendship and Alliance[6] would work in practice, the existence of a widespread Chinese diaspora in South-East Asia would provide a ready-made instrument for infiltration should China choose

---

3   'Note on Australian Political Objectives and Methods in India', undated [August 1952?], cited in David Lowe and Daniel Oakman, *Australia and the Colombo Plan: 1949–1957* (Barton: Department of Foreign Affairs and Trade, 2004), 483.
4   Ibid.
5   Statement on Foreign Policy by the Minister for External Affairs, 9 March 1950, cited in Percy Spender, *Politics and a Man* (Sydney: Collins, 1972), 307–29, 315.
6   Signed in 1945 but only made public in February 1950.

that path. Vietnam was the present danger point in South-East Asia, Spender argued, and should communism prevail there, then the rest of the region including Malaya would become the next direct object of further communist activities.[7] As a result of these concerns, Australia had chosen not to recognise the new government of China.

India, by contrast, had recognised the communist People's Republic of China. This was consistent with India's policy of being aligned with neither of the two power blocs, as well as coinciding with Nehru's view that China was like India in that it deserved to take its rightful place in the world after a long period of decline and foreign interference. Nehru's policy of non-alignment, as it came to be called, evolved slowly and was put succinctly in a letter he wrote in 1947 to KPS Menon and Asaf Ali as they prepared to become India's first ambassadors to China and the United States, respectively:

> Our general policy is to avoid entanglement in power politics and not to join any group of Powers as against any other group. The two leading groups today are the Russian bloc and the Anglo-American bloc. We must be friendly to both and yet not join either. Both America and Russia are extraordinarily suspicious of each other as well as other countries. This makes our path difficult and we may well be suspected by each of leaning towards the other. This cannot be helped. Our foreign policy will ultimately be governed by our internal policy. That policy is far from being Communistic and is certainly opposed to the Communist Party of India. Nevertheless, there is a great and growing feeling in India in favour of some kind of a vague socialist order of society. There is much good will for America and expectation of help from her in many fields, especially technical. There is also a great deal of sympathy for the work of the Soviet Union and the remarkable change this has brought about among the people. The Soviet Union being our neighbour, we shall inevitably develop closer relations with it. We cannot afford to antagonize Russia merely because we think that this may antagonize someone else. Nor indeed can we antagonize the USA.[8]

---

7   Spender, *Politics and a Man*, 313.
8   Cited in KPS Menon, *Many Worlds an Autobiography* (London: Oxford University Press, 1965), 229–30.

At the heart of Nehru's policy was a determination to avoid foreign entanglements. Power blocs aligned against each other, in his view, had led to world wars.[9] Peace and freedom were indivisible, and this meant that India would be opposed to colonialism as well as racialism. To be aligned would mean giving up independence of thought, to sink once again into a colonial mentality. India's policy was not 'middle of the road', hedging bets with one bloc or the other.[10] Rather it was a positive and constructive policy deliberately designed to avoid hostility to others. Although he called his policy at this point, 'one of neutrality'[11] he was later to repudiate this in favour of 'nonalignment' as a more positive term. Stalin did not understand this in 1948 just as the United States secretary of state in the Eisenhower administration, John Foster Dulles, failed to grasp this later.[12]

Crocker was Australian high commissioner to India twice, from 1952 until 1955 and then from 1958 until 1962. Although he was head of mission in five other posts,[13] he thought of his years observing India as the highlight of his career. At the time of his initial appointment he was professor of international relations at The Australian National University. He had wide experience in international affairs, including in the International Labour Organization, the United Nations Secretariat and the British Colonial Service in Nigeria.[14]

Crocker rapidly established a reputation as an excellent reporter on India. Sir John Crawford, secretary of the Department of Commerce and Agriculture, complimented Arthur Tange on the 'particularly useful' reporting Crocker had been sending to Canberra.[15] Crocker was told that the main purpose of his mission was to improve relations with Nehru

---

9   Nehru, 7 September 1946, in ibid., 2.
10   Nehru, 22 March 1949, in ibid., 45.
11   Nehru, 8 March 1948, in ibid., 30.
12   Sarvepall Gopal, *Jawaharlal Nehru*, vol. 2, *1947–56* (London: Johnathan Cape, 1980), 45.
13   Indonesia (1955–57), Canada (1957–58), the Netherlands (1962–65), Kenya (1965–67) and Italy (1967–70).
14   Crocker's new colleagues in the Department of External Affairs welcomed his appointment. Keith Waller, for instance, then in the Australian High Commission in London, wrote to him: 'Your predecessors, although men of great ability, have had no interest or understanding in the problem of India or the Indian approach. This unawareness has separated us in a tragic fashion from the kind of sympathetic contact we could have had with the Indians'. Letter, 18 March 1952, Crocker Papers, Barr Smith Library, University of Adelaide (AUL): 10/5/3.
15   Letter, Crocker to Tange, 28 June 1954, NAA: A1838, 169/10/6 PART 1. By 1954, Tange was secretary of the Department of External Affairs.

personally and with the Government of India generally.[16] Later he wrote that his job was to watch Nehru; he was the focus of Crocker's working life and inevitably he saw a lot of him.[17]

By the time Crocker took up his post in New Delhi, the views of the Menzies Government on the threat of international communism were well known in India.

Krishna Menon noted that India and Australia did not see eye to eye on issues such as the recognition of China. Nonetheless, both countries, he commented, were interested in the peace, stability and freedom of South-East Asia, and Menon hoped that Crocker's appointment would lead to greater understanding between the two governments.[18] Many in the Indian Government thought of Australia as an 'insignificant power' if divorced from the United States or the United Kingdom. It would take 30–40 years with an increase in population and the discovery of more resources for it to become 'a strong and solid power'.[19]

Crocker presented his Letter of Commission to President Rajendra Prasad in May 1952, by which time, Australia's security treaty with the United States and New Zealand (the ANZUS Treaty) had come into force. Australia was now in a formal sense part of the linked alliances that constituted containment. After presenting his letter,[20] Crocker commented in his diary that 'I personally and my country were of little importance to him'.[21] This harsh judgement was to be proven substantially correct over Crocker's first posting.

In reporting on India's views, Crocker noted there was an awareness and apprehension about communism as a factor in international affairs, but it 'does not touch the deeper feelings of Indians'.[22] Despite 'neutralism', communism took second place to issues of colonialism and racial discrimination. Indeed, many Indians believed that communism abolished

16   Despatch, Acting High Commissioner to Canada, New Delhi to Ottawa, 7 July 1959, National Archives of Canada (NAC): RG25, vol. 3726, file 5860.40 part 1. This reference was courtesy of Associate Professor Chris Waters.
17   Walter Crocker, *Nehru: A Contemporary's Estimate* (London: George Allen and Unwin, 1966), 15, 18.
18   Memo, 21 June 1952, NAA: A1838, 169/10/1 PART 2.
19   Annual Political Report for 1951, undated [early 1952?], National Archives of India (NAI): 3(31) – R&I/52.
20   Crocker was the first high commissioner to present a Letter of Commission in a formal ceremony, a step in India's recognition of high commissioners as the equivalent to ambassadors.
21   Crocker Diaries, 12 May 1952, AUL.
22   Memo, 26 October 1952, NAA: A462, 618/2/6.

racial distinctions and thus, there was some predisposition to see some good in communism on this account alone. Nationalism coupled with anti-colonialism could often be mistaken for a communist attitude. Despite this, External Affairs Minister Richard Casey's published journal[23] shows his awareness that India would resist communist aggression, although Krishna Menon, who gave him this assurance, told Crocker that Casey had a phobia about communism.[24] In a dispatch written early in 1953, Crocker commented that the main barrier to the success of the communists in India was Congress, which for the foreseeable future would be dominated by Nehru.[25] Indians disliked 'the police-state aspect' of communism. In fact, Nehru, Crocker wrote, was more opposed to Hindu revivalism than communism seeing it as a greater threat to the state and to the commitment to a secular state. Were there to be a showdown between East and West, India would without question be 'in the western camp'.[26] Towards the end of his first posting Crocker, in one of his valedictory dispatches, noted that Indian foreign policy had become more realistic and self-interested since independence and its emotionalism and abstract idealism had lessened. Coexistence might still be the central point in Nehru's international outlook, Crocker wrote, but he was placing greater emphasis on national security and was thus more wary about international communism.[27]

Nonetheless, the two countries drifted further apart as the Cold War in Asia became more intense. Casey visited India in June 1954 and suggested to Nehru that what was needed in the context of the instability in Indochina in particular was 'the mobilisation and firm expression of eastern and western public opinion against any further Communist advance in South-East Asia' as well as a 'collective security arrangement with teeth in it to deter the Communists'. Casey noted that both objectives would be much more effective were India to participate. After all, a guarantee of the collective autonomy of the Indo-Chinese states was 'essentially one for free Asia, although relevant Western countries could not avoid responsibilities'.[28] Nehru did not disagree with this but he preferred to wait until the outcome of the Geneva conference was known.[29]

23   TB Millar (ed.), *Australian Foreign Minister: The Diaries of R. G. Casey, 1951–60* (London: Collins, 1972), 12 June 1954, 155.
24   Crocker Diaries, 16 December 1954, AUL.
25   Despatch 3, 'The Long-Term Prospects for Communism in India', 31 January 1953, NAA: A5954, 2271/2.
26   Despatch 4, 'On Nehru', 9 February 1953, ibid.
27   Despatch 18, 6 December 1954, NAA: A5954, 2271/3.
28   Millar, Australian Foreign Minister, 10 June 1953, 153.
29   The Geneva Conference (April to July 1954) met to solve the conflicts in Indochina and Korea. The outcomes of it were termed 'the Geneva Accords'.

The negotiations over the Southeast Asia Treaty Organization (SEATO)[30] were, for the United States, an answer to this gap. For Australia, SEATO also represented another means of involving the United States in the region. Unfortunately, like ANZUS, it lacked an explicit trigger to invoke a response to armed attack and, much to Casey's disappointment, its reference to joint military planning was vague. Nonetheless, when Casey introduced SEATO for ratification in parliament, he noted that although it had support from few members from the region, it did at least provide a basis to develop a regional security system to deter communist expansion.[31]

In the Lok Sabha, Nehru outlined his opposition to SEATO, more in sorrow than in anger. India had been invited to Manila but attendance would have implied a retreat from non-alignment. Moreover, it would have compromised India's position as chairman of the three Indo-Chinese commissions set up as part of the Geneva Accords, aimed at resolving outstanding issues resulting from the Korean War and the French retreat from Indochina. These had provided some hope and peace to the region, which SEATO was now putting at risk. While he could 'understand the fears in the Asian countries roundabout, in Australia and in New Zealand' the treaty did not create more security but only added to tension. He especially objected that the defensive area of the treaty could be expanded by the parties to it as they decided. This seemed to him akin to the colonial concept of a sphere of influence. While the motives of the parties might be good, the treaty suggested that internal events within the region might provoke intervention, thus compromising the independence of 'this area'.[32] Eden, according to Crocker, wrote to Nehru about this, which partly mollified him.[33] This affected the independence of countries in the region.[34] Nehru was, of course, angered in particular that Pakistan had joined the treaty parties.

---

30 The South-East Asia Collective Defence Treaty, sometimes called the Manila Treaty from the city where it was signed in September 1954, brought together Australia, New Zealand, France, Britain, Pakistan, the Philippines, Thailand and the United States, in an international security agreement meant to deter communist aggression in South-East Asia. See Peter Edwards with Gregory Pemberton, *Crises and Commitments: The Politics and Diplomacy of Australia's Involvement in Southeast Asian Conflicts, 1946–1965* (North Sydney: Allen and Unwin, 1992), 153–59.

31 Commonwealth, *Parliamentary Debates*, House of Representatives, 27 October 1954, 2382–89 'South-East Asia Collective Defence Treaty Bill 1954' (RG Casey MP).

32 Cable 218, Australian High Commission in India to Department, 30 September 1954, NAA: A5954, 2271/3.

33 Cable 215, 28 September 1954, AUL: MSS 327 C938p, Crocker Papers, Series 10/2/2, Reports and Correspondence India, 1954.

34 Cable 218, Australian High Commission in India to Department, 30 September 1954, NAA: A5954, 2271/3.

The Colombo Plan

The SEATO Treaty included a section to encourage economic cooperation within the region, but the main focus of the government's aid effort was to remain the Colombo Plan, which was of particular interest to Casey. In his briefing discussions with Crocker in Canberra, Casey had asked him to review the operation of the Colombo Plan. It had only been in place since July 1951, but there had been teething problems and Casey had received blunt assessments of it, not least from Gollan. Crocker's first report substantially confirmed the high commission's view that India did not appreciate the work of the plan. His views were not to change throughout his first posting.[35]

In short, after consulting the staff, he thought it was a mess. The hopes Australia had for the plan had not been fulfilled. Australia's efforts were not appreciated mainly because they barely rated a mention in the press. The Indian minister for finance told Crocker that Australian aid was 'marginal'.[36] A few projects would be more administratively simple than the current scattergun approach, which seemed to be inspired by Australia's trade interests. The Indians wanted wheat and money to lessen its deficit. They did not need many experts and Australia should be careful to take trainees only in areas really needed by India. Nonetheless, Crocker added in a letter to Casey, 'the only political value which Australia has got out of its Colombo Plan efforts has been from the students'.[37] In his memoirs he commented that Australia's participation in the plan had been to correct the 'prejudices and phobias behind the White Australia Policy'. It at least put Australia on the map for Asia and vice versa and made a sizeable dent in Australian provincialism.[38]

Much of Crocker's criticism of the plan concerned its implementation. Although the reception of students had greatly improved, 'the ham-handed proceedings of the Immigration Department' needed work. Apprentices could be trained under the plan, but despite having training awards they would not be permitted entry. There was a lack

---

35 Crocker Diaries, 20 December 1952, AUL.

36 Letter, Crocker to Plimsoll, 3 February 1954, AUL: MSS 327 C938p, Crocker Papers, Series 10/2/2.

37 Letter, Crocker to Casey, 11 November 1953, AUL: MSS 327 C938p, Crocker Papers, Series 10/2/1.

38 Walter Crocker, *Travelling Back: The Memoirs of Sir Walter Crocker* (South Melbourne: Macmillan, 1981), 179.

of coordination—'Australia's foreign and immigration policies must be integrated lest both be compromised'.[39] It was important to ensure that training given was actually relevant to India. While in 1950 Australia had been strongly associated with the plan, its focus on providing gifts of small items meant that by 1952, Canada and New Zealand were more top of mind for the Indian public, having chosen to concentrate on only one or two projects. Some of Australia's suggested gifts, such as knitting wool or an Australian book on learning English, 'have covered us with ridicule'. While there might be administrative delays in India, there were too many administrative steps in Australia to guarantee efficiency.[40]

By 1959, during his second posting in New Delhi, India had become the main recipient of Colombo Plan aid, absorbing over a third of the total allocation to the plan by Australia. Crocker thought the plan had become inflated and the defects he had pointed to before, with the exception of the efficiency of Australian procedures, had not been addressed. In particular, he emphasised that the plan was irrelevant in combatting communism and had a small impact on economic development compared to the large amounts spent on it. There was a lot of waste. India's attitude was one of indifference and Australia's role not known; the plan thus had only a slight effect on increasing goodwill towards Australia. India believed that it had a right to aid from the West and such an attitude was not conducive to increasing goodwill. Above all, Crocker was concerned about the disproportionate amount of time the department's officers at home and abroad spent on administering programs under the plan. It had in fact done harm to the department.[41]

Casey, however, had wider objectives. Increasingly in the 1950s he sought to align the work of the plan with the anti-communist objectives of the Australian Government.[42] India was not a focus of this campaign, which instead included encouraging countries such as Malaysia and Thailand to send police for training in Australia or supporting the army of the Republic of Vietnam. A conscious program of publicity was developed that included films and books focusing on the plan's success stories. In this

---

39   Despatch 41, 25 July 1952, NAA: A4231, 1952/New Delhi.
40   Ibid.
41   Memo, Australian High Commission in India to Department, 17 October 1959, NAA: A1838, 3004/11/36 PART 2.
42   Christopher Waters, 'A Failure of Imagination: R. G. Casey and Australian Plans for Counter-subversion in Asia, 1954–1956', *Australian Journal of Politics and History* 45, no. 3 (1999): 347–61, 352, doi.org/10.1111/1467-8497.00069.

regard, the Colombo Plan was in the end so successful a scheme that it swamped the popular imagination in Australia over all other programs of training aid and the large number of privately funded students.[43]

Was Australia a Part of Asia?

The Bandung Conference of April 1955 tested Canberra's preparedness to identify with local geography and with a decolonising world rather than with familiar Western allies. From New Delhi, Cocker argued for Australia to attend the meeting of Asian and African countries at Bandung in 1955. He thought it expedient:

> If the signs are that the conference is likely to go in for anti-colonialism or Racialism, I still feel that consideration should be given to the expediency of reminding them at some stage that Australia is in the South East Asian region and is vitally interested in its well-being and is disappointed that she has not been invited to such a regional conference.[44]

Crocker tried for some months to interest Canberra in attending, suggesting that attendance at the conference might prevent discussion on questions such as Dutch New Guinea that could run counter to Australian interests. He thought a hint to Indonesia that Australia considered itself 'sufficiently a part of Asia to be worth inviting' would be a gesture that would gratify and surprise it, even if Australia were not to be invited.[45] It would be a test of whether Asian nations thought of Australia as a part of the region. For now, however, Crocker's advice was put on hold and was not to be considered until the agenda became known. Nonetheless, his arguments, shared with the New Zealand High Commission in Canberra, provoked New Zealand to seek clarification of Australia's intentions. The New Zealand high commissioner was blunt: New Zealand would not wish to participate as an 'Asian country'.[46]

---

43   See David Lowe, 'The Colombo Plan and "Soft" Regionalism in the Asia-Pacific: Australia and New Zealand Cultural Diplomacy in the 1950s and 1960s' (Working Paper No. 1, Alfred Deakin Research Institute, 2010).
44   Telegram 286, 15 December 1954, AUL: MSS 327 C938p, Crocker Papers, Series 10/2/2.
45   Minute on the Asia-Africa Conference by WR Crocker, 2 September 1954, NAA: A1838, 3002/1 PART 1.
46   Letter from the New Zealand High Commissioner, 22 November 1954, ibid.

In contrast, within the Australian External Affairs Department there was considerable debate revolving around the central issue of how Australia should relate to Asia: to those who had served in the region, attendance seemed a sensible way of flagging Australia's relevance. Opinion in posts overseas was divided, although more were opposed. Significantly, Alan Watt, commissioner in Singapore,[47] was cautious. Crocker told him that although he did not say Australia should necessarily attend or seek an invitation, 'Australia has not less interest in the region than Syria or Lebanon'.[48] Casey was doubtful about the value of the conference. He thought it would be a propaganda exercise and embarrassing for Australia to attend.[49] In a personal letter to Crocker he noted:

> I don't much like this Afro-Asian Conference. No doubt you'll be keeping us informed. I can imagine, as you say, that Nehru doesn't like it much. It seems quite clearly to be a product of 'colour' – ganging up of the Asians etc. against the Europeans. The Indonesians seem to have cashed in on it – as the flying buttress for their West New Guinea affair.[50]

Menzies, as might have been anticipated, was also opposed. With both Menzies and Casey doubtful of the value of the conference, and both the British and United States governments opposed,[51] there was little chance that Crocker's views would prevail.[52]

India's view on whether Australia should attend seemed confused. An article in *The Times*[53] had suggested Nehru wanted the conference to include the South Pacific, meaning Australia and New Zealand, but Crocker, following up in New Delhi, reported that this was not Indian policy, only an idea that had been floated in the Ministry of External Affairs. Pillai explained to Crocker that Australia and New Zealand were omitted from the guest list because they were outside the geographic area.[54]

---

47 Formerly Secretary of the Department of External Affairs.
48 Crocker to Watt, 21 October 1954, NAA: A1838, 3002/1 PART 1.
49 Letter, Casey to Pearson, 28 January 1955, NAC: Lester B. Pearson Papers, MG26, vol. 2, file pre-1958. This reference was courtesy of Associate Professor Chris Waters.
50 Letter of 31 December 1954, NAA: A1838, 555/10/4 PART 1.
51 See, for instance: British High Commissioner in Canberra, 18 January 1955, The National Archives of the United Kingdom (TNA): DO35/6096.
52 Crocker Diaries, 8 February and 3 March 1955, AUL.
53 24 December 1954, 'The Djakarta Conference'.
54 Cable 10, Australian High Commission in London to Department, 4 January 1955, NAA: A4534, 46/14/2, PART 1.

Later, at a press conference, Nehru noted that the Colombo powers would not object to the participation of Australia and New Zealand. Indonesia, however, seemed more reluctant.

Keith Shann, who was head of the United Nations branch of the department, was designated as an observer at the conference and by the time the conference was held, Crocker was ambassador in Jakarta. His closeness to Nehru was useful: during the conference Nehru briefed him on the proceedings and this added considerably to Shann's excellent reporting as the formally accredited 'observer'.

In his final speech at the conference Nehru appealed to Australia and New Zealand to draw nearer and become a part of Asia; both countries were 'nearly in our area … We don't consider these matters on any racial basis'.[55] As the Burmese premier put it, if Australia considered itself to be a part of Asia it ought to be represented at Asian/African talks. This was the point: did Australia regard itself as a part of Asia or not? Despite the warmth towards Australia at Bandung, Krishna Menon, for his part, did not think Australia was a part of Asia and thus should not attend future meetings.[56] Despite this evidence of a difference of opinion in India, it was clear that if Australia wanted to attend meetings of this sort in the future, it had only to ask; it could not expect Asia to take the initiative. Shann, for his part, having observed the conference from the sidelines, now thought that Australia would have had considerable influence on the work of the conference and gained much while losing little. The rule of unanimity under which the conference operated would have meant Australia could have vetoed anything it did not like. The great majority of members of the conference would have been prepared to have Australia attend.[57]

Immigration

Despite Crocker's lack of success in persuading the government to participate in Bandung, he remained well regarded. Menzies thought him 'an extremely able ambassador and, I think, one of the ablest reporters of local conditions that we have had'.[58] Of the department's senior people,

55   Report on Asian-African Conference – Bandung by KCO Shann, NAA: A5462, 2/1/1A PART 1.
56   Australian High Commission in India to Department, 8 May 1955, ibid.
57   Report on Asian-African Conference—Bandung by KCO Shann, ibid.
58   Heather Henderson (ed.), *Letters to my Daughter: Robert Menzies, Letters, 1955–1975* (Millers Point: Pier 9, 2011), 10.

Menzies unreservedly praised only Plimsoll, Macintyre and Crocker. Nonetheless, Crocker did not manage to shift the deeply held positions about India within the department, still less the government. Writing to Tange in May 1955 after discussions with Casey in Australia, Crocker noted he had argued for the reassessment of some Australian policies.[59] This was consistent with the ideas he had pushed since taking up the posting in India: for all the attempts to take Indian views into account, there would be no major shift in the relationship until some basic Australian assumptions had changed.

It was during Crocker's first term in India that Australia's immigration policy became a major issue between the two governments. The tension was instigated by the public statements of General Cariappa, India's high commissioner in Australia from 1953 to 1956.[60] Cariappa had made a series of comments calling for a relaxation of Australia's immigration policy to allow the controlled migration of Indian ex-servicemen into the country. Crocker was well equipped to deal with this contretemps, having been trained in demography. His reporting to the Department of External Affairs had showed how central was the grievance over past racial discrimination in India. He thought of it as the 'primum mobile of emotion in India'.[61] In his first dispatch from India on the topic, he argued that if Australia were to understand India it had to accept that communism did not touch the deeper feelings of Indians, whereas colonialism and racial issues did. Racial discrimination was a preoccupation and led sometimes to unbalanced views, for example, on colonial matters or Nehru's ambivalence on Indochina or Korea. Australia's immigration policy was always in the background in exchanges with Indian officials. The attitude to Canada was friendlier because of that country's introduction of a quota for Indian immigration, a face-saving gesture that removed the total bar against Indians. Racial questions had the potential to blur traditional loyalties to the Commonwealth and, thus, make the Soviet Union a more attractive partner to India.[62] He put the issue succinctly in a subsequent dispatch: 'no policy dealing with India which does not give a prior place to this pre-occupation [with racial issues] can be soundly based'. Geography

59 Letter to Tange, 28 May 1955, AUL: MSS 327 C938p, Crocker Papers, Series 10/3/5.
60 See: David Walker, 'General Cariappa Encounters "White Australia": Australia, India and the Commonwealth in the 1950s', *Journal of Imperial and Commonwealth History* 34, no. 3 (2006): 389–406, doi.org/10.1080/03086530600826017.
61 New Delhi Despatch No. 18, 14 July 1953, NAA: A1838, 169/10/1 PART 2.
62 'Indian Feelings on Race Relations', 26 October 1952, NAA: A462, 618/2/6.

could not be denied and the goodwill of Asia must be a 'cardinal item' in Australia's foreign relations; the current immigration policy was the chief obstacle to this goodwill.[63] In his farewell dispatch at the end of his first posting, Crocker noted that Australia was beginning to count for little more in Nehru's mind 'than the country with a disapproved immigration policy'.[64]

Crocker noted that immigration was always raised when he spoke to the press or to community groups and, in a country highly sensitised to issues of racial discrimination, was a shadow in his interactions with the Government of India. India never lobbied Australia to change the policy despite the incautious public statements of General Cariappa. Crocker, along with other Australian high commissioners, argued for a quota system. This small gesture would not only diffuse the issue, but also was necessary if Australia were to be listened to seriously in Delhi. When Canada introduced a quota in 1951, having had a discriminatory policy, it had an immediate positive effect on its relations with India. Crocker, home on briefing in 1963, stated in a departmental meeting that the White Australia policy was 'resented by all Asians, especially Indians'; although it was not possible to point to it having had direct policy consequences, it underlay the relationship.[65]

Casey was aware, from his travels, that there was a great deal of feeling against the policy in India in particular, but was unwilling to raise the matter in any forceful way. Menzies had made his position clear. In 1955, prior to the Bandung meeting, Casey tried to have provisions in both federal and state legislation, which 'could offend Asian susceptibilities', removed: Menzies opposed this on the grounds that to do so would only provoke debate and, in any case, 'Asians' had not complained.[66]

Conclusion

By the end of Crocker's initial posting in New Delhi, Australia's standing in Indian circles had diminished. Issues of race to do with Australia always made the headlines, whereas similar issues involving Canada would be

---

63 Despatch 1, Crocker to Casey, 5 January 1954, NAA: A4231, 1954/New Delhi.
64 Despatch 18, Crocker to Department, 6 December 1954, NAA: A5954, 2271/3.
65 Policy Intelligence Bulletin, undated [1963?], NAA: A1838, 169/10/1 PART 6.
66 Casey to Menzies, 5 April 1955 and Brown to Casey, 21 September 1955, NAA: A1209, 1957/5056.

in small print in an obscure part of the newspaper. Few Indians would deny the reasonableness of Australia controlling immigration, but 'the implication of inferiority due to skin colour and the total exclusion of non-whites' rankled with politically minded Indians.[67]

Canberra's inability to develop policies that might make India interested in Australia was in contrast to the sophisticated, nuanced view of India that most of the high commissioners developed. Much of this had to do with the character of the responsible minister, Casey. By the time of his second posting to India, Crocker was frustrated at the lack of direction from Casey. He had thought on his first posting that Casey had nothing to say when he visited India: Casey 'notes nothing, sees nothing, listens to nothing. He has one concern—publicity'.[68] Nonetheless, as Crocker wrote later, 'we were grateful for his hard work, his support, his open mind and his spirit which was always honourable, considerate and generous'.[69] There was the wider concern of whether Cabinet was interested in the issues that preoccupied Casey, let alone the manner of Casey's approach to Cabinet, which was to bore its members with rambling comments and consequently have little influence.[70] As Crocker commented, ministers 'were disconcerted by changeableness and inconsistency, at times by a certain shallowness'.[71] He seemed to have no taste for the inevitable fights with Treasury and in Cabinet, which he might have won if he had applied himself. He was genuinely interested in Asia, as John McEwen, minister for trade, told Crocker while on a visit to India, but he was inclined to reduce policy to personal relationships, and with India this approach had worn thin.[72] While he remained minister for external affairs, Crocker had direct access to him through long association. This, however, counted for little in terms of policy. When they met they discussed administrative matters. Not having the confidence of Cabinet meant that foreign policy was marginalised, too often seen as secondary to defence or trade policy because those ministers were stronger.

By the end of his second posting to India the tone of Crocker's dispatches and letters was weary and cynical. His reaction in cables and dispatches to the Indian invasion of Goa in 1961 went far beyond the rather muted

---

67 Despatch 23, Crocker to Department, 6 December 1954, NAA: A5954, 2271/3.
68 Crocker Diaries, 22 March 1955, AUL.
69 W Crocker, 'Richard Casey', *Overland* 107 (1987): 41–52.
70 Paul Hasluck, *The Chance of Politics* (Melbourne: Text Publishing, 1997), 82–88.
71 Crocker, 'Richard Casey', 48.
72 Crocker Diaries, 11 September 1958, AUL.

statements of the government. 'Nehru showed a Machiavellianism which had nothing to learn from such classical models as Bismarck or Hitler or Stalin.'[73] In his farewell dispatch he noted that Indian foreign policy had moved away from Gandhian values and was now 'ruthlessly self-interested' and would resort to force or fraud if expedient. The 'Hindu mentality' led to ambivalence in foreign policy and dissimulation was 'rarely uncongenial … to the oriental mind'. On the bilateral relationship with Australia his damning comment was that it was 'normal rather than cordial' and that although the main lines of Australian policy were sound, Australia must expect resentment over the White Australia policy: 'the main feeling is indifference tinged with hostility'. Australia, for its part, was too ignorant and complacent about India in particular, but also about its foreign relations in general.[74]

He had, however, notched up some significant achievements, one of which was to secure a piece of prime land for the permanent Australian High Commission in New Delhi in the new diplomatic enclave, next to Britain and Pakistan and opposite the United States and China. He had also achieved a status as a diplomat in Delhi far higher than might have been expected for a country with such few interests in India. This meant he was better informed than most of his colleagues. During Chou's visit to Delhi in 1954, Nehru personally took Crocker up the line of the welcoming corps to meet Chou and talk with him.

Crocker set a high standard of representation and diplomatic reporting in the High Commission in New Delhi, which his successors maintained. Given that one of his major tasks was to watch and report on Nehru, we could conclude that he performed very successfully: his dispatches were piercingly accurate if occasionally also acerbic, and, as David Lowe discusses in Chapter Eleven, his book on Nehru remains one of the most lucid and perceptive accounts of one of the key political figures of the twentieth century. In his diary, Crocker left an insider's view of India in a crucial period of its formation as a modern state, as well as some wonderfully mordant views of Australia's development of its diplomatic profession. He was never posted home to the department and given a key policy role. He remains thus the brilliant observer, arguing his points of view from afar and he could easily be ignored when it suited.

---

73   Despatch No. 5, 30 December 1961, NAA: A4231, 1961/New Delhi. Also see: Crocker, *Nehru*, 119–27.
74   Despatch No. 1/62, 'The Years Observing India', NAA, A4231, 1962/ New Delhi.

Despite Crocker's talents, he could not bridge the gap between New Delhi and Canberra that appeared to widen during the 1950s and early 1960s. Menzies remained detached and impatient at Nehru's reluctance to 'commit' to the anti-communist cause. Casey, while never giving up the hope that Nehru could be steered into a more anti-communist version of non-alignment, weakened his cause through signing on to SEATO—a security treaty that threatened to militarise Asian issues (and included Pakistan)—and not managing to interest Cabinet in foreign policy matters. Not all the obstacles in Australian–Indian relations were of Canberra's making. While Nehru dominated Indian foreign policy, public opinion, mobilised easily on issues of immigration, intruded in complicating ways, and at critical times such as Australia's status in relation to the Bandung conference, there were mixed messages from New Delhi. The Indian capital was becoming an intensely interesting but also testing place for negotiation.

4

The Ambassador Extraordinary and the Formidable Public Servant: Sir James Plimsoll and Sir Arthur Tange, 1963–69

Peter Edwards

In a discussion of Australian diplomatic representation in India, it is entirely appropriate to discuss both Sir James Plimsoll and Sir Arthur Tange together. Not only did the two men serve consecutive terms as high commissioner in Delhi, but their careers also had much in common, as well as some striking contrasts.[1]

To start with the similarities, both men had been trained as economists, in the days when an arts degree with a major in economics was seen as good training in public policy. After graduation, both men joined what was perhaps the first important think tank in Australia. Known officially as the Economics Department of the Bank of New South Wales and colloquially as 'Davidson's kindergarten', this was the brainchild of Alfred Davidson, the general manager of the bank, who was also Tange's brother-in-law.

---

1   This chapter is based predominantly on Peter Edwards, *Arthur Tange: Last of the Mandarins* (Sydney: Allen & Unwin, 2006), especially Ch. 9; Jeremy Hearder, *Jim Plim: Ambassador Extraordinary: A Biography of Sir James Plimsoll* (Ballarat: Connor Court, 2015), especially Ch. 6; Meg Gurry, *Australia and India: Mapping the Journey 1944–2014* (Melbourne: Melbourne University Press, 2015). References to the primary sources cited will be found in these books.

Both Tange and Plimsoll were among the cohort of bright young diplomats recruited to the Department of External Affairs in the late 1940s, the best and brightest of whom advanced very quickly to senior positions as Australia's foreign office and diplomatic service expanded rapidly in the 1950s and 1960s. Others of their generation included Peter Heydon, Keith Waller, Patrick Shaw, Keith 'Mick' Shann and Laurence 'Jim' McIntyre, all of whom, like Tange and Plimsoll, received the ultimate accolade for a public servant in the Menzies era, a knighthood. Plimsoll and Tange exchanged the positions of high commissioner in Delhi and secretary of the department. In short, they were seen as two of the most highly regarded officers of their day.

Within that cohort, they also made a sharp contrast. Plimsoll achieved almost legendary status for his abilities as a diplomat. In the words of Alexander Downer, Australia's longest serving foreign minister who had served under Plimsoll as a junior diplomat: 'There never was a greater Australian diplomat than Sir James Plimsoll'.[2] On the other hand, he was far less successful as an administrator. The stories of his brilliance in overseas posts are matched by numerous anecdotes of his quirks as departmental head, with unattended files piling up in his office. His long career was spent in a succession of nearly all the most important missions open to an Australian of his time. Much of his later career was frustrating as he was not treated wisely or well by successive prime ministers. The most notable occasion was when Gough Whitlam pulled Plimsoll out of Washington just as he was helping to rescue the Australian–American relationship from its greatest crisis.

Arthur Tange, by contrast, has generally been seen as a powerful and effective departmental head, but not a great diplomat. The high commission in India was his only head of mission appointment. He had previously served 11 years as departmental secretary, before which his only two diplomatic posts had been as first secretary to the mission to the United Nations in New York, in the formative years of the new international organisation, and as deputy head of mission in Washington, trying with little success to persuade the ambassador, Sir Percy Spender, that he was no longer the all-powerful minister. After his term in India, Tange served for a decade as the secretary of the Department of Defence, playing a leading role in major administrative and policy reforms.

---

2   A Downer, 'Foreword' in Hearder, *Jim Plim*, viii.

It is for his managerial roles as head of External Affairs and later of Defence that he is principally remembered today. This, however, should not lead us to underestimate his impact on foreign policy, not least the relationship with India. Meg Gurry's recent history refers to a 'Tange era' in the bilateral relationship, including not only his five years as high commissioner, but also the preceding decade as secretary.[3]

James Plimsoll

James Plimsoll was appointed to Delhi from his position as Australia's permanent representative (as the ambassador was then styled) at the United Nations Mission in New York. His biographer regards this post as the high point of his long and distinguished diplomatic career.[4] Plimsoll's ability to understand the individual concerns of the numerous players involved in United Nations negotiations, and thus to create a favourable atmosphere in which to advance Australian interests, was quite remarkable. Before New York, his only posting was, as a young but highly influential diplomat, on the United Nations Commission for the Unification and Reconstruction of Korea during the Korean War.

India was Plimsoll's first bilateral appointment (1963–65). He was removed from New York and dispatched to Delhi in some haste, because it was thought that he could bring a new degree of confidence to Australian–Indian relations after India's 1962 border war with China. Garfield Barwick, who had been external affairs minister since late 1961, believed a groundswell of interest in Australia had arisen in India since the war.[5] In addition, Plimsoll, it was thought, was uniquely suited to the task of using the shock of the war to bring the Indians towards greater sympathy for the West and the anti-communist, and therefore anti-Chinese, nations of South-East Asia.[6]

---

3   Gurry, *Australia and India*, 74–75.
4   Hearder, *Jim Plim*, Ch. 5.
5   See: a briefing for the minister, undated but probably in 1963, 'Australia-India Relations', National Archives of Australia (NAA): A1838, 169/10/1 Part 9.
6   Gurry, *Australia and India*, 87.

Figure 4.1. High Commissioner James Plimsoll, after presenting his credentials, with Indian President Dr Radhakrishnan, 10 March 1963.
Source: Australian Department of Foreign Affairs and Trade: HIS 0274, D237t.

Plimsoll was helped in this task, early in his posting, by the visit to Australia of the Indian minister for economic and defence co-ordination, T.T. Krishnamachari, whose aim was to discuss long-term defence assistance as well as political cooperation between the two countries.[7] Nehru had written to Menzies to suggest that India and Australia could work together in South-East Asia to prevent Chinese expansion.[8] Krishnamachari returned to India with a positive view of the potential for this cooperation, even suggesting a regional defence alliance, although the Department of External Affairs was cautious about this, noting it would require a considerable shift in Indian policy.[9]

The success of the Krishnamachari visit continued to pay dividends. He suggested to the Indian Ministry of External Affairs that Indian and Australian posts in South-East Asia should cooperate more closely.[10]

---

7   See: the brief for the visit to Australia of TT Krishnamachari, 22–27 April, 1963, NAA: A1838, 169/10/1 Part 6.
8   Letter of 23 March 1963, NAA: A1838, 169/10/1 Part 1.
9   See: Cable 245, 30 April 1963, and Memo, 19 July 1963, Department to Australian High Commission New Delhi, NAA: A1838, 169/10/1 Part 6 and Part 7.
10   Savingram 22, 5 June 1963, NAA: A1838, 169/10/1 Part 7.

There was even a request from India that Australia should undertake the sensitive task of representing Indian interests in South Africa, as India had withdrawn its mission. Plimsoll recommended that Australia agree but South Africa thought it would damage its relations with Australia and the proposal lapsed.[11]

If these hopes were not achieved, it was not for lack of effort or skill on Plimsoll's part. The moment when Indians lost their self-confidence, and might have been receptive to Western overtures, passed quickly. Both Britain and the United States sent special representatives with a similar mission, but their efforts also gained little, and may even have been counterproductive.

Plimsoll's term also coincided with Australia being torn between the contrasting attitudes of the allies that Menzies called its 'great and powerful friends', Britain and the United States, towards two developing crises in South-East Asia. Britain was seeking help in supporting another member of the Commonwealth, the new Federation of Malaysia, against the 'Confrontation' announced by Indonesia's President Sukarno. At the same time, the United States was pointing to the deteriorating political and military situation in South Vietnam as the crucial theatre in South-East Asia's Cold War. After the 1962 shock, India returned to its customary anti-imperialist sympathies, although it is worth noting that Indian Army officers told Plimsoll that they wanted the United States to remain engaged in Vietnam, provided a stable government in Saigon could be achieved, as this kept the Chinese preoccupied.[12] In short, while Australia was trying to keep both its great Western allies engaged in South-East Asia, India was returning to proclaiming its role as leader of the non-aligned movement. A substantial meeting of minds was never likely.

Within these constraints, Plimsoll did achieve considerable success in establishing strong relationships with a number of leading Indians in his own characteristic way. He travelled widely across the country, with minimal pomp or ceremony, forming links with professionals in a wide variety of fields. His technique was to work from a shared interest in cultural matters towards political links. Plimsoll's interest in Indian culture was deep and genuine. He enjoyed discussions with intellectuals,

---

11   Cables, Department of External Affairs to Capetown, 6 February 1964 and 24 March 1964, NAA: A1838, 169/10/1 Part 7.
12   Hearder, *Jim Plim*, 172.

he frequently visited galleries and museums on his travels, and he displayed many of his personal acquisitions for the rest of his career. He promoted reciprocal interest between those interested in Australian and Indian literature, even giving lectures on Australian writers, and similarly encouraged scientific and technological exchanges.

During Plimsoll's term, Australia was drawn into the counsels of the Indian Ministry of External Affairs on matters of some sensitivity, in particular foreign involvement with the northern border countries. British India had regarded the border countries as buffer states between India and China, and Tibet had been seen as the primary buffer. Now that the Chinese army was on the border with India, since the annexation of Tibet, the security of the remaining buffer states, the Himalayan tier—Nepal, Sikkim and Bhutan—was of great concern. Plimsoll visited Bhutan in October 1963 at the suggestion of the Indian foreign secretary who thought it wise for Bhutan to have contacts with friends of India who would not do anything inimical to India. Plimsoll was clear that Australia's interest in the Himalayan tier 'lay solely in the security and welfare of India and in countering Chinese expansion'.[13] He kept India fully informed about his contacts with Bhutanese officials and proposed a small aid program, of which India approved. Plimsoll was more than a foreign observer in Bhutan; his opinion was sought on the number of visitors to the Kingdom as well as the diplomatic contacts it might have. Australia also had a small aid program in Nepal and Plimsoll was sympathetic to India's problems in dealing with this landlocked country, which wanted to expand its relationship with China.[14]

If he had been allowed to stay longer than just two years, as he himself wanted, Plimsoll might well have been able to develop these political, cultural and scientific links into a broader relationship. As it was, the Indians, like many from other nations in his long career, clearly distinguished between the individual, whose abilities and insights commanded great respect, and the representative of an Australian Government, and especially an Australian prime minister, whose outlook on many issues was antithetical to those of Jawaharlal Nehru and his government. A remarkable tribute to his ability to see other nations' problems from their own point of view, and to give them sound advice

---

13 'Bhutan', attachment to memo 851 of 1 June 1964, NAA: A1838, 169/10/1 Part 7.
14 'Nepal', Despatch 3/63 of 2 July 1963, NAA: A4231, New Delhi/1963.

on that basis, came in 1977 when Plimsoll was ambassador in Moscow. After the unexpected electoral defeat of Indira Gandhi, the Russians asked him for advice on how to handle their relations with India.[15]

Plimsoll achieved as much as could have been expected, or more. In hindsight, it was probably a mistake to pluck him out of New York and send him at some speed to Delhi. Having sent him, it was a mistake to pull him out too soon. These were the first in a long series of examples of the Australian Government failing to make the best use of one of its greatest diplomatic assets.

Arthur Tange

As noted above, when Gurry spoke of the 'Tange era' in Australian–Indian relations, she is referring not only to the five years when Tange was high commissioner in India (1965–70), but also the preceding 11 years when he was secretary of the Department of External Affairs (1954–65). It is therefore appropriate to look briefly at that earlier period.[16]

Arthur Tange was appointed secretary of External Affairs in 1954, at the age of 39. There is some evidence that Menzies, and perhaps some of his ministerial colleagues, intended to rotate this post, at roughly three-year intervals, with head of mission appointments among other members of his cohort, such as Plimsoll, Waller, Shaw and McIntyre. Apparently, no-one conveyed this message to Tange, at least in terms that he felt compelled to acknowledge, and he chose to disregard the increasingly blunt hints from Menzies that he should move on. Eventually, after 10 years as secretary, he agreed to depart, and even then, the transfer did not take place for another year.

It was apparently his choice to accept India as his next posting. This made it easy for the government, as Menzies and his Cabinet wanted Plimsoll to succeed him; but it also delayed the transfer, as Plimsoll had only arrived in early 1963 and argued that it would be discourteous to his hosts to move in less than two years. Whether Tange had in mind this implication of the exchange of posts is a matter for speculation.

---

15   Hearder, *Jim Plim*, 278–79.
16   Gurry, *Australia and India*, 74–75.

Tange's long term as secretary witnessed major reforms of the department, which did much to turn a disparate collection of talented individuals into an effective foreign office and diplomatic service. But while his career at both External Affairs and Defence is generally associated with administrative reform, he clearly saw himself as an important adviser on policy. Soon after becoming secretary he wrote not only a major paper on administration, but also another on policy—a sort of one-man white paper. It heavily emphasised the importance of relations with Asia, while giving less salience to the alliances, notably the Australia, New Zealand and United States (known as ANZUS) Treaty and the Southeast Asia Treaty Organization (SEATO), to which Menzies, with evident support from the electorate, attached great significance. From the mid-1950s onwards, Tange argued that the price of Australia's relationship with Western allies, especially the United States, was suspicion towards Australia in many Asian countries. In his view, ministers such as R.G. Casey and Sir Garfield Barwick took the point, but Menzies did not.[17] This marked the start of the tradition that has lasted to the present day of debate on Australian foreign policy revolving around the poles of global alliances and regional relationships. Most practitioners have argued that these are not polar opposites but mutually beneficial, provided Australia can find the appropriate means to balance and reconcile them. Tange, like many foreign policy professionals then and since, always acknowledged the value of the United States alliance, but also sought to give primacy to relations with major Asian powers, not least India.

This, then, was the mental baggage that accompanied Tange when he arrived in Delhi in 1965. Soon afterwards he reported to his minister, Paul Hasluck, that there was fertile ground for the bilateral relationship, but no-one knew what seeds to plant. He blamed both sides for the failure to establish a good relationship, but attributed more fault to Australia than to India. Senior Australian policymakers, in his view, simply did not understand the impact of Australia's racially based immigration policies on the Australian image in India. Comparisons with the policies and attitudes of the apartheid regime in South Africa—the country in which Mahatma Gandhi, the revered leader of the independence movement, had grown up—were far too prevalent. Tange thought that Australia needed a much greater understanding of Asian issues and views, but he did not see any signs of this emerging from Menzies or those around him. He wrote in

17   Gurry, *Australia and India*, 76–77.

his diary that: 'The "lesson of Munich" underlies pacts, commitments and responses to the civil wars of Asia because we have no other inherited principles of action'.[18]

The contrast was all the more severe because Tange's term in Delhi coincided with the escalation and turning point of the American and Australian commitments to the Vietnam War. Menzies's last pre-departure instruction to Tange was to try to gain Indian support and understanding for Australian policy towards both the Indonesian Confrontation of Malaysia and the Vietnam War. In the event, the Confrontation ended before there was any need to discuss that conflict, but there was never much chance of bridging the gap between the Australian and Indian perspectives on Vietnam. As Tange told Menzies, the best that could be achieved was to encourage India to keep its hostility towards the American and Australian commitments as restrained as possible. While Australia was seen as a leading 'hawk' on Vietnam, India, along with communist Poland and western Canada, was the third member of the International Control Commission established by the 1954 Geneva Agreement. India was supposedly neutral and non-aligned, but many in high places in Delhi clearly had more sympathy for Hanoi than for Washington.

It is worth noting also that Australia linked its Vietnam commitment to SEATO, of which Pakistan was a member. In fact Pakistan contributed nothing to the anti-communist cause in Vietnam, and very little to SEATO as a multilateral alliance, but the connection was hardly an aid to relations with India. Even if only symbolic, SEATO meant more to Canberra than the relative importance of India and Pakistan.

The Australian focus on South-East Asia led many Australians at the time, and historians since, to overlook the fact that Tange's arrival coincided with the 1965 India–Pakistan War. Before the war, both countries had been armed by Western countries; both were then disappointed that they were driven to a ceasefire by the cut-off of arms supplies from the West. Consequently, during the late 1960s, both turned away from the West, India towards the Soviet Union and Pakistan towards China. Tange urged Canberra not to 'tilt' towards Pakistan, or even to regard India and Pakistan as 'Siamese twins', to be treated identically, as if they were of equal importance in the world. There is little evidence that he had much influence.[19]

18 Ibid., 2, 75–76.
19 Ibid., 85, 90.

While Plimsoll had used his personal contacts and cultural interests to develop relationships, Tange's efforts centred on traditional institutional tools, including visits by ministers and if possible prime ministers; annual consultations at official or ministerial level; and intelligence exchanges. He had contributed even earlier. During Plimsoll's term in Delhi, Tange had visited in order to give advice on policymaking structures, which led to the Indian Government establishing a Prime Minister's Secretariat, now known as the Prime Minister's Office. There is no little irony here, given Tange's deprecation of efforts by the Prime Minister's Department in Canberra to shape foreign policy.

In March 1966 Hasluck made a successful visit to India. The two governments then accepted Tange's proposal for annual ministerial consultations, alternating between capitals, which have continued to the present day. Exchanges at the prime ministerial level were more difficult to establish. Tange accompanied Indira Gandhi on a visit to Australia in 1968. This was, he felt, less successful. Although Menzies had departed in early 1966, and John Gorton was now prime minister, Tange felt that too many senior Australians still idealised British experience and deftness in international affairs and American power and generosity, and displayed little understanding of the attitudes of India and other Asian nations that had recently gained their independence from Western empires.

Tange endorsed an Indian proposal to establish an exchange of intelligence, but this seems never to have been taken up. It was a regrettable failure, as Australia could have provided valuable intelligence about South-East Asia in return for Indian insights on China and South Asia. A broader concept of a triangular relationship between Australia, India and Japan was occasionally floated, essentially as a means of containing China, but the differences in outlook between the three nations were too great to allow it to come into effect.

By his own account, Tange did not enjoy 'the fatuous ideological pronouncements of the foreign affairs community', although his then deputy, and later successor, Rob Laurie recalled that he relished vigorous discussions with Tikka Kaul, the formidable Indian diplomat. Tange was particularly dismayed by his encounters with the anti-American *éminence grise* of Indian diplomacy, Krishna Menon, who habitually greeted Tange by asking 'What has Australia done for the Americans today?' and once introduced him to a public audience as a spokesman for the Americans. Tange was deeply frustrated by this deliberate misrepresentation of his own views and advice to his political masters.[20]

By contrast, Tange did enjoy discussions with Indian military and defence officials, often outside Delhi. Tange always said that he had no idea that his next posting would be as secretary of the Defence Department, where he spent the last 10 years of his official career as the focus of a revolution in defence organisation and strategic policy. Nevertheless, Tange's discussions with the Indian defence establishment would have a major influence on the reorientation of Australia's defence in the 1970s. One example was the idea of a tri-service academy, in which officer cadets of all three armed services would undertake university-level studies together, rather than in single-service institutions, and thus develop greater mutual understanding and ability to cooperate. Senior Indian officers said that such tri-service education had proved valuable during the 1965 war with Pakistan. Their testimony contributed to Tange's significant role in helping to create, against considerable opposition, the Australian Defence Force Academy.[21]

In directing the high commission's political reporting, Tange made a point of ensuring that the Australian diplomats covered the Lok Sabha closely. He believed, with some justification, that this ensured that Australia was ahead of the pack in two respects. First, Australia was among the first to realise that Indira Gandhi was not merely Nehru's daughter who was being manipulated by the Congress hierarchs, but was an able and substantial political leader in her own right. Indeed she was: she would lead India for 15 of the next 18 years. Secondly, the high commission, and consequently policymakers in Canberra, foresaw the split in the Congress Party before most other observers.

As a trained economist, Tange was well prepared for the pressure applied by a number of Indians, who argued that, because India suffered from a shortage of wheat, while Australia had a surplus, Australia should donate tonnes of wheat to its poorer neighbour. Tange retorted that Australia had a surplus of wheat in the same way that Switzerland had a surplus of watches or Germany had a surplus of Mercedes Benz cars: that is, it was a commodity produced to gain export income. The real answer to India's shortage of wheat and similar products was, as Tange surmised, the green revolution.

---

20   Edwards, *Arthur Tange*, 159.
21   Ibid., 247.

Tange shared Plimsoll's enjoyment of extensive travel outside Delhi, but in a decidedly different style. He unashamedly enjoyed the trappings of travel as His Excellency the High Commissioner. He would travel in a convoy of vehicles, complete with the ambassadorial silverware. He travelled with his wife, Marjorie, and sometimes their son and daughter, who long remembered their rides on elephants and the ventures into hunting, shooting and fishing. On one occasion when the British minister Lord Carrington visited India, he stayed with Tange rather than the British high commissioner: they had become friends in Canberra in the 1950s when both men had been in senior positions when remarkably young, Carrington as British high commissioner and Tange as secretary of external affairs. In India the two men went on a hunting expedition together, where Carrington proved a decidedly better shot. Nonetheless, Tange prized a photograph of himself with a brace of game birds he had shot. Tange also combined two of his favourite recreations, writing and fishing, by penning as essay 'On Trout Fishing in Kashmir'. When he left India, he passed on his shotgun and his fishing waders to Rob Laurie.

Tange thoroughly enjoyed his five years as high commissioner in Delhi. He oversaw the building of a new chancery and improvements to the residence. He drove his staff hard. Communication between the high commissioner and his staff was by a telephone with a buzzer. The staff discovered that no-one was better than Tange at communicating his personality and management style by means of a buzzer. His driving, dominating style was long remembered: after he took off at the end of his term, the entire staff had a party to celebrate. At the same time, they respected his work ethic and his firm but fair assessments of their abilities and output.

Tange's final dispatches from Delhi repay reading even today, and not only for diplomats posted to India. They recommended a realistic approach to India and its relations with Australia. India should not be romanticised as the democratic alternative to communist China, nor condemned for taking a different stance in the Cold War.[22]

---

22   Ibid., 162.

5

The Buildings and Their Locally Engaged Staff

David Lowe

This chapter examines the Australian High Commission in New Delhi in terms of its local grounding. Part of this grounding is material and geographic. There is a case to make for the high commission being one of the most integrated of all Australia's overseas posts, with its locale and with an era defined by a particular architecture. This case unfolds according to both the shaper of the buildings and grounds, and also the people who most constantly occupied them.

Postwar city-building, including the expansion of New Delhi, was marked by new modes of architectural expression, including forms of modernism in dialogue with local heritage and environmental sensibilities. As apostles of the international modernist movement, foreign-born architects left their mark on post-independence India, and Le Corbusier's imprint on the Punjab capital of Chandigarh remains a much-discussed example. But none responded to the Indian landscape and design over decades and remade modernism within an Indian framework in the way that American-born Joseph Allen Stein managed.

Certainly, none of those whose work punctuates the growth of New Delhi is more celebrated than Stein; and Stein's first major commissioned work in the capital, in 1955, was the Australian High Commission chancery and residence. The high commission's stature as both exemplar of architectural innovation and part of a bigger legacy Stein left in New Delhi invites further consideration, especially in the context of the recent emergence of scholarly interest in the geographical and material circumstances of diplomacy, and their connections to the vast, swirling debates on soft power and public diplomacy. It presents a good opportunity to take up the challenge put by Naoko Shimazu who argues that integrating place with the diplomatic process is a necessary task, consistent with the changing nature of the state and increased popular participation in political processes over the course of the twentieth century. She suggests that 'Studies of diplomacy need to integrate "the people" more centrally to their analyses and interpretations as befitting the social reality of contemporary world' by paying closer attention to places.[1]

The other dimension to the high commission's 'local grounding', and one that also addresses Shimazu's call, is an exploration of the presence of large numbers of locally engaged staff (LES) in the high commission. While this is not distinctive to the post in New Delhi—most overseas posts depend heavily on LES—the size of the post makes it an important feature, and again, one that has not received significant scholarly attention. To what extent are LES 'invested' in Australian national interests, as they construct them? How does a career at the high commission, often much longer than the three-year rotations of Australian-based staff, enable different perspectives on the work of the post? And in what ways do LES observe and reflect on changes over time? A series of interviews conducted with LES of the high commission in February 2016 help to address these questions and underpins the second section of the chapter.

The Buildings and the Legacy of Stein

Given the huge costs and the heightened symbolic attachment to embassy/ high commission buildings, it is not surprising that the architecture of diplomacy is an emerging subfield of the history of architecture. Chanceries are symbolically charged and speak to both the imagined futures in diplomatic relationships and stylistic trends of a particular time. The enduring qualities of buildings should not be underestimated

1   Naoko Shimazu, 'Places in Diplomacy', *Political Geography* 31, no. 6 (2012): 336, doi.org/10.1016/ j.polgeo.2012.03.005; and for a collection on the politics and diplomacy of postwar furniture in official buildings see Fredie Floré and Cammie McAtee (eds), *The Politics of Furniture: Identity, Diplomacy and Persuasion in Post-War Interiors* (Abingdon: Routledge, 2017), doi.org/10.4324/9781315554389.

as a potential counter to the fluctuations in relations between nations. In the words of architectural historians Isabelle Gournay and Jane Loeffler, foreign missions:

> become fixtures that stand as symbols of national commitment and expectation. They also provide snapshots of key moments in the history of a diplomatic relationship and insight into the changing meaning of architecture.[2]

The location, the dimensions and the features of foreign missions can speak to national identity, a bilateral relationship, a shared presence with other foreign missions and local architecture, and a sense of the future, to varying degrees. They also speak to changing external conditions. In the last three decades, for example, the need for enhanced security has increasingly imposed on the forms and points of access in foreign missions, including for the Australian High Commission in New Delhi.

International politics was a constant factor in foreign mission–building in independent India, and especially so as the Cold War deepened. Not surprisingly, this was particularly notable in United States buildings. In the mid-1950s, when plans for Australia's High Commission in New Delhi were drawn up, the American approach to building overseas missions was turning from the more internationalist form of modern sleek 'skin and bones' buildings, to more conspicuously nationalist expressions. US Secretary of State John Foster Dulles established a new policy body in the State Department in 1953, the Architectural Advisory Panel (AAP), to oversee the expansion of United States representation abroad in ways that eschewed any one particular style, but designed buildings that had a 'distinguishable American flavour'.[3] The AAP held ongoing discussions on the limitations of mere functionalism and the need to represent, amid any historical architectural sensibilities, pride in the power and richness of American life. Edward Stone, the architect chosen to design the new American Embassy in New Delhi and an influential member of the AAP, stressed the importance of permanence and endurance in design, 'the idea that the United States had a long and solid stake in the host country, through the use of explicit symbolism and monumental architecture'.[4]

---

2   Isabelle Gournay and Jane C Loeffler, 'Washington and Ottawa: A Tale of Two Embassies', *Journal of the Society of Architectural Historians* 61, no. 4 (2002): 480, and 480–507, doi.org/10.2307/991870.
3   Quoted in Ron Theodore Robin, *Enclaves of America: the Rhetoric of American Political Architecture Abroad, 1900–1965* (Princeton: Princeton University Press, 1992), 150.
4   Ibid., 152 and 136–66.

Stone's New Delhi embassy, constructed in 1954–58, dominates its 28-acre site, an imposing rectangular block that incorporates local-style lattice masonry. It attracted, and continues to attract, praise in India but also mixed feelings from those working there, including United States Ambassador John Kenneth Galbraith, for whom its expense and grandeur (a 'modern Taj Mahal') triumphed in both a positive and negative way over practical living and working spaces.[5] Stone's was one of the many expressions of generously funded American embassy-building projects in the second half of the 1950s that required a strong degree of 'Americanism' moulded with a continued embrace of modernism—a Cold War framework within which there could still be diversity in individual styles.[6]

Delhi sat at the crossroads of the Cold War and decolonisation during the 1950s and these geopolitical currents informed the spatial as well as the human politics of the Indian capital. For foreign missions, the decade was a transitional one, marking the building, or at least commencement, of new foreign missions. The makeshift premises of the 1940s, several of which were formerly princely residences, gave way to purpose-built embassies and high commissions in a new diplomatic enclave, Chanakyapuri, the first major extension of the capital beyond Luytens's design boundaries, to the south. During the 1950s and 1960s this highly planned area sprouted embassies, hotels and international schools, connected by wide avenues and punctuated by green areas, including Nehru Park, which was designed for the pleasure of diplomatic families in 1969.

Australian High Commissioner Walter Crocker acquired land under a perpetual lease at 1/50 Shantipath, Chanakyapuri, in 1953. This would be the site of the first overseas mission built for Australian purpose since Australia House in London was opened in 1918. Other missions had, up to this point, been content to locate in existing buildings.[7] The novelty for Australia thus chimed with the excitement of a new space being developed according to the modernising plans and activities that Nehru,

5   Ibid., 163–64.
6   See: Jane C Loeffler, 'The Architecture of Diplomacy: Heyday of the United States Embassy-Building Program, 1954–60', *Journal of the Society of Architectural Historians* 49, no. 3 (1990): 252–78, doi.org/10.2307/990518; and Loeffler's *Architecture of Diplomacy: Building America's Embassies* (New York: Princeton Architectural Press, 1998), 187–95.
7   See: Philip Goad, 'Designed Diplomacy: Furniture, Furnishing and Art in Australian Embassies for Washington DC and Paris', in Floré and McAtee, *The Politics of Furniture*, 179–98, doi.org/10.4324/9781315554389-11.

in particular, championed during the 1950s, and with the contributions of a broad range of architects and designers recruited to the tasks. Further, the site negotiated by the Australians, a block at the corner of Shantipath and Panchsheel Marg, was extraordinary for its being at the geographic centre of the new diplomatic enclave. Across the road would be the British High Commission. In one direction along Shantipath would be the US Embassy, the Embassy of France, the Pakistan High Commission (abutting the Australian block and thereby elevating the level of security measures needed), and the Soviet Embassy, now Embassy of the Russian Federation. In the other direction would rise the Embassy of the People's Republic of China. All of these missions were within a 500-metre radius of Australia's.

The Cold War also intruded in the form of competitive grandiosity, as the Soviets jostled with Europeans and Americans to leave their marks on the landscape. One of the leading American architects making multiple contributions was Joseph Allen Stein, a rising architect who had, to the mid-1950s, leaned towards the left politically, yet during this period also benefited from close relations with the Rockefeller and Ford foundations, regarded by many as cultural instruments of American foreign policy.

Joseph Stein's architectural influence in New Delhi is so striking that his Australian high commission buildings often come well down a list of achievements. One of the best known and most admired is the India International Centre (IIC), a focal point for local and visiting intellectuals, politicians and civil servants, artists and writers, with a rich program of conferences, concerts and other events. It was conceived in 1958 when Stein was commissioned, and completed in 1962, adjacent to the Lodi Gardens, a part of New Delhi in which Stein would leave his most significant legacies. Stein fully embraced the liberal international idealism behind the IIC's mission 'to promote understanding and amity between the different communities of the world'.[8] With a sensitivity for which he would become renowned to connections between stone, earth, water, garden and the work of the people at the IIC, Stein stressed the importance of simplicity and relationships as being at the heart of his project.[9] He said:

---

8   'About IIC', India International Centre, www.iicdelhi.nic.in/User_Panel/UserView.aspx?TypeID =1025, accessed 20 May 2018.
9   Ibid.

it is a place where a certain kind of relationship exists—between the garden and the building, and the water and the earth and the sky, and the learning and activities that take place, and the things that can happen.[10]

In 1962 another of Stein's commissioned works, the American International School, was completed in its first phase, which was followed by the Headquarters for the Ford Foundation on the Lodi Estate (1968), the Master Plan for Lodi Park (1968), a Memorial Plaza on the Lodi Estate (1970), the Ethiopian Embassy (1970), a Conservatory for the Lodi Gardens (1971), a Guest House for the Ford Foundation (1972), a Child Development Centre at Lady Irwin College (1976), the Headquarters for the United Nations Children's Fund on the Lodi Estate (1981), the Headquarters for the World Wide Fund for Nature—India (1990), and the huge, multipurpose India Habitat Centre adjacent to the Lodi Estate (1993). The Habitat Centre's completion meant that roughly one continuous kilometre of building in the Lodi was owed to Stein. It is known affectionately today as 'Steinabad'. This list does not include the many works he designed elsewhere in India from the 1950s through 1990s.

As others have recalled in greater detail than can be attempted here, Stein's blend of modernism, his environmental sensibility and his uses of concrete, for reasons of cost and through his ongoing attachment to its different forms and uses, feature in these much-celebrated buildings in New Delhi.[11] That Stein chose to stay in India and remain engaged with iconic projects such as the IIC (to which several Stein-designed additions were made) contributes to his celebrated standing in modern Indian architecture. Throughout his career he repeatedly stressed the importance of collaboration with others and of building an environment conducive to human interactions. 'I suppose that the real thing that one strives for in architecture' he later reflected, 'in the end … is to achieve an environment that encourages fellowship'.[12]

---

10   Joseph Allen Stein, NH Ramachandran and Geeti Sen, 'The India International Centre: Concept and Design: Joseph Allen Stein in conversation with N. H. Ramachandran and Geeti Sen', *India International Centre Quarterly* 22, no. 4 (1995): 128.

11   This section draws in particular on Stephen White, *Building in the Garden: The Architecture of Joseph Allen Stein in India and California* (Delhi: Oxford University Press, 1993); Jeffrey M Chusid, 'Joseph Allen Stein's Experiments in Concrete in the U.S. and India', *The Journal of Preservation Technology* 48, no. 1 (2017): 23–31; and Stein, Ramachandran and Sen, 'The India International Centre', 118–28.

12   Stein interview of 1987, quoted in White, *Building in the Garden*, 52.

Stein's early designs marked the transition from war to postwar in a manner that seemed to translate well to an India transitioning from colonial rule to independence. Many of his key design features emerged in California in the 1940s, when he was involved in designing affordable prototypes for war and postwar housing. Although one of the most ambitious programs for large-scale affordable cooperative housing fell over before Stein and his colleagues could fulfil their aims, Stein's designs became well known. His own Californian house featured interlocking concrete panel walls, a concrete floor and a thin concrete roof. Every room opened onto a part of the garden. Both the openings to garden and the avoidance of wood spoke to a concern for the environment that would later be seen in his New Delhi designs, including the Australian High Commission chancery and residence. As Stein reflected, with reference to his time in California, 'I had the good fortune to live in a beautiful part of the world at a time when it was just beginning to be threatened by development'.[13]

Stein's arrival in India in 1952 owed a good deal to the Cold War. In California in the late 1940s he, like many of his colleagues, had embraced left-wing politics and, according to the FBI, had joined the Communist Party. With some of his close friends, he and his family left the United States suddenly in 1951, at the start of what would become known as the era of McCarthyism. He arrived in Bengal in 1952 to a teaching position at the Bengal Engineering College in Calcutta, after spending time in Mexico, Italy and Switzerland. During his three years at the college, he and his students designed simple houses for mass production in factory towns such as Durgapur. He then moved to Delhi in 1955 to work on two commissioned projects with another former Californian architect, Benjamin Polk—the Australian high commission and a pavilion for Delhi University. Thus, the Australian project, completed in 1958 (residence) and 1966 (chancery), was the start of a particularly distinctive period of work by Stein, with partners such as Polk, and two with whom he would form an enduring commercial partnership, Jai Rattan Bhalla and Balkrishna Doshi.[14]

---

13   Stein, Ramachandran and Sen, 'The India International Centre', 121.
14   Stein, Doshi and Bhalla joined in the mid-1950s to found the highly successful architectural consultancy, 'SDB Consultants'.

The circumstances around Crocker's commissioning of Stein and Polk to design the Australian chancery and High Commissioner's residence are not clear from the archival record, but Crocker's diary does list the many meetings about progress in the late 1950s. Not unusually, conversations around delays, troubles with builders and inefficient practices loom large in these entries. Indeed, Crocker grew impatient with delays to both buildings, and with what he thought were, 'Stein's changing and reversing his views, recommendations + his consternation + his long windedness'.[15] The Australian high commissioner was supportive of Stein's design, however, and in 1959 noted, with seeming approval, Stein's distaste for the 'exhibitionism' of other missions being constructed in Chanakyapuri and his verdict on the 'ugly' American embassy.[16]

In the buildings of the Australian high commission, Stein displayed a form of modernism that was less exuberant and more organic, with its connections to the earth and green spaces. His wife and landscape architect, Margaret Stein, continued to shape the direct connections between indoor and outdoor. Reflecting on this period and subsequent works such as the IIC, Stein spoke of his desire to make good, not great, buildings that catered to the mood of transition from colonial rule to independence and were appropriate to time and place. He also recalled his embrace of the ideals of postwar liberal internationalism, and the need to enable this internationalism to become manifest in different geographical settings:

> Our attempt to blend functionalism and regionalism … At the time we did these things, the weight of architecture was in the direction of the international style, which placed theory ahead of the particular site, or the cultural context. It was part of the concept of One World. Now, I believe very much in One World … I think we will have to have a common language so we can all communicate. But I still think that within the frame of shall I say, the integrity of the logic that modern architecture tried to develop, this search for truth is not incompatible at all with sensitivity for site and even ecological awareness, and sensitivity to nuances of culture.[17]

---

15   Crocker Diaries, 15 May 1959. Also see entries for 13 December 1958, 16 January 1959, 18 July 1959, 30 July 1959 and 22 October 1959, copy held at Deakin University Library (hereafter DUL): 327.94 Crocke Cro/Dos.

16   Ibid.

17   Stein interview from 1987, quoted in White, *Building in the Garden*, 53.

Figure 5.1. Stein's Australian Chancery, New Delhi, 1966.
Source: Commonwealth Department of Works with Joseph Allen Stein and
Associates, National Archives of Australia (NAA): A1200, L89642.

Architectural preservation expert Jeffrey Chusid describes Stein's integration of concrete with a broader 'material vocabulary' in the Australian high commission:

> Most notably, it included a local quartzite that Stein used for piers, stair towers and walls. The stones were cut into rough pentagons and arranged in courses that grouped several rows together. Concrete was used for the basic structural frame: in thin shells that evoked Mughal vaults and domes, in precast floors and roofs, in *jalis* [lattice-style screens], and in the Australian High Commission offices and residence as slender arcade elements. Stein would also use handmade clay tiles and other elements to both support local craftspeople (he hoped) and to reinforce the building's connection to local traditions.[18]

---

18   Chusid, 'Joseph Allen Stein's Experiments in Concrete', 27–28.

Figure 5.2. Chancery building, 1970.
Source: NAA: A1200, L89639.

Generally, commentators distinguish between the two forms of buildings comprising foreign missions, namely chanceries and ambassadorial residences. Chanceries are public buildings that anticipate multiple uses and are filled by offices in which diplomats and staffers conduct work and meet with outsiders in designated public spaces. Residences, on the other hand, are less overtly symbolic and more private, save for events to which guests are invited; but it would be wrong to draw too sharp a distinction for there is generally a high expectation that the head of mission will regularly entertain a range of influential local people. The chancery building of the high commission designed by Stein lasted until 2004 when, controversially, it was demolished and replaced by a larger building that continues to serve the mission today. As outlined for an Australian parliamentary committee, the building was lacking the amenities and safety features required of the modern era. It was also a victim of the successful promotion of Australia for Indian students and visitors—not only was the post increasing in staff numbers, but it was also having to cope with rapidly increasing numbers of visitors and visa applicants. Indeed, if any one area of activity highlighted the chancery building's limitations, it was the rapidly expanding visa section of the high commission, the staffing of which increased rapidly during the first decade of the new century.[19] The brief for the new building, as put before a parliamentary committee in 2003, was technically correct but remarkably silent about what was being torn down. Its noting that 'There are no known heritage issues restricting the development of the proposed new Chancery building'[20] was not a comment likely to have endeared the Australian Government to the many admirers of Stein's New Delhi.

The 'old building', as it is now commonly known, was more intimate and its recalled advantages—working more closely together with other sections and between LES and Australian staff—are mixed with the common nostalgia for a smaller cohort of pioneers who enabled an enterprise to grow. Members coming in and out, or circulating within the building, were more visible to a greater number of fellow staff than is now the case, in conditions that might today be called an 'incubator'. Its generous windows welcomed the exterior more than those of the new building, and helped foster a sense of community and amity—very much along the lines Stein had intended.[21] As one long-term LES reflected, growth in staffing has brought about silos and less exchange. It is much harder now to leverage the knowledge in, for example, the immigration section, by walking past and conversing with those in Austrade, as the new office geography does not allow for it.[22] The old building's disadvantages were the other side of the coin. Working space became too cramped as staff numbers grew, creating occupational, health and safety issues, and the building was not suited to modification allowing for growth.

But Stein's legacy lives on strongly in the High Commissioner's residence. In September 2017, High Commissioner Ms Harinder Sidhu hosted an event at the residence at which architects who worked with Stein reflected on his achievements and legacies. She said:

> Having a residence in Delhi designed by Joseph Stein must be for
> Australians the same as having your home designed by Jørn Utzon,
> the Danish architect who created the Sydney Opera House. It is

19   Interview with LES (h), David Lowe and Eric Meadows, 23 February 2016, New Delhi. In notes that follow, locally engaged staff are not identified, in accordance with interview conditions, but referred to as 'LES (a)', 'LES (b)' and so on.

20   *Construction of New Chancery, New Delhi, India: Statement of Evidence for Presentation to the Parliamentary Standing Committee on Public Works* (Canberra: Department of Foreign Affairs and Trade Overseas Property Office, June 2003), 3, 23.

21   Interview with LES (c), David Lowe and Eric Meadows, 23 February 2016, New Delhi.

22   Interview with LES (e), David Lowe and Eric Meadows, 23 February 2016, New Delhi.

a great privilege, and living here is a daily delight. The things that Stein strove for—a building that is at one with its garden and surroundings, a sense of openness and freedom of movement, of light and air—they are all apparent every moment in this place.[23]

Some of those attending this event bemoaned the sudden demolition of the Stein-designed chancery, but the architectural excellence in the residence, and its place in the bigger Stein firmament of New Delhi ensure that the Australian presence remains easily 'placed' in a venerated story of New Delhi's growth. Joseph Stein's determination to build structures fostering collaboration and fellowship produces ongoing diplomatic warmth towards the High Commissioner's Residence.

Locally Engaged Perspectives

The roles played by locally engaged staff are multiple. LES are generally regarded as of high importance by the many countries that rely heavily on them, even if they have attracted little research attention. 'They provide', according to a 2011 profile of US embassy life, 'the institutional memory for the missions', generally remaining at posts for much longer than their rotating American (or whichever national) colleagues. 'With their intimate understanding of the politics, culture and society of their country, they provide valuable insight into effectively addressing complex situations and overcoming challenges in a cross-cultural environment.'[24] As a recent commentator on modern diplomacy observes:

> Much more than is widely recognised, the local staff, even when cleaving to more than one loyalty, often are responsible for a large degree of whatever success embassies can claim, knowing their own countries and how to get things done much better than do most of the diplomatic staff.[25]

---

23   'Social Architect', *The Pioneer*, 11 September 2017, www.dailypioneer.com/vivacity/social-architect.html, accessed 2 June 2018. The author also participated in this event.

24   Shawn Dorman, 'Profiles: Who Works in an Embassy?' in Shawn Dorman (ed.), *Inside a U.S. Embassy: Diplomacy at Work, All-New Third Edition of the Essential Guide to the Foreign Service* (Lincoln, University of Nebraska Press, 2011), 65, doi.org/10.2307/j.ctt1djmhxq.

25   David M Malone, 'The Modern Diplomatic Mission', in Andrew F Cooper, Jorge Heine and Ramesh Thakur (eds), *The Oxford Handbook of Modern Diplomacy* (Oxford: Oxford University Press, 2013), 123–24, doi.org/10.1093/oxfordhb/9780199588862.013.0007.

Beyond this type of admiring assessment, however, there is little research that takes us further in understanding the impact of LES activities. This chapter does not make grand claims in this direction, but brings together testimonies, memories and personal reflections in ways that are suggestive for our understanding the dynamics of working in a sizeable post such as the Australian High Commission in New Delhi. In fact, it might be considered more unusual *not* to consider seriously the roles played by LES, such has been their growth in numbers over the last three decades in some of Australia's larger posts, and such are their distinctive perspectives. Some members of the High Commission in New Delhi have worked there for more than two decades, and in a couple instances, more than four decades! Given that most Australian-based staff are posted overseas for a term of three years, which is occasionally extended depending on circumstances, it is often the LES who have the longer-term perspectives when reflecting on change and continuity. Sometimes they are the best placed to measure change from different vantage points, according to their varying roles. A history of the high commission according to human movement, for example, with the assistance of long-term LES, would show that the number of movement requisition forms required for any travel by a member of the High Commission in New Delhi grew from around 100 for the financial year 1997–98 to close to 500 for 2015–16. A 'material history' of the high commission might aggregate and extrapolate this information with other indices collected at a less diplomatic and more administrative level of work. As well as growing in size—from less than 100 members in 1997 to nearly 400 in 2016—the high commission grew dramatically in its geographic reach, with members travelling more often, even despite the opening of Consulates General in Mumbai and Chennai during this period.[26]

Overseas postings might be integral to career progression for Australian staff, but careers have progressed in the one location and over a longer term for LES. According to one longstanding LES, the advantage of working in an English-speaking diplomatic post marks out the Australian high commission (and other English-language-speaking embassies and high commissions) as more desirable than others. Career progression could occur more quickly, and levels of responsibility might be reached in the Australian post faster than might be possible in a non-English-

---

26   Interview with LES (d), David Lowe and Eric Meadows, 23 February 2016, New Delhi. All interviewees are de-identified, in accordance with Ethic Committee–approved interviews.

speaking embassy.[27] One of the strongest recurring themes from LES interviewed in 2016 was their appreciation of Australian managers who had encouraged LES to stretch out beyond their formal designations and ranks. These fondly remembered managers had provided informal rewards and opportunities for those LES who work above and beyond their job descriptions. Informal mentoring, sometimes mixed with camaraderie-building social events (such as Bollywood skits involving 'visa villains'), was remarked on by those who had not seen such behaviour at other diplomatic missions.[28]

A career spent at a diplomatic post such as the Australian high commission was, and remains, highly valued relative to other possible vocations in New Delhi. For women, there is the added attraction of career mobility that might be less possible in comparable Delhi workplaces.[29] And both men and women are conscious of the conditions attaching to their employment—hours that are more regular and family friendly than the hours that might be worked at a comparable pay scale elsewhere in New Delhi, and weekends that can be spent with family. They welcome those Australians who are most embracing of their work and they endure others who interact less with them, knowing that the revolving door of overseas postings will soon throw up replacements. The main qualification to these positive views, at least as expressed by longer-term LES, was the recent rise of a more 'corporate culture' at the high commission, in which past service was less valued and had been replaced by the need to constantly negotiate one's standing in the organisation.[30] The new chancery building, while much better suited to the needs of an expanding mission, also compartmentalised and corporatised the feel of the workplace more than previously had been the case.[31]

The intercultural exchange that we imagine is part of the diplomat's bread and butter is even more necessary for the LES. It also lies at the heart of what can be a source of satisfaction: being embedded in the development of Australian–Indian relations. The task of needing to know Australia in order to prosper in New Delhi is one that is, according to

27   Interview with LES (a), David Lowe and Eric Meadows, 23 February 2016, New Delhi.
28   Interview with LES (a), (b), (c), (d), (f), (h) and (i), David Lowe and Eric Meadows, 23 February 2016, New Delhi.
29   Interview with LES (i), David Lowe and Eric Meadows, 23 February 2016, New Delhi.
30   Summary drawn from interviews with LES (a), (b), (c) and (d), David Lowe and Eric Meadows, 23 February 2016, New Delhi.
31   Interview with LES (h) and (i), David Lowe and Eric Meadows, 23 February 2016, New Delhi.

interviewees, readily embraced: 'You have to adopt a little part of that country in order to work, in order to be in the same space'[32] The corollary is that there emerges a local form of authority when LES reflect on Indian attitudes towards Australia on matters of policy priority. Changing the mix of Australian exports to India, for example, is an ongoing challenge, even if volumes have risen steadily. One of the Australian Government's aims has been to grow the export of services, and promote a shift from Indians seeing Australia as primarily a source of commodities. When an LES reflects that 'Somewhere in the psyche of the Indian business community they are not able to see Australia as more than a traditional supplier of commodity goods', this judgement comes with a blended expertise deriving from skill and experience, and a boldness in occupying a cultural joining point between the two countries. Whatever the merits of the judgement, it reflects a preparedness to interpret Indian conditions through the lens of Australian national interests.[33] The word 'we', used repeatedly in interviews as a short-hand by LES to describe Australia and Australian interests, is at one level merely logical, but at another level, goes to their personal involvement in the ongoing project of drawing India and Australia closer together. As one member put it, it is 'a good feeling that you are working to achieve something—in this case, Australian–Indian relations'.[34]

Strong collaborative relationships between LES and Australian members underpinned some of the fondest memories expressed in February 2016. These touched on both areas of work and the social life of the high commission. To have been drafting cables in recent times that were based on their independent research for particular policy questions was a source of pride. (The Americans, it was suggested, did not grant LES the same licence.)[35] LES research officers might not see the final version in which their labour bears fruit, but to know that their work passes through a respected hierarchy of officer and sometimes head or deputy head of mission, is important.[36] To have watched sporting events grow stronger and broaden from a high commission cricket team to regular soccer, tennis and badminton events provided one longstanding LES great satisfaction. In the case of another, non-sporting member, it was her son who loved

32 Interview with LES (d), David Lowe and Eric Meadows, 23 February 2016, New Delhi.
33 Interview with LES (e), David Lowe and Eric Meadows, 23 February 2016, New Delhi.
34 Interview with LES (g), David Lowe and Eric Meadows, 23 February 2016, New Delhi.
35 Interview with LES (f), David Lowe and Eric Meadows, 23 February 2016, New Delhi.
36 Interview with LES (c), David Lowe and Eric Meadows, 23 February 2016, New Delhi.

playing with the high commission cricket team.[37] In all cases, the mixing of LES and Australian staff was a key ingredient to what was regarded as success. Similarly, the high commission's Social Club was a common focal point, and its vitality—including a happy hour—contributed to the general sense of sociability and the crossing of boundaries, ethnic and bureaucratic power, in well-recognised and celebrated ways.[38]

Discussion of LES logically invites consideration of power relationships between them and Australian-based staff. Australia-based staff carry more responsibility and wield more power, thereby creating potential for exploitation or possibly a roller-coaster ride from one Australian manager to the next one. As one LES put it, you only get to know your boss well in year two, and after the third year they are gone. The best approach was a mixture of friendliness and wariness:

> I tell my staff when we get a nice boss, do not get used to them, because the next one might be tough and you won't be able to work with them.[39]

Exploring this with current LES is fraught, with understandable reticence to engage in ways that may damage reputations and risk stories circling back to current members of the mission. But to the extent that we can report, then, with one exception—recollection of one Australian manager who seemed to exude race-inflected superiority—the relations of power seem to have been negotiated adroitly.[40] And the creation of well-known work events in which power boundaries were periodically relaxed, such as social and sporting events, seems to have been a mostly successful feature of Australian–LES relations. Inspiring Australian staff mentors coming and going featured more strongly than the less well-loved ones.

Conclusion

This chapter has taken up the invitation in recent scholarship to introduce a stronger sense of geography, both physical and human, to the study of overseas missions. While more work awaits, the case of the Australian High Commission in New Delhi provides strong evidence of the value

---

37   Interview with LES (h), David Lowe and Eric Meadows, 23 February 2016, New Delhi.
38   Interview with LES (a), David Lowe and Eric Meadows, 23 February 2016, New Delhi.
39   Interview with LES (d), David Lowe and Eric Meadows, 23 February 2016, New Delhi.
40   Interview with LES (i), David Lowe and Eric Meadows, 23 February 2016, New Delhi.

in this approach. Architecturally it was, and remains, distinctive. It was the first purpose-built Australian mission in Asia, and Australia's only commissioned overseas mission between Australia House's opening in London in 1918 and the Bates, Smart & McCutcheon–designed embassy in Washington in 1969. As one of many missions being built in the new Chanakyapuri area, it inevitably took shape in comparison with others, and in the landscape of Cold War and postcolonial politics jostling with Nehru's vision for modern India. The work of the high commission's chief architect, Joseph Allen Stein, rode these themes over four decades, while Stein cumulatively laid a legacy in concrete, gardens and environments receptive to human interactions across New Delhi, thereby folding the Australian buildings into a bigger story that continues today. Moreover, the 'locating' of the high commission begs consideration of its longer-term workers who are, not surprisingly, locally engaged staff. A focus on LES, as shown here, does not necessarily dilute a concern for 'Australian national interest', that fuzzy and malleable phrase that guides much discussion of Australian diplomacy. In fact, the work of LES helps to add clarity to the concept in some ways, enabling us to reflect on the policies, priorities and growth of the high commission over time, and to hear from those who see themselves as small, human bridges in the bigger story of Australian–Indian relations.

6

The Bangladesh Crisis Seen from New Delhi

Ric Smith

Introduction by Eric Meadows

The author of this chapter, Ric Smith, has had a distinguished career in Australian diplomacy and public service. After various postings including at Tel Aviv, Manila and Honolulu, and senior appointments in the Department of Foreign Affairs and Trade in Canberra, he held ambassadorial positions in China and Indonesia before being appointed secretary of the Department of Defence.

At the time of the events that he describes in this chapter, which follows, Smith was on his first posting in New Delhi (1970–73), and was thus well placed to report on the evolving crisis in East Pakistan. His chapter gives a firsthand account of a major military and diplomatic crisis and the different perspectives of Australian diplomats in New Delhi and in Islamabad.

The Bangladesh crisis had its roots in the Partition of colonial India in 1947. This created two independent states based on confessional lines: a largely Hindu India and a mostly Muslim Pakistan, which itself was divided into two separated by the bulk of India. West Pakistan held the political power; the Muslim elites of pre-independence India had mostly moved there at Partition. East Pakistan was Muslim Bengal and had the greater economic power of the two parts.

Since independence, Pakistan had had a series of military dictatorships, but in 1970 national elections were held in which the Awami League, a Bengal-based party led by Sheikh Mujibur Rahman, won a clear majority. Pakistan's military dictator, General Yahya Khan and the leader of the Pakistan Peoples Party, Zulfikar Ali Bhutto, which had won the majority of the seats in West Pakistan, refused to accept the outcome: for them power in Pakistan could only come from the western half of the country. The Awami League for its part had made no secret of its policy of autonomy for the east, and the creation of a federation. In 1966 it had published its 'Six Points' which made that abundantly clear.

Talks between the leading parties failed to resolve the impasse and by early March 1971 Yahya started moving troops to the east. Student groups in the east had called for independence, and at the end of March Yahya launched a ruthless military crackdown, which became increasingly brutal; Sheikh Mujibur Rahman was arrested but not before he issued a declaration of independence. A Bangladesh government in exile was created based in India. India began helping a guerilla movement, the Mukti Bahini, which was leading the resistance to the Pakistan Army. At first India provided arms, supplies and safe refuge, and resisted domestic pressure to be more involved. As the fighting increased and the refugee flow became greater, India started providing training facilities for the guerillas and covering fire support for actions in the border areas. Eventually Indian commandos were sent into combat with the guerillas.

There is no agreement on the number of civilians killed in the war, which has been dubbed by some 'genocide'.[1] What is not disputed is the savagery of the Pakistan Army's crackdown, in particular, against the intelligentsia, the press and the Hindu minority.[2] A huge flow of refugees into India, up to 10 million people by the end of the war, created a major humanitarian crisis.[3] In August a 'Concert for Bangladesh', the first rock event to raise money for an international humanitarian crisis, was held in New York. It did much to raise awareness internationally of the scale of the refugee problem.

---

1   For the best history of the war, see: Srinath Raghavan, *1971: A Global History of the Creation of Bangladesh* (Cambridge, MA: Harvard University Press, 2013). He avoids a definitive statement on the number of casualties; Bangladeshi sources put the figure at 3 million, but others say it was up to 100,000.

2   See: Gary J Bass, *The Blood Telegram: Nixon, Kissinger, and a Forgotten Genocide* (New York: Alfred A Knopf, 2013).

3   See: PN Dhar, *Indira Gandhi, the 'Emergency', and Indian Democracy* (New Delhi: Oxford University Press, 2001), 146–86.

The United States was unwilling to put pressure on its ally, Pakistan, to stop the savagery of its military action, despite having eyewitness reports of the brutality of the Pakistan Army's action in Dacca from its consulate-general. Nor did it pressure Pakistan to reach a political agreement with the Awami League on the future of the east. The Nixon administration ignored its own advisers. There was a much bigger strategic objective: Yahya was acting as the main channel of communication between the Nixon administration and the government of China as Kissinger sought to lay the ground for his own secret visit to Beijing in July 1971. Détente with China was of far greater strategic consequence to the United States than intervention to stop Pakistan's actions.

Other governments initially viewed the conflict as an internal matter and were also unwilling to pressure Pakistan. India, feeling isolated, finalised a Treaty of Peace and Friendship with the Soviet Union in August 1971. The Indian Government sent out envoys, including to Australia, to put its side of the dispute; the plight of the refugees was a powerful persuader of international public opinion.

Full-scale war between India and Pakistan broke out in early December when Pakistan attacked India in the west. The war was all over in less than two weeks with Pakistan's surrender. But, in a twist to the tail end of this crisis, the United States deployed the Seventh Fleet into the Bay of Bengal, ostensibly to be ready to evacuate American citizens. The threatening nature of this symbolic act only spurred the Indians to reach Dacca with greater speed, but it left a lasting legacy of distrust of the United States in India.

India's war aims had always been modest, despite the frantic imaginings of Kissinger and Nixon who seemed to think India had wanted to destroy Pakistan. Its aims were the withdrawal of Pakistan's troops from the east leading to eventual independence for Bangladesh and the return of the refugees.[4] In this, India was successful. Australia's recognition came early and, as Smith points out, the view that the Australian Government took of the crisis stands as an example of independent thinking that had no adverse effect on its relations with the United States. Moreover, it reflected an Australian foreign policy that gave priority to Australia's long-term interests in the region.

---

4   See: Raghavan, *1971*, 236 and 262.

* * *

The following is an extract from Ric Smith's monograph, *India, the United States, Australia and the Difficult Birth of Bangladesh* (pages 44–77 and notes from pages 83–85), published by the Australian Institute for International Affairs in 2019, in their 'Diplomatic History' series. This publication also benefited from support provided the Australian Department of Foreign Affairs and Trade.

Untold History: An Independent Australian Policy

26 March 1971: In the late afternoon Don Hook, the Australian Broadcasting Commission's New Delhi–based South Asia correspondent, is talking to Sheikh Mujibur Rahman at his home in Dhaka when news comes that the army will shortly be coming for Mujib. Hook departs by a back door; a veteran in his field having reported on Indochina and Papua New Guinea for 20 years, he had taken the iconic photograph of Mujib, from behind, addressing a million Bengalis at Dhaka Racecourse on 7 March.

Driving back into Dhaka, Hook calls by the university. All is quiet, his contacts nowhere to be seen; the army has been there already, only bodies are to be found. Back at the Intercontinental Hotel, after a short sleep interrupted by gunfire and explosions in the adjoining streets, he is invited to a press conference at Dhaka Airport. Escorted there, he finds all the other foreign correspondents waiting; they are placed on a Pakistani aircraft and flown out to Karachi, via Colombo (where *The New York Times*'s Sydney Schanberg unsuccessfully seeks political asylum).

Hook's reception at Karachi airport is unfriendly as the army seize his notebooks, maps and several precious rolls of film taken by the legendry ABC cameraman, Willie Phua, of the brutality of the Pakistan Army in Dhaka's streets. A day later Hook is released and placed on an Air France flight to New Delhi.

Figure 6.1. ABC correspondent Don Hook with Bengali refugees, Calcutta, 1971.
Source: Image supplied courtesy of Don Hook.

Back at the Intercontinental, Peter Rodgers, third secretary at the Australian Deputy High Commission, had been awakened by the sound of gunfire. He has been in Dhaka for a month as the Department of Foreign Affairs, anticipating the crisis, enhanced its presence in East Pakistan. This is his first overseas assignment.

Looking down from his hotel window, Rodgers is stunned to see Pakistani soldiers shooting up a newspaper office across the street, and then setting fire to the building. Later that day in the ruins he sees the charred bodies of a least a dozen people, presumably staff of the newspaper. The incident is reported in a cable to Canberra. None who read it fail to be shocked. Thus, from an early point in the crisis the Australian Government has firsthand advice of the depredations that have been unleashed.[5]

My own experiences of the early days of the crisis are not as direct or vivid as those of Don Hook or Peter Rodgers, but the Australian High Commission in New Delhi, my home from 1970 to 1973, nevertheless proves a privileged vantage point from which to view the tumultuous

---

5   Peter Rodgers, interview with author, 2015.

events of 1971. It was also incidentally the first haven for Bengali officers of the adjoining Pakistan high commission who, after months of harassment, began literally to jump the wall in about August 1971.

* * *

From an early stage, the Australian Government showed a realistic appreciation of the situation in the subcontinent as it unfolded in late 1970 and early 1971. An assessment prepared by the Department of Foreign Affairs (DFA) in early March 1971 concluded that the division of Pakistan into two states was 'nigh inevitable', though the prospects for an independent Bangladesh were not considered bright. The paper also noted the challenges that the emergence of a new, impoverished nation of 70 million people in South-East Asia would pose for Australia, as well as for Japan, the wealthiest countries in the region.[6]

In April 1971 Prime Minister William McMahon wrote to Pakistani President Yahya Khan, urging him to consider releasing the Awami League leaders as a step towards a political solution. McMahon also wrote to Prime Minister Indira Gandhi assuring her that he was seized of the gravity of the refugee problem and making the point that 'the transfer of power to elected representatives of the people offers the best hope of progress towards a solution'.[7]

Government statements reflected this concern about Pakistan's disregard of the election outcome, and about the impact of the outflow of refugees. Siddhartha Shankar Ray, a senior Cabinet minister close to the prime minister and himself a West Bengali, visited Australia in June as one of a number of envoys sent abroad to explain India's position. He was well received, made a good impression and helped consolidate the case for more humanitarian aid. On his return to New Delhi, he noted the evident sympathy in the Australian community for India's position. Foreign Minister Leslie Bury remarked to him 'you are in a hell of a jam'; for the beleaguered Indian Government, this idiomatically expressed judgement was taken, rightly, to reflect understanding and even sympathy.[8]

---

6   Policy Planning Paper of 9/3/71 held in the National Archives of Australia (NAA), cited in Raghavan, *1971*, 170.
7   McMahon to Gandhi, 3 June 1971, NAA: A1838, 169/10/1 PART 18.
8   Quote cited in Raghavan, *1971*, 171.

The crisis attracted strong parliamentary and media interest in Australia, as abroad. Kim Beazley senior, a leading figure in the opposition Labor Party, visited India and East Pakistan and spoke on the issues in parliament and publicly. The ABC had covered the crisis in detail from an early stage, with its South Asia correspondent, Don Hook, active in New Delhi, along the borders and in occasional visits to Dhaka. Australian current affairs program, *Four Corners*, had also run in-depth pieces on it, and Gerald Stone had done thoughtful interviews with Prime Minister Gandhi and Zulfikur Ali Bhutto that had attracted interest in Australia and beyond. Other Australian correspondents, including the foreign editor of *The Australian*, drifted in and out of the region, some visiting from Vietnam. And of course the international mood as reflected in the Concert for Bangladesh on 1 August carried through to the Australian media and public opinion.

The Role of the Diplomats

Australia was well served during this period by its high commissions in New Delhi and Islamabad, headed respectively by Patrick Shaw and Francis Stuart, both senior and very experienced diplomats; and by small but professional deputy high commissions in Dhaka, headed by Jim Allen, and in Calcutta by Doug Sturkey. Allen's parents had been missionaries in Bengal before the Second World War; he was born in Noakhali and spoke Bengali, and had been secretary to Richard Casey during Casey's time as governor of Bengal (1944–46).

From the outset, Patrick Shaw in New Delhi emphasised India's concerns about the refugee inflow and the political and economic challenges it engendered. Drawing on his access to Indian ministers and officials, he also reported on the Indian Government's disappointment with the UN and the non-aligned movement's responses to the crisis, and—reflecting his close contact with the US ambassador—on India's concerns about American policies.

Shaw advocated busily for Australian aid to help India cope with the refugees. An amount of A\$500,000 was announced on 27 May, followed by another A\$500,000 on 8 June. Following a visit to refugee camps in West Bengal in July, and the experience of others of us elsewhere, Shaw reported that the Australian-provided poly-fabric was being well used as shelter and that this, and the medical supplies being delivered, had been welcomed by Indian authorities on the ground, but that our aid to date had amounted to less than 2 per cent of all international aid. He urged another aid tranche, which was forthcoming.

Shaw reported that 'Australia's timely refugee assistance has been greatly appreciated ... Apart from its humanitarian aspect ... our contribution has had favourable impact on Indo-Australian relations generally, out of all proportion to its magnitude'. He noted that the fact that the supplies had been delivered directly (by RAAF C-130 aircraft) had added much to its value and to the Indian Government's appreciation of it.[9]

From Islamabad, Francis Stuart shared the department's judgement about the likely demise of Pakistan and the poor prospects for an independent state in East Pakistan. On 8 April he reported that:

> the evidence of the last month has confirmed [Canberra's] view that the present state of Pakistan will split into two ... the Army will almost certainly be forced to withdraw itself from the East Wing.[10]

Figure 6.2. Dacca family fleeing the city with their staff and luggage piled on an oxcart on the way to the countryside, 29 March 1971.
Source: Image supplied courtesy of Associated Press/AAP Image.

---

9   Shaw to Minister, 6 August 1971, Despatch 7/71, NAA: A4231, 1971/ASIA DESPATCHES. The Royal Australian Air Force undertook seven C-130 relief supply flights directly into India, most to Calcutta but at least one to Agartala, on 24 or 25 June. In addition, one flight came from Butterworth to assist the repair of an aircraft that became unserviceable in Calcutta. The last of them flew into Calcutta in late August. QANTAS aircraft were also used to carry relief supplies.
10   Stuart to DFA, 8 April 1971, NAA: A1838, 144/10/1 PART 1.

This of course was a sound judgement shared in Canberra, but different at that time from the view held in Washington, at least in the White House.

But Stuart was gloomy about the viability of a successor state, and this remained a theme in his reporting as the crisis unfolded. He reported on 15 July that 'I see diminished prospects of East Bengal being able to rule itself under any arrangements', a view that was apparently consistent with the assessment of Australian intelligence agencies.[11]

Shaw and Stuart met to exchange assessments on three occasions during the crisis. After their second meeting, in Islamabad on 22 July, they reported that:

> it is our judgement that the Pakistan Government will be unlikely to maintain its control over East Pakistan for very long ... In the long term, the Pakistan Government will have to abandon East Pakistan, and perhaps to its advantage.[12]

But as 1971 progressed, Shaw and Stuart developed different perspectives on some key issues. The events of July and August—Kissinger's visit to China and the Indo–Soviet Treaty—took Australia's diplomatic missions (and most others) by surprise.

In New Delhi, the high commission had been aware that an agreement of some sort had been under discussion with Moscow for some time. But they did not know that the negotiations had come to embrace a mutual security component. Nor of course was the high commission aware of the conversation between India's ambassador in Washington, Lakshmi Kant Jha, and Kissinger on 17 July in which Kissinger, seemingly contradicting earlier advice, had said that in the event that China became involved in a conflict between India and Pakistan, India could not expect support from the United States.

Shaw wrote sympathetically to Canberra about the treaty's context, pointing out that India maintained a deep anger toward the United States for not cutting off military supplies to Pakistan. He reported to the minister that 'in certain places, particularly Articles VIII, IX and X, the document bears the signs of hasty drafting'. He said the 'immediate effect

---

11   Quoted by Shaw, 6 August 1971, Despatch 6/71, NAA: A4231, 1971/ASIA DESPATCHES.
12   Shaw to Minister, 6 August 1971, Despatch 6/71, ibid.

of the [treaty] was to relieve internal pressure on the Indian Government … Mrs. Gandhi showed that India had a powerful friend in a time of need. The security articles … were taken as a warning to Pakistan'.[13]

Shaw and Stuart disagreed on the treaty's impact. Shaw contended that the 'effect of the Treaty had been to reduce the possibility of war'. But Stuart felt that with India's confidence now restored, it was more likely. In the end this difference was essentially one about the timing of any conflict. As Shaw put it, Mrs Gandhi has been able to 'buy time in which to consider what she can do to relieve the financial burden on India and the political pressure on herself'.[14] As the distinguished historian Margaret MacMillan wrote in discussing the treaties concluded between the European powers in the years before WW1: as 'so often in international relations … what is defensive from one perspective may appear a threat from another'.[15]

Most fundamentally, Shaw and Stuart also differed over India's motives and ambitions. Stuart—who had served in New Delhi earlier in his career—considered that India was pursuing a long-held strategic ambition to dismember Pakistan, so weakening it as a state and placing India in a situation of supremacy in the subcontinent. He felt strongly that it was all part of India's aspiration for great power status.

From New Delhi, Shaw was aware of India's growing support for the Mukti Bahini and its cross-border operations. But he nevertheless rejected the notion that India's aspirations went beyond resolving the situation in the east. He saw no evidence within the government of any more ambitious agenda. He was aware of what Indian hawks and jingoists were saying, but did not consider these views to represent mainstream Indian opinion, and took at face value the assurances of Indian Government spokesmen about India's limited objectives. Shaw's opinion was supported by, among others, James Plimsoll, who had been Australia's high commissioner in India from 1962 to 1965, secretary of the Department of External Affairs from 1965 to 1970, and, in 1971, ambassador to the United States.

Prime ministers McMahon and Gandhi met in Washington on 4 November 1971 while on respective official visits. McMahon told Mrs Gandhi he was concerned that the United States did not understand what was happening, and that the administration did not sufficiently appreciate

---

13   Shaw to Minister, 20 August 1971, Despatch 8/71, ibid.
14   Ibid.
15   Margaret MacMillan, *The War That Ended Peace* (London: Profile Books, 2013), 546.

that the basic problem was within East Bengal, not between India and Pakistan. He told her he would write to Yahya again, expecting, he said, that his 'message might have added weight coming from Washington'.[16]

In this letter to Yahya—his fourth[17]—McMahon again urged a 'political settlement based upon negotiation with the Awami League and its leaders, particularly Sheikh Mujibur Rahman'.[18] In this, he was reflecting advice from Foreign Minister Nigel Bowen and his department, and from Jim Allen in Dhaka, which consistently emphasised that the 'release of Mujib' was the key to resolving the crisis.

Following the declaration of war on 4 December after the Pakistan Air Force attacks in the west the previous evening, Foreign Minister Bowen said in a formal statement that Australia 'deeply regrets that events in the Indian subcontinent have led to full-scale warfare between India and Pakistan'. Australia, he said, regretted that its:

> repeated efforts to try to influence the leaders of Pakistan and India in the direction of reaching a political settlement … have been unsuccessful … Our view is that the first requirement is an agreed ceasefire with a disengagement and withdrawal of opposing forces. This must be accompanied by a political settlement directed towards removing the underlying causes of conflict. Meanwhile, Australia's position, as a friend of both Pakistan and India, will continue to be that of a neutral.[19]

Staff and families of Australia's deputy high commission in Karachi were evacuated on 8 December, after the Indian Armed Forces agreed to an Australian request through the high commission in New Delhi for a temporary halt in the bombardment of Karachi airport to allow a Qantas aircraft to land and fly out 154 Australian and other foreign citizens. Families of Australian staff in Islamabad moved up to Kabul early in the war, and all but Allen and his wife, Marion, and one staff member were evacuated from Dhaka to Singapore. There were no evacuations from Australian missions in India.

---

16   Australian Embassy in Washington to DFA, 6 November 1971, Prime Minister to DFA, NAA: A1838, 169/10/1 PART 19.
17   The official record indicates four, but McMahon told Mrs Gandhi it would be his fifth.
18   McMahon to Yahya Khan, 4 November 1971, NAA: A1838, 169/10/1 PART 19.
19   Press Statement, Foreign Minister Bowen, 7 December 1971, *Current Notes on International Affairs* 42, no. 12 (1971): 629.

Shaw was unconcerned by Pakistani threats to slice through to New Delhi with an armoured blitzkrieg. He was confident that India's war aims were limited and that the war would be over within in two weeks. Once again, there was disagreement with Stuart who contended on 6 December that 'Pakistan has been the victim of calculated and graduated aggression'. India, Stuart argued, would probably ensure the 'complete annihilation … of the Pakistan Army [in Bangladesh]' and 'then turn its forces to the West and seek to destroy Pakistan's Western Army'.[20] This judgement was consistent with that of the White House.

Australia was not a member of the UN Security Council at the time and so did not have to take a position on the December resolutions. When the matter was referred to the General Assembly on 8 December, Australia supported a resolution that called for a ceasefire and the withdrawal of troops. The resolution was adopted by a vote of 104 to 11, with 10 (including the UK and France) abstaining. In response to Indian expressions of regret about Australia's vote, which was seen to be inconsistent with our earlier more sympathetic positions, it was explained simply that it was not possible to avoid supporting a call for a ceasefire in a war.

'Not Just Any Ship'

14 December 1971: I answer the phone in my high commission office to hear the stentorian but furry tones of Peter Hastings: 'The Yanks have gone nuts! They've sent in the bloody Enterprise! Not just any ship—the "Big E"! We'll all be nuked!'

Hastings, *The Sydney Morning Herald*'s veteran foreign editor, is in New Delhi covering what he has assumed is an intraregional scrap. His more measured report in the *Herald* on 15 December reflects a busy day among the diplomats in Chanakyapuri.[21] 'Some foreign missions', he writes, 'are strongly convinced that President Nixon has threatened US intervention … unless India accedes to the UN call for a ceasefire and troop withdrawal … those who are convinced that Mr. Nixon has threatened US intervention are unwilling or unable to say what this threatened action is and under what circumstance'.[22]

---

20 Stuart to DFA, 6 December 1971, NAA: A1838, 169/10/1 PART 20.
21 The Diplomatic area of New Delhi.
22 *The Sydney Morning Herald*, 15 December 1971.

> Suddenly the crisis has gone global. And while the high commission does not share Hastings' initially apocalyptic tone, we are surprised and a little concerned about what direction the war might now take and begin to wonder whether our World War II-like contingency preparations—papered-over windows, buckets of sand and water in every room, makeshift air-raid shelters under dining room tables—will be adequate. Nor can our friends in the US Embassy across the road shed light on what it is all about.

President Nixon had ordered the *Enterprise* battle group to the Bay of Bengal on 10 December, and it was revealed by *The New York Times* on 12 December (the news reaching New Delhi on 13 December).

While it did not comment publicly, the Australian Government was taken by surprise.[23] A cable sent to Ambassador Plimsoll in Washington on 15 December instructed him to seek advice about the decision (among other matters).[24] The senior State Department official to whom Plimsoll spoke told him that decisions were being made elsewhere (meaning the White House, Plimsoll noted) and that he could throw little light on the deployment other than to note that it might be part of a contingency plan for the evacuation of Americans. Plimsoll reported no reference to the far more significant geopolitical dimensions to the crisis that had driven Nixon and Kissinger.

Of particular note was Foreign Affairs Secretary Keith Waller's record of the view of Foreign Minister Bowen, who commented on 16 December that 'if the presence of the Seventh Fleet in the Bay of Bengal was purely humanitarian, then it was clearly excessive. If it were gun-boat diplomacy, it was deplorable'.

---

23   On 7 January 1972, in response to a media report of an American decision to maintain a task force in the Indian Ocean, Nigel Bowen stated: 'We have no official confirmation yet of this apparent announcement … but a development of this kind would be consistent with American objectives as the Government knows them and we should naturally welcome it'. This statement was not related to the *Enterprise* deployment three weeks earlier, which the foreign minister and his department clearly saw in a different context. Rather, it reflected Australia's persistent concerns, canvassed, for instance, during Prime Minister McMahon's visit to Washington in November 1971, about the Soviet naval presence in the Indian Ocean.

24   DFA to Plimsoll, 15 December 1971, NAA: A1838, 169/10/1 PART 20; Waller to Anderson, 16 December 1971, ibid.

Figure 6.3. Recognise Bangladesh Rally in Trafalgar Square, 8 August 1971.

Source: Image supplied courtesy of Keystone Press.

The cable to Plimsoll had also asked him to follow up reports from New Delhi 'about [the US] invoking treaty obligations with Pakistan if India seized territory in Pakistan-occupied Kashmir'. In fact, as Kissinger was reportedly surprised to learn, the US did not have any treaty obligations to Pakistan—SEATO (the Southeast Asia Treaty Organization) and CENTO (the Central Treaty Organization) did not apply. In a subsequent letter to the deputy high commissioner in London, Waller—a former ambassador to the United States, and generally measured in his language—recorded his view that the Americans had 'behaved with egregious stupidity, especially so far as the last gesture of sending half the Seventh Fleet to the Indian Ocean'.[25]

Within days of the war ending, Bowen began to review the events and to think ahead. On 20 December, he cabled Shaw and Stuart to say that he had 'concerns about the isolation of India from many of her traditional friends, and in particular the breach with the United States', and sought their views. 'Can we build on [our positions to date] and our aid to refugees to reinforce in Indian minds the picture of a friendly and

---

25 Waller to Pritchett, 22 December 1791, NAA: A1838, 144/10/1 PART 2.

understanding country?' he asked. Shaw thought we could, and so did Plimsoll, but Stuart was 'sceptical of Australian ability to bring India back [sic] to the West'.[26]

Later, in January, Bowen asked Waller's advice on whether Australia 'should not in present circumstances be thinking of some new initiative with the Indians, such as proposing a treaty of friendship'. Waller's view—with which First Assistant Secretary David Anderson quickly concurred—was that 'we should let matters rest for the time being, as such a gesture would be somewhat contrived'.[27] The matter was taken no further.

Recognition of Bangladesh

Shaw, Allen and Plimsoll advocated early recognition of the new state, both to capitalise on the goodwill Australia had attracted by its policies, and to help ensure that the field in Dhaka was not left to the East Europeans and other communist governments. Stuart was concerned about how Pakistan might react, and anyway remained sceptical about the new state, describing Bangladesh as 'a hopeless case'.[28] He had earlier predicted that it 'will be well on the way to becoming a communist-dominate [sic] trouble spot and [will] add to our South East Asian worries'.[29]

The government addressed the question of recognition soon after Mujib returned to Dhaka.[30]

Waller told Anderson on 11 January that he thought Australia should recognise Bangladesh 'fairly soon' and was prepared to take a 'bit of a risk' on it. He said he had already had some pressure on the matter from Prime Minister McMahon, though the minister (Bowen) was not attracted to the idea of precipitate recognition.[31]

On 14 January, McMahon told Waller he was not unduly perturbed by the possibility that Pakistan might cut off diplomatic relations if Australia recognised Bangladesh (as it had with a number of East European early

---

26 Cable exchange, Bowen-Shaw-Stuart, 20/21 December 1971, NAA: A1838, 169/10/1 PART 20.
27 Minute, Waller to Anderson, 11 January 1972, ibid.
28 Stuart to Minister, 21 December 1971, NAA: A1838, 199/10/1 PART 20.
29 Stuart to DFA, 6 December 1971, NAA: A1838, 169/10/1 PART 20.
30 Don Hook recalls that Jim Allen was among the first people Mujib greeted on this arrival back in Dhaka airport, embracing him warmly and thanking him. Australia's recognition was of course welcomed in Dhaka and New Delhi, and also by South-East Asian governments that recognised the importance of Canberra's independent view of a regional issue.
31 Waller to Anderson, 11 January 1972, NAA: A1838, 144/10/1 PART 2.

movers). 'We have done a lot already. These people will be important to us in the future', he said.[32] Nor, apparently, was he concerned by advice from the British that Kissinger had warned their ambassador in Washington that it would be 'premature' to recognise Bangladesh before the president's visit to Beijing (scheduled for May), and would be 'taken amiss'.[33]

In the event, Australia announced its recognition of Bangladesh on 31 January 1972, a couple of weeks later than first contemplated. It was delayed by the desire to move in company with 'like-mindeds'. The United Kingdom and others were canvassed—in what now would be described as an 'activist middle power' diplomatic initiative—but for various reasons they all delayed and so Australia moved with only New Zealand and Fiji to become the ninth, and first non-eastern bloc, government to recognise the new state.

The announcement was applauded in Australia. Amidst favourable editorial comment, *The Canberra Times* stood out: the recognition of Bangladesh, it said, was:

> possibly the most significant exercise undertaken by this country since it befriended Indonesia in 1945 … Australia, by its early recognition, has enlivened its reputation as an independent participant in the affairs of the region.[34]

Australian Policy: An Analysis

While Canberra's policy responses in the early days of the crisis might have been spontaneous, by the end of 1971 they had become quite deliberate. Australia's position was distinctive among usually 'like-minded' governments. Early in the crisis, in light particularly of the tone and content of McMahon's correspondence, a British official had remarked that the Australian position 'went rather further than anything we had said to the Pakistanis'.[35] Raghavan notes the more cautious approaches of, among others, the United Kingdom and Canada, each of whom was more reluctant to come out against Pakistan, lest they risked the effective use of the leverage they believed they had in Islamabad.[36]

---

32 Record of a telephone conversation between Waller and McMahon, 14 January 1972, ibid.
33 Australian High Commission in London to DFA, 10 January 1972, ibid.
34 *The Canberra Times*, 1 February 1972.
35 Raghavan, *1971*, 171.
36 At a 2015 conference on Australia–India relations, it was remarked that, contrary to what has come to be expected in more recent times, on this issue Canada was closer to the United States and Australia more distant.

In short, two strands of Australian policy had emerged quite early: acceptance of the reality that East Pakistan was finished, and well-founded humanitarian concern. Realpolitik and moral right don't always coincide, but on this occasion, for Australia, they did. Although there were occasional criticisms of India, and the traditional line about the need to balance the relationship between the two countries was not formally repudiated, in the broad our position was more sympathetic to India than those of most other Western governments. Future high commissioners would note how it was a position remembered and respected in New Delhi in the decades that followed, albeit other issues—in particular, ironically, that of India's nuclear tests—arose to affect the relationship more seriously over the following three decades.

As the crisis unfolded, the nature of Australia's policy interests broadened. Concern about India's potential isolation and the determination to recognise Bangladesh early in order not to leave the field to communist governments reflected a mature sense of the sort of role Bowen, at least, saw for Australia in the world. His pride in this was evident when he told parliament in May 1972 that Australia had 'taken not simply an active interest but also a positive role, and in some aspects a leading role'.[37]

New Delhi's appreciation of Australia's position was evident in the access that continued to be available to the high commissioner and visiting Australians, and was reflected particularly when Bowen visited India in May and was warmly received by Indian Minister of External Affairs Swaran Singh.

Nor did Australia's activism on behalf of Bangladesh end with the McMahon Government. Australia's first ambassador to the People's Republic of China, Stephen FitzGerald, records in his memoir that in his first meeting with Premier Zhou Enlai after taking up duty in Beijing in early 1973, he 'explain[ed] Australia's recognition of Bangladesh and urges China to do the same'. Zhou, he says, 'repli[ed] that China will refuse to recognise Bangladesh while it fails to carry out two UN resolutions on the repatriation to Pakistan of POWs'. FitzGerald records that a Chinese vice minister later asked why Bangladesh had aroused such interest in Australia, and that when Prime Minister Whitlam visited China in October 1973, Bangladesh was one of only two issues on which there were 'sharp disagreements'.[38]

---

37 Commonwealth, *Parliamentary Debates*, House of Representatives, 9 May 1972, 'Australian Foreign Policy', 2218 (NH Bowen MP).
38 Stephen FitzGerald, Comrade Ambassador: Whitlam's Beijing Envoy (Melbourne: Melbourne University Press, 2015), 100–02, 111.

In short, Australian policy in response to the events of 1971 placed Canberra at odds with both Washington and Beijing.

Australian and US Policies: 'Markedly Divergent'

Australia's policy responses through this crisis were different from those of the United States from the outset. This was acknowledged explicitly by Foreign Minister Bowen when he said, in a letter to US Secretary of State William Rogers on 22 December: 'I have noticed that during the past few weeks differences have developed between American and Australian policies in relation to the present crisis on the Indian sub-continent'. In strong language that seemed to capture Australian policy thinking rather better than those used in DFA's cable to Shaw and Stuart two days earlier (see below), Bowen went on:

> I know you feel that attempts being made by the United States to produce a political settlement were wrecked by India … it cannot be overlooked that the Government of Pakistan by its repressive actions in East Pakistan caused the deaths of hundreds of thousands of its own citizens and the flight into India of about 10 million more. Pakistan's military regime by many acts of brutality created a situation which was intolerable for its own people. It was Pakistan that mounted the pre-emptive air attack on India.[39]

Plimsoll took the letter to Rogers, who pointed out that the United States, as a matter of principle, was opposed to breaking up states. Plimsoll responded that sometimes states do nevertheless break up, and in this case 'the people had broken away and this had to be recognised'.[40] Again, Rogers did not allude to the global or geopolitical context in which Kissinger had come to see the crisis. Later, in his embassy's Annual Review for 1971–72, Plimsoll reported that the East Pakistan issue was 'the only issue on which Australian and US policies have diverged markedly'.[41]

Three questions arise. Did the United States notice or care about these differences between its positions and those of its ally? Did Australia influence the United States in any way, or attempt to? And why were the positions of these two allies so different?

---

39   Bowen to Rogers, 22 December 1971, NAA: A1838, 144/10/1 PART 1.
40   Plimsoll to DFA, 22 December 1971, ibid.
41   Jeremy Hearder, *Jim Plim: Ambassador Extraordinary: A Biography of Sir James Plimsoll* (Ballarat: Connor Court, 2015), 235.

Figure 6.4. 'Once we've worked out how to recognise them, let's try it out on China!' Stewart McCrae, *Courier Mail*, 1971.

Source: National Library of Australia: nla.gov.au/nla.obj-145844331.

On the first question, the differences would have been noted within the State Department and would have been referred to in the briefing prepared for Nixon's meeting with McMahon on 4 December (though in the event the matter was apparently not raised in that meeting). But overall, as matters relevant to the security relationship between the two countries were not considered to be in play, the reality is that Canberra's position did not matter much to the Nixon administration. Indeed, Kissinger notes in his memoir that 'the President would be reluctant to confront Yahya, but … the White House would not object to other countries' efforts to dissuade him from using force'.[42]

As to whether Canberra sought to influence Washington, it is easy to think that any advocacy would have been ineffectual given that policy was being made in the White House, where the attitudes of the president and his national security adviser were firmly entrenched. Plimsoll did, however, try.

42   Henry Kissinger, *White House Years* (Boston: Little, Brown and Co, 1979), 852.

Jeremy Hearder, in his biography of Plimsoll, records that, in an oral history recorded in 1981, Plimsoll had said he spoke to Secretary of State Rogers and other officials 'to try to hold them back from any violent support for Pakistan', though he could not be sure that his message was getting through to the White House. Plimsoll may have been referring here to an occasion on which, he told his staff, he had received a personal message from Mrs Gandhi asking him to intercede with Kissinger to try to persuade him to a more balanced view of India's position.[43]

Yet Hearder also adduces some tantalising evidence that Plimsoll's modesty at the time might have been misplaced. He notes that Plimsoll said in his 1981 oral history that, at a function at the White House in 1973, the president had said to another guest that Plimsoll had been 'of great value to us in recent troubles in India and Bangladesh'. And Nixon told Plimsoll on another occasion that: 'I will never forget what you did for us on Pakistan, India and Bangladesh. I will always be grateful. We owe you a great deal'.

In recording this later, Plimsoll said he was unsure what the president was referring to, but he speculated that if the United States had been contemplating some sort of military intervention in support of Pakistan, then 'what I had been saying to people may have held them back'.[44]

Why the Difference?

The remaining question then is this: why were the Australian and US positions so different on an issue where they might otherwise have been seen to have shared interests? The question is especially pertinent given that this was a conservative (Liberal/Country Party) coalition, the direct successor to one on whose behalf Prime Minister Harold Holt had famously said that Australia was 'all the way with LBJ'. It is all the more intriguing because Australia was still engaged in Vietnam alongside the United States. There are three plausible explanations.

---

43   Hearder, *Jim Plim*, 235.
44   Ibid. In advocating constraint on the part of a powerful ally, it can be said that Plimsoll had undertaken precisely that diplomatic role that Denis Stairs subsequently endorsed in his salutary work *The Diplomacy of Constraint: Canada, the Korean War, and the United States* (Toronto: Toronto University Press, 1974), doi.org/10.3138/9781487574260.

1. Unaligned Interests

The first and most evident explanation is that the two countries' interests were not the same. From the outset, American interests were shaped in good part by the impending rapprochement with China and Kissinger's planned visit to Beijing, of which the Australian Government knew nothing until two hours before it was announced. And later, as the crisis reached its denouement, the eyes of the White House were very much on what Nixon and Kissinger saw as the geopolitical stakes. The Australian Government did not see things or operate at that level, and indeed may not have agreed that so much needed to be at stake.

In short, Australia's view of the issues was simpler and less cluttered (including by personal perceptions) than that of the United States, probably more akin to what Kissinger had identified as the regional view taken by the State Department. As a result it was easier for Australia to base its positions on judgements about the moral issues and South Asian realpolitik than to take contrary positions.

2. Impact of the Diplomatic Voice

Yet there seems to have been more to it than this. Australian policy in regard to the subcontinent since 1947, frequently articulated and argued for by the Department of Foreign Affairs, had been to try to maintain a balance between India and Pakistan: to treat each the same. This hyphenation had its origins in the need to ensure neutrality on the Kashmir dispute, but it had come to pervade all areas of Australian interest in the two countries. While at the highest levels there was more sympathy for India, within the department at least the inclination was still to apply the template with apparently little consideration of the merits of the issues in play in 1971.

In August, First Assistant Secretary David Anderson had advised Foreign Minister Bowen that 'our first concern is a reluctance to adopt a position which either openly or by implication would appear hostile to Pakistan'. And as late as 17 September, Peter Henderson, the assistant secretary responsible for South Asia, told the Indian high commissioner—who had called to thank Australia for its aid to the refugees and to request Australia to again urge Pakistan to seek a political settlement in the east—that:

> We should be careful to remember that in the context of exerting political pressure, there was a delicate balance to be struck; we needed to maintain a position in which we were listened to by both parties.[45]

The postwar cable of 20 December in which Bowen had sought the views of Shaw and Stuart again reflects the 'delicate balance' theme. Presumably drafted in the department, it took care to distribute blame in an even-handed way, noting at the outset that:

> both sides have made serious mistakes. Pakistan by its brutal military regime in the East … and the pre-emptive strike on 3rd December … [while] India by its flagrant support for the Mukti Bahini contravened UN Resolutions she herself had helped to draft, and seriously jeopardised international attempts to produce a reasonable political settlement.

(As suggested above, it is interesting to compare these words with those used in Bowen's letter to Secretary Rogers just two days later.)

At this level then, the commitment to balance or even-handedness seems to have been firmly embedded. At the same time, however, more senior officials, including at the permanent head level, had been thinking more broadly about Australia's interests in the subcontinent. Keith Waller said after his retirement that, in coming to the office of secretary of DFA in 1970, one of his three main objectives had been to 'change the emphasis in our attitude to India and Pakistan', where, he said, we had been 'quite unrealistic' in favouring Pakistan over India.[46]

Arthur Tange, one of Waller's predecessors in DFA, who was by now secretary of the Defence Department and had served as high commissioner in New Delhi, had told Minister for External Affairs Paul Hasluck in 1966 that the 'delicate balance' approach had had a 'stifling effect on the development of policies to further our interests'. Tange criticised what he called 'the over-simplified concept of parity … the two countries

---

45   Record of Conversation, 17 September 1971, NAA: A1838, 169/10/1 PART 19, quoted in Meg Gurry, 'A Delicate Balance: Australia's "Tilt" to Pakistan and Its Impact on Australia–India Relations', *Australian Journal of International Affairs* 67, no. 2 (2013): 141–56, doi.org/10.1080/10357718.20 12.750641. Gurry argues in this thoughtful article that Australia had in fact 'tilted' to Pakistan over the years and was perceived in India to have done so.
46   Keith Waller, *A Diplomatic Life: Some Memories* (Nathan: Centre for the Study of Australia-Asia Relations, Griffith University, 1990), 45.

are not equal'.[47] Plimsoll, Waller's predecessor and now ambassador in Washington, held very similar views.[48] And of course Shaw became a vocal and respected advocate from New Delhi of the need to deal with the present issue on its merits and not through the prism of balance.[49]

It may be then that these—the real mandarins at the time—were the people whose views had most influence with the prime minister and his foreign ministers. McMahon had been foreign minister; he was known for his tendency to simplify issues and was certainly responsive to media and public interest. Leslie Bury, foreign minister from March to August 1971, was not particularly effective but did listen to Waller and read the cables during his brief spell in office. Nigel Bowen, who succeeded Bury in August, was not noted for flair, but he was a thoughtful and thorough man—'a hard and methodical worker', according to Waller[50]—who approached issues with an open mind and with compassion.

None of these had any investment in the notion of balancing relations between India and Pakistan. While taking conventional advice from the Department of Foreign Affairs, they are likely to have approached the events that followed the Pakistani crackdown as a new issue in its own right, and to have seen both the realpolitik and the moral considerations of the day without the baggage of policy history: or the complexities that influenced the positions of other governments.

3. The Prime Minister's Call?

There may also have been a third factor shaping Australia's policies. Customarily in Australia the prime minister of the day 'owns' the relationship with the United States, and that seems to have been the case for McMahon's three Liberal Party predecessors.[51] That being so, it might have been expected that the prime minister would have been sensitive to

---

47   Gurry, 'A Delicate Balance', 90–91. With considerable prescience, Tange's parting advice to his successor as high commissioner, Patrick Shaw, in 1970 had been not 'to echo the American point of view … [it] destroys respect for Australia as an independent nation'. See: Meg Gurry, *Australia and India: Mapping the Journey 1944–2014* (Carlton: Melbourne University Press, 2015), 77.

48   For example, see: Gurry, *Australia and India*, 88; and Hearder, *Jim Plim*, 234.

49   This was also the view of most of those who served as Australian high commissioner in New Delhi, including Peter Heydon, who became secretary of the Immigration Department but died in May 1971 as the crisis was playing out.

50   Gurry, 'A Delicate Balance', 96.

51   Indeed, when John Gorton became prime minister following Harold Holt's disappearance, Waller, then ambassador in Washington, asked his minister Paul Hasluck whether he should step aside to allow Gorton to appoint his own person to the job. See: Geoffrey Bolton, *Paul Hasluck: A Life* (Crawley: University of Western Australia, 2014).

Washington's positions, and concerned not to let Australian policy get too far from them. But McMahon himself was quite active on the issue, for instance in writing—as we have seen—to Yahya four times in fairly forthright terms, meeting with Mrs Gandhi in Washington when their visits coincided in November and then pressing for early recognition of Bangladesh.

In this, McMahon may have been moved by no more than his own appreciation of the situation and what he was hearing from his most senior officials. But there is likely to have been another consideration. McMahon was not reputed as a strategic thinker, but he was shrewd, media-sensitive and, according to his contemporaries, not inclined to let loyalty get in the way of his own interests. Having been embarrassed by Nixon's sudden move to engage China, and with Vietnam looming as a toxic issue in the election due in 1972, he may well have judged it useful to maintain some distance from Washington on the South Asian issue.

Also, McMahon seems to have been feeling some pressure from the Labor opposition, led by Gough Whitlam, who was vocal about the need for Australia to adopt a more independent foreign policy. On the eve of his visit to Washington in November 1971, McMahon was reported to be 'at pains to stress that he would not relegate Australia to the status of "echo or satellite" of the United States',[52] and it is possible that he saw the crisis in the subcontinent as an opportunity to give some substance to this position.

Consistent with this, following McMahon's visit to Washington and his meeting with Mrs Gandhi, one of the travelling press party, John Stubbs, presumably reflecting on a briefing from either McMahon himself or a senior adviser, wrote:

> Mrs. Indira Gandhi found a new and active ally in Washington last week. Not President Nixon, who made no concessions to her case against Pakistan. The Indian Prime Minister's ally is Mr McMahon, who is expected to argue in [his forthcoming visit to] London that international pressure should be applied to Pakistan.

---

52 *Melbourne Herald*, 4 November 1971, cited in James Curran, *Unholy Fury: Whitlam and Nixon at War* (Melbourne: Melbourne University Publishing, 2015), 109.

> [Mr McMahon] appears to have taken a calculated position that runs counter to his Government's strongly maintained policy of non-interference in the politics of other countries … On most topics he seems determined to adopt new and more independent approach than Australian Prime Ministers [visiting London] have done in the past.[53]

The superficial nature of this posturing on McMahon's part was of course evident in the fact that he used his visits to Washington and London to seek closer engagement with both governments in response to what he saw as the danger of the Soviet naval presence in the Indian Ocean, among other things. The day after Australia announced its recognition of Bangladesh, McMahon wrote to Yahya Khan again saying that 'Our recognition in no way detracts from the importance we attach to our friendship with Pakistan', and expressing the 'hope that good relations would continue'.[54] But in a short-term sense, it had suited McMahon well for Australia to take positions on the India–Pakistan issue that differed from those of the United States.

In reflecting on Australia–US relations during this crisis, it is also worth noting that there is no indication in the available archival records or commentaries on this crisis to suggest that the McMahon Government was consulted or advised about what Kissinger described as a 'decision to risk war', or was even aware of the 'decision', notwithstanding that the US facilities in Australia would have played a part in any US–Soviet conflict.

Reflections and Reverberations

1985: Following a promotion in the Department of Foreign Affairs, I attend the obligatory week-long management course that is intended to prepare me for the level to which I have been elevated. Each course participant is required to do a project on an issue relevant to their department. The new secretary, Dr Stuart Harris, who had come to the department from The Australian National University, believed that dissent within the department about Vietnam policy in the sixties and early seventies had not been sufficiently heard, and wanted to ensure that dissent of this kind, from whatever level, would be properly considered in the management of future policy issues. Conscious of this, I decide that my project would be the creation of a 'policy dissent mechanism'. Harris likes the proposal, and the progressive chairman of the Public Service Board, Dr Peter Wilenski, hears

---

53 *The Sydney Morning Herald*, 8 November 1971, by-line John Stubbs.
54 *The Sydney Morning Herald*, 1 February 1972.

of it and, himself the product of the pre-Vietnam generation in external affairs, also likes it. The birth of this imaginative piece of policy machinery is thus promulgated through a departmental 'administrative circular'. In the event, the mechanism is very little used, handling, as I recall, only one case (an eccentric one at that) while it quietly withered.

Incongruities and Ironies

The East Pakistan–Bangladesh crisis and its aftermath were laced through with incongruity. The greatest of these was the fact that the autocratic, communist Soviet Union supported democratic India and urged Pakistan to respect the will of its elected representatives, while the democratic United States supported Pakistan's military regime. For some at least, there are lessons here about the role of values in foreign policy when harder interests are engaged.

Irony is evident, too. At the strategic level, the United States is now more concerned than ever about the stability of Pakistan as it faces challenges from Islamic forces whose influence grew after the fall of Bhutto's regime in 1977. Increasingly uneasy about the relationship between Pakistan and China that it had used so adroitly in 1971, and in response to the rise of China, the US has been courting India as a counterweight or balance to China in Asia.

India is even more concerned about China's relationship with Pakistan and is especially wary of the extension of Beijing's 'One Belt-One Road' strategy into Pakistan. India continues too to be concerned about America's continued close relationship with Pakistan. Yet now, four decades on, with the rise of China, the passing of the post-independence Congress-influenced generation and the advent of the Modi Government, India has found common ground with the United States and worked its way past the reservations fostered by US policies of the 1960s and 1970s.

The Soviet Union meanwhile died in the year the Indo–Soviet Treaty expired, though the treaty had ceased to have any meaning long before then. Mrs Gandhi, unhappy about the Soviet Union's invasion of Afghanistan in 1979, declined to visit Moscow in 1981 to celebrate its tenth anniversary; any remaining chance of the treaty's renewal in 1991 was formally ruled out by President Yeltsin,[55] though by then there was no chance of India wanting to extend it anyway.

---

55   Shyam Saran, interview with author, 2 March 2015.

The ironies have compounded in other ways, too. At the level of international norms, India could not have won international support for any kind of humanitarian intervention in 1971, but when the concept of the 'Responsibility to Protect' (R2P) was developed by the International Convention on Intervention and State Sovereignty (ICISS) in 2001, the Pakistan Government's brutal intervention in East Pakistan was one of the cases on which it based its ground-breaking work. Indeed, former Australian foreign minister Gareth Evans, as co-chair of the ICISS, wrote later that:

> [India's] intervention was ostensibly (and not entirely incredibly) a self-defence response to a pre-emptive air strike by Pakistan; but, in fact, the action was taken primarily to ensure that mass murder and displacement, especially of the Hindu population, would not continue.[56]

Figure 6.5. Sheikh Mujibur Rahman pictured in Dacca, Bangladesh, 3 March 1971.
Source: Photo by Michel Laurent for the Associated Press, supplied by AAP Images.

---

56   Gareth Evans, *The Responsibility to Protect: Ending Mass Atrocity Crimes Once and For All* (Washington DC: Brookings Institution Press, 2008), 23.

'R2P' was subsequently endorsed by the UN General Assembly in its World Summit Outcome document in 2005. We can only speculate about what Washington's position might have been had 'R2P' been an internationally endorsed concept in 1971.

Finally, irony of a tragic kind extended as well to the *dramatis personae*. Of the four key players in the saga in the subcontinent, three died violently. Only Yahya Khan, who had instigated it all by calling an election whose result he could not manage, died in his own bed. Zulfikar Ali Bhutto replaced Yahya as president on 20 December 1971, then in 1973 became prime minister; displaced by a vengeful military leadership in a coup in 1977, he was then put on trial and executed. Sheikh Mujibur Rahman became prime minister and then president of Bangladesh, but in 1975 was assassinated in a coup from which Khondakar Mostaq Ahmed, the foreign minister of the Bangladeshi government in exile through whom the United States had sought to establish an alternative channel to the Bengali leadership in 1971, emerged as president. Indira Gandhi, who lost office in 1977 and was re-elected in 1980, was assassinated by Sikh nationalists in 1984.

Diplomatic Lessons

Reflection on the events of 1971 suggests a number of lessons for diplomacy, in particular for Australia. The history of the 1971 crisis and the differing policy responses to it underline an overarching policy lesson of the 'keep it simple' kind. Australian policy was framed in an uncomplicated context: rarely in international affairs do morality and realpolitik coincide as easily as they did in this case. As well, for Australia the crisis was seen as a regional issue of a kind best resolved among the countries immediately concerned. American policy by contrast was more complex: it brought into play interests external to the immediate issue that cut across the values and interests that the United States might otherwise have pursued in the subcontinent; and, in the White House at least, the crisis was quickly placed in a geopolitical framework, which greatly complicated its handling and raised the stakes very significantly.

A second lesson is about the Australia–US relationship: it is possible to shape Australian policy on the basis of our own understandings and judgements and to differ from Washington without exciting a diplomatic crisis in the alliance relationship. Washington's apparent lack of interest in our views is a reminder that the United States doesn't always care if we differ. At the same time, however, if we evaluate the evidence of Plimsoll's influence on American policy, the least that can be said of it is that his efforts were respected. In historical terms, his endeavours are a reminder that there can be a role for Australia: as a respected ally of the United States; in urging constraint on the use of its power; or 'speaking truth to power', in the modern argot.

Third, there is a lesson about the role of diplomatic and consular missions. Throughout this crisis, Australia's missions in South Asia, and indeed those in other capitals, not only reported fulsomely on the events as they unfolded, but also stimulated robust debate about Australian policy and participated actively in it. For those looking for lessons that might be relevant today, this is an important one: overseas missions can be critical not just in informing government and advocating Australia's interests, but also in contributing to the development of sound—and authentic— policy.

Significantly, Australia had a mission on the ground in Dhaka led by a diplomat who understood the mood and politics of East Pakistan and reported frankly on the events of the year as he saw them. This contrasts with, for example, the situation in East Timor in 1974, from which the Australian Government withdrew its consular mission in 1971 and was thus less well informed about the situation on the ground in the province leading up to the Indonesian invasion.

The role of Australia's missions was of course made easier by the more open policy framework within which they worked. The US Consulate in Dhaka was presumably at least as well informed as its Australian counterpart and certainly spoke plainly to Washington, but it was operating in a constrained policy framework. This was the context in which, amidst the chaos in East Bengal in April 1971, and with White House–led policy trending in ways that made it inconvenient to recognise the awfulness of what the Pakistan Army was doing, Consul General Archer Blood signed off on his 'policy dissent' telegram, and his career. For diplomats to conclude that challenging policy is fatal to their careers would be very much the wrong lesson to draw from the 1971 crisis!

The final lesson in all of this might well be about the importance of policymakers knowing their history: the more we educate ourselves about the past, the more easily we can make sense of the present and thus manage its challenges.[57]

Nor does the process of historic discovery necessarily have an end—had the accounts of Nixon and Kissinger been the end of the story, understanding of American policy might have been different—but the opening of Washington's archives has shed further light on the perfidy of the White House in 1971. Access to Canberra's well-maintained archives has shed a better light on Australian policy and, in doing so, served a useful purpose in itself.

Four Decades On

As Australia's mandarins had rightly foreseen, in the long term India was always likely to be a more significant player in world affairs than Pakistan, and its relative importance grew as a result of the vivisection of Pakistan. In the short term though, while Australia's sympathetic position was well remembered in New Delhi for some time, the Australia–India relationship benefited little from the new promise it had briefly shown in 1971–72.

It was not until after the Cold War had ended and a process of economic reform began that India was able to begin to translate its importance onto a wider international canvas. Forty years after the 1971 crisis, with India having been through another round of nuclear tests, with the rise of China suggesting a new level of shared interest, and with India's economic reforms beginning to show real returns, the Australia–India relationship began to realise the potential that wiser heads had foreseen in 1971.

Epilogue: Bangladesh

Meanwhile, the scars of 1971 remain evident on the South Asian body-politic, and the politics of Bangladesh in particular are riven with tragic reminders of events of 46 years ago. The political parties that emerged in this turbulent democracy were defined originally by the country's early history after independence. One major party—the Awami League—

---

57 Coincidentally, Australian journalist Laura Tingle published a thoughtful essay in 2016 arguing that a significant factor in the weakness of recent Australian governments has been 'political amnesia': a failure to know and learn from the past.

is led by Mujibur Rahman's daughter, Sheikh Hasina Wajed, the other, the Bangladesh Nationalist Party, by Sheikh Khaleda Zia, the widow of General Ziaur Rahman, who succeeded Mujib after the coup in which he was assassinated in 1975 (and was himself assassinated in 1981). Both Hasina and Zia have served periods as prime minister, but neither can let go of their personal history.

Thus, in 2009, Sheikh Hasina's newly re-elected government tried and executed nine military officers for their parts in Mujib's 1975 assassination. And in 2010, her government established two International Crimes Tribunals to prosecute crimes committed by Pakistan military personnel and others—including Bangladeshis—during the 1971 civil war. As a result of the tribunals' trials, at least 26 people have been convicted on charges of genocide and crimes against humanity, and four Bangladeshi nationals have been executed, including a member of Sheikh Zia's party.

As well as these personally vengeful touch points, the issue of how many Bengalis died in 1971 has, if anything, grown in importance in the poisonous political discourse. As *The New York Times* has put it, the belief that there were 3 million victims of the 1971 genocide is 'totemic' and a 'foundational element' for the ruling Awami League. In 2016, the Bangladesh Law Commission opened consultation on a draft law called the Liberation War Denial Crimes Act. The proposed law would outlaw any 'inaccurate' representation of the civil war's history, and as reported would almost certainly be used to prosecute anyone who questioned the 3 million figure.[58]

Increasingly, connections to 1971 go beyond personal party politics. Those executed since 2010 have also included members of Jamaat-e-Islami, a party that because of its commitment to Islam is seen to be closer to Pakistan. Thus, through a linkage to 1971, the modern politics of Islam has come to provide another overlay in the machinations of the political elites in this struggling nation.

---

58   *The New York Times*, 5 April 2016.

7

Mediating Middle Powers: Shaw, Grant, Curtis and Upton, 1972–83

David Lee

In the years from 1972 to 1983, Australia's relations with India entered a new phase. In this period, Australia adopted a more independent path in foreign policy, including a high-profile stance against racial discrimination. Particularly from the 1970s, Australia increasingly saw itself as a 'middle power' because of its regional leadership in the Pacific and its activism in multilateral forums such as the United Nations on whose Security Council Australia was a non-permanent member in 1973 and 1974. India was also a non-permanent member of the Security Council in 1972 and 1973 and, for somewhat different reasons, also saw itself as a middle power. As the dominant power in South Asia, India considered that it had the same 'senior' status in Asia, including South-East Asia, as did China and Japan.[1] It pressed its claims for 'middle power' status most conspicuously by entering the ranks of the nuclear weapon states in 1974.[2] In the years from 1972 to 1983, four Australian high commissioners to India, Sir Patrick Shaw, Bruce Grant, Peter Curtis and Gordon Upton, sought to

---

1   Submission from Sir Keith Waller to Minister for Foreign Affairs, 'India–Regional Cooperation', 29 May 1973, National Archives of Australia (NAA): A1838, 169/10/1 PART 23.
2   JD Sethi, 'India as Middle Power', *India Quarterly: A Journal of International Affairs* 25, no. 2 (1969): 107–21, doi.org/10.1177/097492846902500201; Charalapos Efstathopoulos, 'Reinterpreting India's Rise through the Middle Power Prism', *Asian Journal of Political Science* 19, no. 1 (2011): 74–95, doi.org/10.1080/02185377.2011.568246.

help the Australian Government to strengthen a bilateral relationship that had never managed to live up to its early promise. Although all of these high commissioners struggled valiantly and in different ways to mediate between the two middle powers, domestic and geopolitical factors conspired against the ambitions for the relationship that two prime ministers, Gough Whitlam and Malcolm Fraser, shared.

In 1972, in the year of the election of the Whitlam Government, Sir Patrick Shaw was the Australian head of mission in New Delhi. Shaw was born on 18 September 1913 in Kew, Melbourne, fourth child of Patrick Shaw, a physician. He was educated at Scotch College and the University of Melbourne. Shaw joined the Commonwealth Public Service in 1936 and was posted to Tokyo as a third secretary in 1940. When Japan entered the Second World War in December 1941, Shaw was interned for some months until exchanged for Japanese diplomats in 1942. From 1956 to 1959 he was ambassador to the Federal Republic of Germany and to Indonesia from 1960 to 1962. As head of mission in Jakarta, he recommended accommodation with Indonesia on the issue of West New Guinea and the retention of friendly links between the two countries.[3] In 1965 he was appointed permanent representative to the United Nations in New York, and after that was appointed to head Australia's mission in New Delhi. Commencing in India in 1970, he was still in India when the first federal Labor Government in two decades was elected in December 1972. By all accounts, Shaw was expecting to end his long and distinguished career with his posting in India. These plans changed with the election of the Whitlam Government.

On his first day as prime minister, E.G. Whitlam articulated a new thinking on foreign policy that presaged changes in Australia's relationships with all its regional neighbours. 'Our thinking', Whitlam declared:

> is towards a more independent Australian stance in international affairs and towards an Australia, which will be less militarily oriented and not open to suggestions of racism; an Australia, which will enjoy a growing standing as a distinctive, tolerant, co-operative and well-regarded nation not only in the Asian and Pacific region but in the world at large.[4]

---

3 David Lee, 'Shaw, Sir Patrick (1913–1975)' in John Ritchie and Diane Langmore (eds), *Australian Dictionary of Biography: Volume 16* (Carlton: Melbourne University Press, 2002), 220–21.
4 Commonwealth, *Parliamentary Debates*, House of Representatives, 24 May 1973, 2643, 'International Affairs' (EG Whitlam, MP).

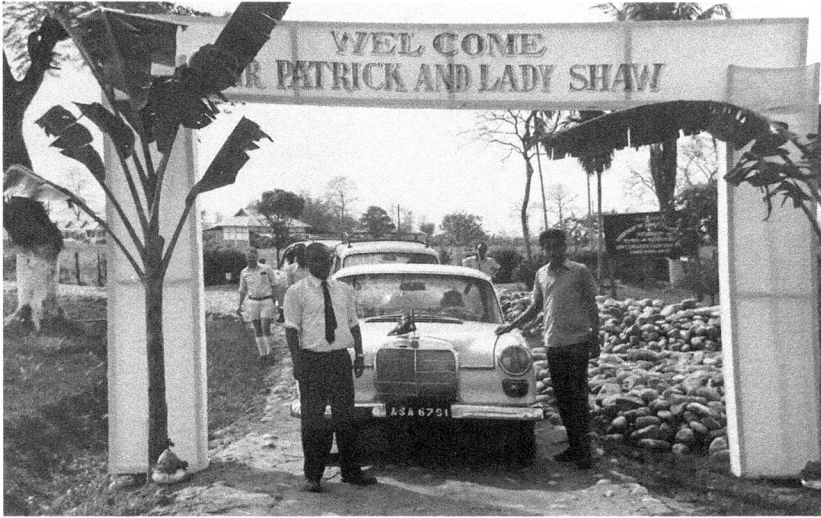

Figure 7.1. Photo of the welcome for Sir Patrick and Lady Shaw, Assam, March 1973.

Source: Photo by E Meadows.

The Whitlam Government moved quickly to recognise and establish diplomatic relations with the People's Republic of China and to initiate work on a new treaty with Australia's major trading partner, Japan. In the early period of the new government, Whitlam and his ministers also announced the removal of the remnants of Australia's discriminatory immigration policy—the White Australia policy—and foreshadowed that it would pass the *Racial Discrimination Act*, a law making discrimination on the grounds of race illegal. Whitlam's ministers further announced that they intended to accelerate the timetable for the independence of Papua New Guinea—the Australian external territory that would eventually achieve its independence in 1975.[5]

The Indian Government responded positively to the shift in both the policy and rhetoric of Australian foreign policy under Whitlam. At that time, India was reassessing its role in South-East Asia as a large Asian power in its own right. It was conscious of doubts, particularly in Western countries, about its historically strong relationship with the Soviet Union and was also disappointed by its exclusion from the supervision of the

---

5   Meg Gurry, *Australia and India: Mapping the Journey 1944–2015* (Carlton: Melbourne University Press, 2015), 102–3.

ceasefire arrangements and from the international conference convened to try to end the Vietnam War. The Indians were also aware of the special importance that Australia was giving to Indonesia and had noticed that India had been replaced by Indonesia as the main foreign recipient of Australian aid.

These were part of the reasons why, on Australia Day in 1973, the Indian minister for external affairs issued an invitation, through Shaw, for Whitlam to visit India.[6] Whitlam accepted immediately, later remarking that he was 'horrified' to learn that no Australian prime minister had visited India since 1959. Whitlam himself had visited the country before becoming prime minister and was keen to return to India as soon as possible in the life of his government. In New Delhi, Shaw helped to lay the ground for Whitlam's visit by making a major speech on Australia and Asia at the India International Centre in New Delhi, that placed the Whitlam Government's 'independent' foreign policy in historical context.[7] Whitlam's visit to India from 3 to 6 June 1973 served a concrete objective: to demonstrate, notwithstanding the sea change in Australia–China relations in 1972, that Australia was not excessively oriented towards China at the expense of other major Asian countries, such as India, Japan and Indonesia. Whitlam adopted the view that, although Australia was on the United Nations Security Council as a member of the 'Western Europe and Others' grouping, Australia would coordinate its activities in New York as far as possible with the Asian members of the council, especially India and Indonesia. As Whitlam told the Indian media:

> never again [in the United Nations] are we going to be in the position of finding ourselves siding with Britain, France, Portugal, South Africa and the US, while all our neighbours are on the other side.[8]

Whitlam was accompanied to India by a party of officials, including Sir John Crawford, the recently retired vice-chancellor of The Australian National University, and Bruce Grant, his unofficial adviser on foreign policy. Whitlam's choice of Crawford, a former secretary of the Department of Trade and then Canberra-based academic, as companion was deliberate

---

6   Cablegram, Department of Foreign Affairs to Minister for Foreign Affairs and Cablegram, Department of Foreign Affairs to Australian High Commissioner in New Delhi, NAA: A1838, 169/10/11/2/5 PART 1.

7   Shaw, 'Notes for Talk Given at India International Centre,' New Delhi, 22 May 1973, NAA: A1838, 169/10/1 PART 24.

8   Quoted in Gurry, *Australia and India*, 102–03.

and symbolic. After Crawford left the public service to join The Australian National University, he took part, in 1964–65, in the World Bank economic mission to India. Crawford subsequently made regular visits to India to assist in the development of his strategy for Indian agricultural development.[9] By 1972 Crawford had become a trusted friend of India and of Indian Prime Minister Indira Gandhi, who insisted that Crawford should never visit India without calling on her.[10] The high esteem in which Crawford was held in India reflected the priority that India was giving to achieving self-sufficiency in food production. However, although in 1971 India had hoped to achieve both self-sufficiency in food production and zero net aid, in 1974 a confidential report by the World Bank indicated that India would need at least 10 million tons of imported grain over the second half of the 1970s.[11]

Australia had historically made a significant mark in India during such episodes as J.B. Chifley's support for India to remain in the British Commonwealth despite its Republican status, and, as examined in Chapter Two, in Australia's participation in 1949 in a regional conference in New Delhi convened to support Indonesia's independence, positioning Australia alongside regional Asian states against European colonial powers.[12] Whitlam took the opportunity of his first visit to India as prime minister to forecast the eventual emergence of a new and widely representative association for Asia and the Pacific.[13] He made this forecast in a prerecorded speech broadcast on an all-India radio network prior to his arrival in New Delhi.[14] Whitlam remarked that he did not expect the concept to come about overnight. 'Rather', he said, 'we believe that the concept should be allowed to mature slowly and gradually, by close consultation and discussion among all those interested, until a consensus in its favour begins to emerge naturally among the nations of the region'.

9   W David Hopper, 'An Interlude with Indian Development', in LT Evans and JDB Miller (eds), *Policy and Practice: Essays in Honour of Sir John Crawford* (Canberra: Australian National University Press, 1987), 158–73.
10   JDB Miller, 'Crawford, Sir John Grenfell (1910–1984)', in Diane Langmore (ed.), *Australian Dictionary of Biography, Volume 17* (Carlton: Melbourne University Press, 2007), 265–68.
11   Bernard Weintruab, 'India Seeks to Change Her Beggar Image', *The New York Times*, 24 March 1974.
12   Frank Bongiorno, 'British to the Bootstraps? H. V. Evatt, J. B. Chifley and Australian Policy on India's Membership of the Commonwealth', *Australian Historical Studies* 36, no. 125 (2005): 18–31, doi.org/10.1080/10314610508682909; see also David Lee (ed.), *Documents on Australian Foreign Policy 1937–49*, vol. 15, *Australia & Indonesia's Independence: The Transfer of Sovereignty 1949* (Canberra: Australian Government Publishing Service, 1998).
13   Gurry, *Australia and India*, 105.
14   John Slee, 'PM Forecasts New Links for Asia, Pacific', *The Sydney Morning Herald*, 4 June 1973.

In his 1973 speech in New Delhi, however, Whitlam could not help noting that there was 'something missing in recent years in the relationship between the two countries'.[15] Whitlam speculated that Australia's focus on Indochina in the 1960s and 1970s and the 'fascinating possibilities Australia had before her in her relations with China' might have meant that relations with India did not receive the attention that they deserved. He added:

> The anomaly I find is this: here are two great democracies—bordering the Indian Ocean, both members of the Commonwealth, both deeply dedicated to world peace, both with Federal systems, both holding great institutions in common: and yet we haven't forged the very close relations I believe we should have.[16]

Notwithstanding Whitlam's foreshadowing of a regional organisation, some of his advisers were sceptical about how quickly the bilateral relationship between India and Australia could be developed and about how readily India might fit into an Asian regional grouping. Patrick Shaw, for example, warned that the Australian Government should be mindful that many of India's policies were not popular with its South-East Asian neighbours and that none of the countries of the South-East Asian and East Asian region have much interest in encouraging Indian participation in their affairs. Shaw also reported that, while Whitlam had established excellent relations with top-level Indian policymakers, Australia still had to add substance to sentiment:

> India ... is not simply the 'pitiful helpless giant' described [elsewhere]. India is one of the great Asian powers and the one with which we share perhaps the greatest common background although not the greatest economic interest. We share a common geographical concern in the Indian Ocean ... we [must] strengthen our influence here [with] a modest investment of attention.[17]

The secretary of the Department of Foreign Affairs, Sir Keith Waller, also warned Whitlam that both Indonesia and Malaysia had indicated that they did not wish India to be part of any new regional organisation. Waller recommended that Gandhi should be informed that 'decisions will

---

15 Speech by Whitlam in New Delhi, *Australian Foreign Affairs Record* 44 (June 1973): 393–94.
16 Ibid., 395.
17 Shaw to the Department of Foreign Affairs, 10 June 1973, NAA: A1838, 169/10/11/2/5 PART 3.

be made from within the South-East Asian and East Asian region itself'.[18] Senior official in the Department of Foreign Affairs Michael Cook agreed with Shaw that:

> India has always been recognised as of major importance to Australia—a recognition often honoured, perhaps more in the breach than the observance, but nevertheless a basic constituent of Australia's foreign policy thinking, particularly in respect of Asia. At least while our policies on current issues continue to coincide, there will be scope for increasing the amount of direct attention we pay to India, but this will of course have to compete with numerous other major concerns.[19]

In a significant reshuffle of senior diplomats in the year of his speech, Whitlam moved Sir James Plimsoll, a former high commissioner in New Delhi and ambassador to the United States, to Moscow; designated Shaw from New Delhi to replace Plimsoll in Washington; and then appointed Australian journalist Bruce Grant to succeed Shaw in India. Born in 1925 and educated at the Perth Modern School and then the University of Melbourne, Grant joined the staff of *The Age* in Melbourne in 1949 and in 1957–58 was a Nieman Fellow at Harvard University. Author of a number of books on Asia, Grant was a strong supporter of the Whitlam Government and of greater 'independence' in Australian foreign policy. Indeed, Grant had been an unofficial foreign policy adviser to Whitlam in 1971 and 1972 in the lead-up to the 1972 election. Whitlam had considerable regard for Grant's knowledge of the Asian region and for that reason took him with him on his trip to India.[20] Chapter Eleven examines Grant's published writing about India.

Before he took up his position in New Delhi, Grant told an Australia–India Society Meeting in Melbourne in October 1973 that Australia's relations with India, although friendly and useful, lacked substance.[21] Trade between the two countries in 1973 was actually declining and general economic relations could 'most courteously be described as minimal'.[22]

---

18   Submission from Waller to Whitlam, 14 May 1973, NAA: 1838, 169/10/11/2/5 PART 2; Gurry, *Australia and India*, 106–7.
19   Letter from MJ Cook to Patrick Shaw, 18 April 1974, NAA: A1838, 169/10/1 PART 27.
20   See: Bruce Grant, *Subtle Moments: Scenes on a Life's Journey* (Clayton: Monash University Publishing, 2017).
21   Cablegram from Department of Foreign Affairs to High Commission in New Delhi, 29 October 1973, conveying text of remarks of Bruce Grant at the Australia–India Society, Melbourne, on 26 October, NAA: A1838, 169/10/1 PART 25.
22   Ibid.

Grant remarked that he had been urging Australia to improve its relations with India and that the independence of Australia's new foreign policy depended on keeping a balance between the three great Asian states: China, Japan and India. 'It would be a mistake', Grant concluded, for Australia to become economically dependent on Japan and it would be a mistake to become uncritical in our relations with China, 'replacing the old myth of the "bad" nation with a new myth of the "good" nation'.[23]

Don Willesee, who succeeded Whitlam in the portfolio of Foreign Affairs, gave strong encouragement to Grant by urging him to:

> seek to convince the Indian authorities that Australia is a sophisticated and independently minded country with wide interests and having a useful network of international contacts … that it would be an advantage to India to develop the habit of exchanging views with us on major international issues.[24]

In his first address to the Indian National Press Club on 20 December 1973, Grant asserted that the Whitlam Government had 'removed forever the psychology of dependence' and that the government had taken away 'all official sanction of racial discrimination'.[25] The government, he explained:

> has made a conscious effort to show that, officially, racial prejudices will not be tolerated. So we have taken clear positions on South Africa and Rhodesia. We have signed long-neglected human-rights conventions. We have removed the racial implications from our immigration policy.[26]

He continued:

> [Australia] will look to Asia as the crucible of an independent foreign policy. Our relations with the nations of Asia are primary. They necessarily underpin the structure of Australian foreign policy … we regard India as one of the great nations of Asia, with whom we would like a relationship no less essential to an independent foreign policy than those we have with China and Japan.[27]

---

23 Ibid.
24 Willesee to Grant, 2 January 1974, quoted in Gurry, *Australia and India*, 109–10.
25 Address by Australian High Commissioner, Mr Bruce Grant, to the Press Club of India, 20 December 1973, NAA: A1838, 169/10/1 PART 26.
26 Ibid.
27 Ibid.

Not long after taking up the position in New Delhi, Grant reported optimistically to Canberra that 'for a robust middle power' like Australia, 'there is now a region of special application … where we are more deeply involved … the three great Asian states of Japan, India and China'.[28] In his first dispatch to the minister for foreign affairs, Don Willesee, in February 1974, Grant confirmed that Australia was being more highly regarded in India; and that India, as a major regional power, 'was important to Australia because good relations with it can help to underpin an independent Australian policy'. In the past, he noted:

> Our relations [with India] were determined primarily by broad international concerns, such as the Commonwealth, the Cold War, containment of China etc. Today we can perhaps begin to see India in a new way: as an object of Australian foreign policy. If India retains roughly its present importance in international affairs, the requirements of Australia's own foreign policy will demand that we seek closer relations.[29]

However, as Meg Gurry has observed, despite Grant's optimism, progress towards a more developed bilateral relationship were slow. Planned ministerial visits were postponed, initiatives in the cultural exchange program were not implemented and Australian aid to India, at A$1.4 million, remained distinctly modest compared to Canada's C$80 million.[30] Then the explosion by India of a nuclear device in the Rajasthani desert on 18 May 1974 emerged as the most significant challenge to the development of the relationship between middle powers. Coming little more than a year after the Whitlam Government ratified the Nuclear Non-Proliferation Treaty, the Indian explosion highlighted the difference in the two countries' notion of 'middle power'. For India the nuclear test showed India's transformation into a modern technological society, non-aligned in foreign policy and equipped to defend its sovereignty against other states such as Pakistan and the People's Republic of China. For Australia, on the other hand, its idea of a middle power was the pursuit of a principled foreign policy through adherence to international norms such as those in the nuclear nonproliferation regime and activist diplomacy in the United Nations. India and Australia were both temporary members of the Security Council in 1973, but by the

---

28 Ibid.
29 Dispatch from Grant to Willesee, 'State of Relations between Australia and India', 11 February 1974, NAA: A1838, 169/10/1 PART 26.
30 Gurry, *Australia and India*, 110–11.

second year of Australia's term, India had also joined the ranks of the small number of states that were nuclear powers. According to Grant, Whitlam was particularly disappointed by the Indian nuclear test because he had placed a great deal of faith in the Nuclear Non-Proliferation Treaty, and now India, to which Whitlam had 'made a point of extending the hand of friendship, had shown up the Treaty's limitations in a particularly blatant way'.[31]

The return to power of the Coalition Government under Malcolm Fraser in November 1975 brought with it a focus on combatting the extension of Soviet power in the Indian Ocean region. In 1976 Fraser reversed a policy of the Whitlam Government by welcoming an American military presence on the small island of Diego Garcia. The Indian Government, which had sided with the Whitlam Government in pressing for the demilitarisation of the Indian Ocean, did not welcome this development, but other aspects of the Fraser Government's policies were more congenial. Fraser pushed ahead with legislating land rights for Aboriginal people in the Northern Territory and adopted as strong a position as Whitlam on opposing racially based regimes in southern Africa. These policies were well received in India. Fraser played an important role in meetings of the Commonwealth in introducing boycotts of South African sporting teams and promoting black majority rule in Rhodesia. This stance helped Fraser to develop a constructive relationship with Indira Gandhi's successor as prime minister, Morarji Desai. Desai and Fraser agreed on the usefulness of regional meetings of the Commonwealth, which had tended, in the 1960s and early 1970s, to concentrate overwhelmingly on African issues. India accepted an invitation to attend a Sydney Commonwealth Heads of Government Regional Meeting in Sydney in 1978. After attending it, Desai commented that the meeting had 'helped to inform and educate Australians about the nature of our region [and confirm India's position] as a well-intentioned and responsible country in the Asian-Pacific area'.[32]

By 1976, the career diplomat, Peter Curtis, had succeeded Bruce Grant as Australian high commissioner to India. Born in Sydney in 1929 and educated at the universities of Sydney and Oxford, Curtis joined the Department of External Affairs in 1957 and was ambassador to Laos and then to Lebanon before succeeding Grant in New Delhi in 1976. As Meg Gurry has written of him in her study of Australia's relations with India,

---

31 Grant quoted in ibid., 111.
32 Ibid., 118.

Curtis, like Shaw and Grant before him, was concerned about the relative lack of priority that Australia accorded to relations with India. As Curtis put it:

> The desire to boost Australia/India relations has been reaffirmed at Prime Ministerial level but there has still been no significant commitment to new resources to give substance to that expressed intent … India should be accorded a higher place in the Australian government's priorities [but] if we continue to be unable to match action to words we will increasingly lose opportunities to improve our relationship with an important regional neighbour … It is ironic … that as opportunities for expanding the relationship have increased … resources have dwindled.[33]

Curtis was farsighted in recommending in 1979 the establishment of an Australia India Foundation along the lines of the pioneer councils established with Japan in 1976 and China in 1978. Curtis hoped in 1978 that Fraser might make the announcement of such a council the centrepiece of a prime ministerial visit to India.[34] However, he backed away from the idea when it failed to attract support in the Department of Foreign Affairs.[35] It would take another 13 years for such a foundation to be established and for Curtis's suggestion to be realised.

Curtis was high commissioner during Malcolm Fraser's first visit to India as prime minister in 1979. The highlight of the visit was an address to the Indian Parliament, the first ever by an Australian prime minister. In announcing his visit to India, Fraser replicated the remarks of Whitlam in 1973. He declared that: '[t]he relationship between India and Australia is an important one but over the years I think it has been taken a little too much for granted'.[36] The reason for the visit, he added:

> wasn't that there were problems between our two nations. It was the fact that we wanted to work positively to promote a better, a closer and a warmer relationship than had existed in the past.[37]

---

33 Curtis quoted in Gurry, *Australia and India*, 119.
34 Letter, Curtis to Tonia Shand, 14 December 1978, NAA: A1838, 169/10/11/2/7 PART 6.
35 For example, IG Bowden, first assistant secretary responsible for the Public Affairs and Cultural Relations Division, commented on 17 January 1979: 'I am opposed to the idea of an Australia–India Foundation. Some over-worked section will get lumbered with the secretariat chores and the Department will have less influence on the development of cultural relations than now'. NAA: A1838, 169/10/11/2/7 PART 6.
36 Prime Minister's Statement for Indian Television, 14 December 1978, NAA: A1838, 169/10/11/2/7 PART 6.
37 Ibid.

Curtis greatly contributed to the success of Fraser's visit. He briefed the prime minister extensively on India's cultural history and suggested that Fraser make contact with leading experts in South Asian history before coming to India. He advised Fraser:

> I cannot stress sufficiently the importance of the Prime Minister getting across to the Indians during his visit that he is aware of and appreciates India's considerable cultural heritage and he recognises that there is much more to this country than the influence of the British Raj and the period since 1947.[38]

Fraser took Curtis's advice and pursued many of the same themes as Whitlam had done in his speeches in India in 1973. Fraser remarked that neither Australia nor India had done enough over the previous 30 years to fulfil the potential of the relationship. It was an important and extremely well-received speech, informed by Peter Curtis's advice that the speech should pay due attention to Indian cultural history. 'No country on earth', Fraser declared, 'has such a long cultural continuity as India. By comparison, Australia is a very young country, one which has created a distinctive cultural identity for itself during the course of the century'.[39] Fraser was at pains to rebut the common perception that Australia was a 'typically western country which happens to be eccentrically located at the bottom right-hand corner of Asia'. He elaborated:

> We are Western with a difference. A country which originated as a colony, whose own physical geography and environment are so distinctive, whose outlook and perspectives are profoundly affected by its location in the South-East Asian region: whose export earnings derive principally from commodities; which is a net importer of capital, cannot be regarded as typically western. Australia is Australia, not an appendage of Europe.[40]

Fraser's visit to India, like Whitlam's, was well received, as was his major theme that India in the non-aligned world and Australia in the Western world were two middle powers that could profitably cooperate together to help solve significant international problems.[41]

---

38 Curtis quoted in Gurry, *Australia and India*, 120.
39 Text of the Australian Prime Minister's address to the Indian Parliament on 27 January 1979, *Australian Foreign Affairs Record* 50 (January 1979): 67.
40 Ibid., 68.
41 Record of Meeting, 8 March 1979, NAA: A1838, 169/10/1 PART 38.

In 1979, when the Soviet Union invaded Afghanistan, however, the realpolitik of the Cold War retarded the closer Australian–Indian relationship for which both Whitlam and Fraser had called. Fraser put Australia firmly in the US camp against the Soviet intervention. However, India, with Indira Gandhi as prime minister again, made it clear that it would not be taking such a position against the Soviet Union, on which India was reliant for trade and arms and in the United Nations on the Kashmir issue. With the United States now recognising the People's Republic of China, India felt that it had more to fear from US relations with Beijing and Islamabad than it did with a Soviet-backed regime in Kabul.

Curtis was succeeded in New Delhi after 1980 by Gordon Noel Upton. Born in Sydney in 1920, Upton was educated at Canterbury Boys High and then the University of Sydney. He joined the Commonwealth Public Service in 1937 and after military service in the Royal Australian Air Force, was appointed to the Department of External Affairs as a diplomatic cadet. He was counsellor in the Australian Embassy, Jakarta, under Patrick Shaw and served as high commissioner in Sri Lanka from 1970 to 1973 and high commissioner in Suva from 1976 until his appointment to New Delhi in 1980. In the year of his appointment, Upton was shaken by a leak of one of his confidential dispatches to the minister for foreign affairs, Andrew Peacock. Upton reported in the dispatch that, after nearly nine months back in office, Prime Minister Gandhi had failed to solve any of India's major domestic problems and that, moreover, the country was at risk of being subject to a military coup. The dispatch was leaked to journalist, Laurie Oakes, and published in *The Age* newspaper. Bruce Grant, at that time, had returned to *The Age* and as a journalist had ironically reached conclusions about India that were similar to Upton's.[42] The leak occasioned some Indian parliamentarians to call for Upton's removal. As Upton confided to a colleague on 18 November 1980, the following two or three weeks would tell him whether he would he could usefully carry on in New Delhi.[43] The top echelons of the Department of Foreign Affairs were also worried. The secretary of the Department of Foreign Affairs, Peter Henderson, at that time was not certain whether the Indian Government would be prepared to go on working with Upton and was worried that the Opposition in India was using Upton's leaked dispatch to attack Gandhi.[44]

---

42   Cablegram from WGT Miller to Upton, 11 November 1980, NAA: A1838, 169/10/1 PART 42.
43   Letter from Upton to WGT Miller, 18 November 1980, NAA: A1838, 169/10/1 PART 42.
44   Minute from PGF Henderson to WGT Miller, 14 November 1980, NAA: A1838, 169/10/1 PART 42.

A personal and magnanimous letter from Gandhi to Fraser illustrates the degree to which the relationship had been strengthened in the 1970s, even if it had not blossomed to the degree that both Whitlam and Fraser desired. Gandhi explained frankly to Fraser that India indeed faced vast problems, but pleaded:

> Can any problem be solved straightaway? At most we can set the country on the right direction in a step by step process which takes us nearer the objective … The administration is recovering from the coma into which it had settled during the last three years. Our next five year plan has been finalized in the shortest time, with the highest ever allocation of funds and very defined priorities. Law and order has been improved but the situation needs to improve further. Similarly the performance of our railways has not improved as it should have. While a lot remains to be done, we are firmly set on a clear direction. We value our friendship with Australia and hope that the Australian people will see India in perspective.[45]

The minister for foreign affairs, Andrew Peacock, annotated to the secretary of his department: 'You should see this remarkable letter. We are talking to PM&C about making a copy available to Gordon Upton, & about intentions in a reply'.[46] After Fraser published a press release regretting the leak, Upton was allowed to remain in his post and reported a year later that there was no reason to feel that the leak had created lasting embarrassment.[47]

Under two prime ministers, Gough Whitlam and Malcolm Fraser, the Australian Government sought a substantial improvement and development of the bilateral relationship between countries that saw themselves, for different reasons, as 'middle powers'. One of these prime ministers, Whitlam, also looked forward to the time when Australia and India were both fellow members of an Asian regional organisation. Four high commissioners, Patrick Shaw, Bruce Grant, Peter Curtis and Gordon Upton, worked hard to try to give more substance to the relationship underpinned by two successful prime ministerial visits to India in 1973 and 1979. The effort put in to developing Australian–Indian relations in the period from 1972 to 1983 was partially successful as was demonstrated

---

45   Letter from Gandhi to Fraser, 11 November 1980, NAA: A1938, 169/10/1 PART 42.
46   Ibid., annotation by Peacock, 26 November 1980.
47   Upton quoted in Gurry, *Australia and India*, 128.

by the magnanimous position adopted by Gandhi after the leak of Upton's dispatch in 1980. However, both domestic and foreign policy developments conspired against the fuller realisation of the ambitions that Whitlam and Fraser shared for the relationship. In Whitlam's case, his domestic problems distracted from his foreign policy agenda and particularly his ability to put in place new regional architecture. In Fraser's case, despite a valiant effort to change Australia's image in Asia and India, the Soviet invasion of Afghanistan underlined the wide disparity between the fundamental positions of non-aligned India and Western-aligned Australia. On top of this, was the relative lack of the economic 'complementarity' between Australia and India that there was between Australia and Japan and would be between Australia and China. Between 1975 and 1983, for example, exports from Australia to India decreased as a percentage of total exports from 0.74 per cent to 0.57 per cent.[48] As Meg Gurry has observed, in the Whitlam and Fraser years, 'a viable multilateral and regional framework still eluded the Australia–India relationship'.[49]

---

48 Gurry, *Australia and India*, 127.
49 Ibid., 129.

8

Arresting the Drift: The Graham Feakes Era

Meg Gurry

Graham Feakes was Australia's high commissioner in India from August 1984 until October 1990. He requested the posting. Both he and his wife Nicky were pleased when asked to stay on for a second term. Feakes later said he regarded it 'as the best period of my whole service'.[1]

This chapter divides the analysis of Feakes's time in India into three sections: first, the years 1984–87; the second looks at 1987–90; and the third tells a story that sheds light on Graham the person. There are many declassified files open in the National Archives of Australia for the first period, but less after 1988. The second and third sections thus rely on more secondary sources and the memories of those who were in India at the time.

The research for this paper included interviews with a number of people who had served with Graham, either in New Delhi, Canberra or other posts around the world. There was little variation on the theme that he was one of the best of his generation, a serious man of depth and integrity who was a pleasure to work with. It should be noted too that Feakes is one of a long line of Australian high commissioners to India whose work is remembered with profound respect.

---

1   Graham Feakes, interviewed by Michael Wilson, 18 October – 24 November 1993, Canberra, National Library of Australia (NLA): Australian Diplomacy Oral History Project.

The First Term: 1984–87

Feakes arrived in New Delhi in August 1984 at a point where the relationship between Australia and India was described as 'good but lacking in depth'. It had been 'a modest year', the review for the previous year stated.[2] Elsewhere it was more candidly described as 'in the doldrums'.[3] These reflections were not new. In 1983, Foreign Affairs Department Secretary Peter Henderson lamented that:

> the bilateral relationship lacks real depth. Neither side looms large in the thinking of the other and we have few illusions about our capacity to influence Indian views where we differ.[4]

Indeed, as outlined in Chapter Seven, in 1979 Prime Minister Malcolm Fraser made an official trip to India, working with Australia's then high commissioner to India, Peter Curtis, to strengthen what seemed an important but little understood regional relationship. It was a well-publicised visit, but with few sustainable outcomes.

This time, five years later and under a new Labor Government, it was High Commissioner Feakes who set out to raise its profile. The new foreign minister, Bill Hayden, was keen to focus on the Indian Ocean region. Department Secretary Stuart Harris wrote to Feakes in December 1984, outlining how Hayden was keen to obtain Cabinet's endorsement to 'lift bilateral relations with India [and of] paying India a great deal more attention'.[5] Feakes knew a lot about India. He had been the senior official in the South Asia branch of the Department of Foreign Affairs (DFA) from 1980 to 1984, and he enjoyed a personal interest: his wife Nicky was born in India and was learning Hindi.[6] Just before his term began, he wrote a speech for Foreign Minister Hayden to deliver in Perth, which outlined a new Australian policy for the Indian Ocean. It referred to the 'drift' that had affected Australia's relationship with India. The term stuck. Before long the new narrative for Australia–India relations was all about 'arresting the drift', a task Feakes accepted with zeal.

---

2   Annual Review, July 1983 – July 1984, National Archives of Australia (NAA): A1838, 169/10/21 PART 5.
3   Maurice to Feakes, 26 November 1985, NAA: A1838, 169/10/1 PART 54.
4   Henderson to Upton, 17 November 1983, NAA: 1838, 169/10/21 PART 5.
5   Harris to Feakes, 28 December 1984, NAA: 1838, 169/10/21 PART 5.
6   Nicky Feakes, interview with author, Sydney, 22 September 2016.

Hayden declared it was time to 'become busier diplomatically and culturally in the [Indian Ocean] region'. There were now, he said, 'unassailable reasons of national self-interest why it should hold a consistent and sensible place in our priorities'.[7] The speech was well received in New Delhi. Feakes said it nicely oiled the wheels for his arrival.[8]

By the end of 1984, Hayden was urging Prime Minister Bob Hawke to endorse a new India strategy. Relations with India, Hayden wrote, had:

> been allowed to drift in recent years … and Australian foreign policy has develop[ed] without a full appreciation of India's present and potential importance … [There would be considerable] material economic benefits from a closer relationship.[9]

To a word, the letter reflected the deeply held belief of High Commissioner Feakes of how the relationship was, could and should be travelling.

A visit to India by Hayden was planned for May 1985, the first of a foreign minister since Nigel Bowen in 1972. Hayden and Feakes wanted to find a 'central core' to underpin the relationship. They identified closer trade and economic links as the path with the most potential.[10] But Hawke was not yet on board the India train. Initially cautious, he pointed out 'the real difficulties' in dealing with India, reminding Hayden of the problems experienced by previous Australian governments. He listed the perennial bilateral roadblocks: India's vast development challenge, its tradition of economic self-sufficiency, its affinity with the Soviet Union and the fact that Australia has closer Asian neighbours where 'the problems are more manageable in scale and the results more immediately evident'.[11]

Hawke changed his mind after meeting Rajiv Gandhi at a Commonwealth Heads of Government Meeting (CHOGM) meeting in Nassau in October 1985. As Hawke put it, 'we just clicked … there's no other leader I have met for whom I have developed such an immediate, deep and abiding affection'.[12] They began cooperating on a Commonwealth campaign of ending apartheid in South Africa. With Prime Minister Brian Mulroney

---

7   Bill Hayden, 'Australian Government's Views on the Indian Ocean', 20 June 1984, *Australian Foreign Affairs Record* 55, no. 6 (1984): 576–84.
8   Graham Feakes, interview with author, Sydney, 17 December 1992.
9   Hayden to Hawke, 19 December 1984, NAA: A1838, 169/10/1 PART 54.
10   Ibid.
11   Hawke to Hayden, date indecipherable but early 1985, NAA: A1838, 169/10/1 PART 54.
12   Hamish McDonald, 'A Testing Time for India—and Australia', *The Sydney Morning Herald*, 3 September 2011.

of Canada, Hawke and Gandhi formed a three-member team, aiming to talk British Prime Minister Margaret Thatcher out of her staunch opposition to sanctions. A productive and warm working relationship was established. Hawke invited Rajiv to visit Australia and he came in October 1986, the first Indian prime minister to come to Australia on a formal bilateral visit since Indira Gandhi in 1968. (The next would be Narendra Modi in 2014.)

By the end of 1985, the Australia–India relationship was attracting both prime ministerial and foreign ministerial interest. But the bureaucratic response was less enthusiastic. The departments of the Prime Minister, of Foreign Affairs and of Trade were scrambling to find an appropriate and workable response. Before Gandhi's visit, the head of the Prime Minister's Department, Geoffrey Yeend, called a meeting of department secretaries. The minutes provide a fascinating insight into just how difficult it was to 'arrest the drift' and find the elusive 'central core'. Yeend was clearly not excited by India. He noted, with obvious disapproval, that the invitation to Rajiv Gandhi had been issued 'without prior consultation'. It may reflect, he conceded, 'the excellent personal relations between Mr. Hawke and Mr. Gandhi', but how many bilateral relationships of the kind Australia was now seeking—with Japan, China, the Association of South-East Asian Nations (or ASEAN) countries—'could be sustained?' Was it even 'feasible', he asked, 'trying to put India on the same footing?'[13]

He suggested there were limits to Australia's capacity to manage India. And one by one all the department secretaries agreed. John Menadue from the Department of Trade noted that trade with India was stagnant and it had not proved possible to build a sustained relationship. He listed the obstacles of India's self-sufficiency and its highly regulated economy, and questioned whether political direction could overcome these problems. The secretary of defence emphasised that India is not within Australia's area of prime strategic interest, and hence, bilateral defence contacts were low key. The secretary for science spoke frankly of the difficulties encountered in cooperating with the Indian bureaucracy under the Science and Technology Agreement of 1975. The secretary of industry and commerce said he saw no sign of Australian industry

---

13   Notes of meeting of departmental secretaries, 13 November 1985, NAA: A1838, 169/10/1 PART 54.

wanting closer contacts with India. The best spin that Yeend could find to mitigate the gloomy outlook was to conclude that 'quick results should not be expected'.[14]

In short, the central core remained out of reach and, to many, out of sight. Just as Prime Minister Malcolm Fraser had attempted in 1979 to add some substance to the bilateral relationship through his warm connection with Indian Prime Minister Morarji Desai—they too had met at a Commonwealth meeting—so Hayden and Feakes tried to combine an encouraging prime ministerial bond with some top-down political energy to move the relationship forward. But within the bureaucracy in Canberra, it was obvious that officials were desperately searching for some 'announceables' to accompany the prime ministerial visit, but were having problems finding what they might be.

Meanwhile, unhappy cables from New Delhi kept arriving. Feakes sounded chronically disappointed. He described Hayden's 1985 visit as 'unproductive'. Hayden had come 'empty-handed', which meant that 'any genuine effort to exploit opportunities for bilateral trade' could not succeed. Contesting the view that India was 'more difficult to deal with than is worth the effort', he asserted that 'others manage it and given our own economic situation, we can no longer afford to ignore a market which others find both attractive and profitable'. He stressed that the 'central importance of trade and aid ... cannot be over-emphasized'.[15]

Feakes's cables questioned the government's commitment to closer engagement. A testy exchange took place between the high commissioner and Ray Greet, first assistant secretary for the South Asia Division. Feakes agreed there was no real interest in Australia coming from the Indian bureaucracy, but he blamed Australian policymakers. He spelt that out, lamenting the small size of the South Asia section where 'there were no more than 2 or 3 people working on the whole of the sub-continent'. He complained that 'there is no one in the Department who has a sense of what is going on in the relations between Australia and India across the board'.[16] Greet had an answer:

---

14   Ibid.
15   Annual Review, July 1984 – August 1985, NAA: A1838, 169/10/21 PART 5.
16   Feakes to Greet, 18 December 1984, NAA: A1838, 169/10/21 PART 5.

one of the problems we have in managing our relations with India [is] the low priority given to India by many in and outside Government. We now have a situation where because of the work of you and your staff ... the Department is coming to accept India's importance ... What is needed now, however, is broad Government endorsement.[17]

Greet agreed more staff were needed: '3 officers, with one officer dealing full-time with India ... but one cannot feel optimistic that an extra body can be seized from the system'.[18] (It was not until late in the term of the Howard Government that India was allocated a section of its own.)

Feakes never lost his sense that relations with India were under-resourced and under-appreciated. In 1986 he wrote to Greet that he believed there 'was a lobby in ADAB [Australian Development Assistance Bureau] which is opposed to aid to India on grounds which do not have to do with the merits of the case'.[19] Until Paul Barratt arrived in 1988 as department deputy secretary, Feakes commented later, there had been an absence of an interested senior public servant looking after India's interests.[20]

The visit of Rajiv Gandhi to Australia in 1986 came with the considerable expectations that prime ministerial visits engender. Both prime ministers were interviewed by newspapers in the other's country; each referred to a new bilateral momentum. Hawke, in an interview with the *Illustrated Weekly of India*, referred to the bilateral 'drift' of recent years, and that he wanted to 'identify areas where bilateral cooperation can be extended'.[21] For his part, Rajiv Gandhi spoke to the *Bulletin*'s Bruce Stannard about Hawke's 'honest, straightforward manner' and lamented that the state-to-state relationship 'hasn't really expanded'.[22] The Indian press covered the trip extensively, focusing on the two men's shared international approach and plans to work jointly on South Africa, the Antarctic Treaty and arms control in the Indian Ocean. Hawke spoke of the 'dramatic new vitality' between Australia and India, evidenced in part by the signing by business representatives of an agreement to establish the Australia–India Business Council.[23]

---

17 Greet to Feakes, 31 January 1985, NAA: A1838, 169/10/21 PART 5.

18 Ibid.

19 Feakes to Greet, 17 January 1986, A1838, 169/10/1 PART 55.

20 Graham Feakes, interview with author, Sydney, 17 December 1992.

21 Nikhil Lakshan, 'Coming Together', *The Illustrated Weekly of India*, 9 November 1986.

22 *Bulletin*, 14 October 1986, 126–28.

23 Hawke's statement in House of Representatives, 17 October 1986, in *Australian Foreign Affairs Record* 57, no. 10 (1986): 954–56.

But the 'new vitality' did not last. In a submission to Hayden, Ray Greet cautioned 'that there are still major obstacles in our path (the trade imbalance, Indian access to the Australian market, and our very different perspectives on some key issues)', concluding that 'the staying power of both sides will be crucial'.[24] By January 1987, Feakes was informing department head Stuart Harris of:

> a climate of opinion within the [Indian] external affairs ministry which is sceptical of any great outcome emerging from current efforts to put flesh on the bones of bilateral relations.

Feakes reported that he and the Indian high commissioner to Australia, Hamid Ansari, were concerned that 'Prime Ministerial attention on both sides will wander off elsewhere'.[25]

The Second Term: 1987–90

Nevertheless, as Feakes's second term began, a number of agreements were reached and some significant bilateral infrastructure established. Following Gandhi's 1986 visit, plans were made for a High Levels Official Group meeting, and the first one took place in New Delhi in April 1987. It had been an idea endorsed by both prime ministers and was aimed at reinforcing Australia's interest in developing a broader-based relationship with India. The files reveal that the meetings were organised around four key issues—trade, coal, science and technology, and cultural relations—which was in keeping with the trade and economics focus that Feakes and Hayden believed was central to the development of a more engaged bilateralism. Following the meeting, the leader of the Australian delegation, Stuart Harris, told Hayden that a potential Australian open-cut steaming-coal-mining project in Piparwar, in Bihar state, had assumed a central importance over the course of the talks. Officials reported that it had been 'an objective of our meeting that India be persuaded to award the major coal mining project to Australia'. It was seen, Harris wrote, as having importance 'in its own economic right, [but also as] a symbol of development in the relationship, and [providing] a basis for the establishment of a joint working group on coal'.[26]

---

24   Greet to Hayden, 19 November 1986, NAA: A1838, 169/10/1 PART 56.
25   Feakes to Harris, 23 January 1987, NAA: A1838, 169/10/1 PART 56.
26   Harris to Hayden, 29 April 1987; Minute paper, DFA, 17 June 1987, NAA: A1838, 169/10/1 PART 38.

Following this meeting, High Commissioner Feakes continued his search for bilateral ballast. A Joint Ministerial Commission was created, an idea that had been mooted at the time of Malcolm Fraser's visit to India in 1979 but dropped in the face of departmental caution. This time it was picked up with more enthusiasm and has held regular meetings ever since.

From 1987 to 1989, Feakes maintained that the future of the relationship was in commerce and that trade/aid packages were the way forward. But by late 1988 the department was observing that 'progress has been less than both sides had hoped'. The Australian Government was awaiting decisions on a number of matters, they reported, 'chief among them Piparwar ... which has become something of a symbol of the relationship'.[27] Feakes felt Canberra was not doing enough to secure the project: he argued that there were limits to the extent to which Australia could keep saying that, yes, India was important to us, but sorry, we don't have the resources to put into it. That limit, he said, had been reached.[28]

To that end, Feakes was successful in securing a prime ministerial visit of Bob Hawke to India in February 1989. Hawke arrived bearing gifts—a three-year tied aid and development program, valued at A$35 million. The program hoped to stimulate two-way commercial activities, which were chosen in sectors where India ascribed priority and where Australia had expertise: energy, mining, telecommunications, food technology and processing. But the most important commercial contact was made with the provision of A$61.5 million in grant aid to the Australian company White Industries to enable it to win the contract for the Piparwar joint venture with Coal India. It was the biggest ever business project between Australia and India, and Australia's largest overseas aid project.[29]

Many decades later, it is interesting to note how much diplomatic energy was invested in the Piparwar project. It was seen by Australian officials—and particularly by Feakes himself—as the 'lynchpin of our efforts to develop a broader and more substantial relationship with India'. If it 'falls through', Australian officials noted, 'it will have a significant detrimental effect, not only at government level, but within the business community'.[30]

27   Burns to Gareth Evans, Ministerial Submission, 31 October 1988, NAA: A1838, 160/10/1 PART 61.
28   Graham Feakes, interview with author, Sydney, 17 December 1992.
29   India Update, Australian High Commission, New Delhi, 21 February 1992.
30   Sturkey, undated but late 1987, 'Relations with India: Discussion between Prime Ministers Hawke and Gandhi at CHOGM', NAA: A1838, 169/10/1 PART 59.

Yet in late 1987, it had seemed a project with no future, with Ministry of Finance officers in New Delhi seeing no urgency in moving it forward. But Feakes kept the issue alive, and was pivotal in bringing the prime minister to India to finalise the deal. Work began in the early 1990s, and finished in 1997. But as evidence of how difficult it was to chalk up commercial successes with India, its promise was not to be realised. Piparwar may have started with huge expectations, but it ended in court. By 1999 White Industries was suing Coal India over a contractual dispute. It took 13 years to resolve, making its way through Indian courts until finally an arbitration tribunal in 2012 ruled in White Industries' favour.[31]

But at the time, Hawke's visit was celebrated as a success. The aid/trade announcements were well received, and the 'friendship' between the two prime ministers was on display. Feakes recalled a private dinner between Rajiv and Sonia Gandhi and Bob and Hazel Hawke at the Gandhis' home in New Delhi, which went long into the night and well over the time that protocol demanded.[32] In retirement Feakes commented that the friendship between Hawke and Gandhi was 'as friendly as both leaders indicated. For once there was [not] political exaggeration of diplomatic fact'.[33]

At this dinner, Hawke, in another act of impetuous generosity— again without 'prior consultation'—invited Rajiv and Sonia to send their children to school in Australia where, he promised, they would be kept safe. He would later chuckle about the 'collective fit' this caused for Australia's security agencies.[34]

Shortly after this sharing of goodwill, however, the relationship was abruptly derailed. In early 1990, Defence Minister Robert Ray announced that Australia was to sell 50 of its obsolete fighter jets to Pakistan. The files remain closed, but some facts are clear. It was at a time of heightened subcontinental tension over Kashmir, hence the Indian Government was furious at the prospect of 50 Mirage jets being sold cheaply (A$36 million) to Pakistan—India's principal enemy since Partition, with whom they shared a long and contested border, had fought three wars, and were locked

---

31   'Protecting your Investments in Foreign Courts', statement from Freehills Patent and Trade Mark Attorneys, March 2012.
32   Graham Feakes, interview with author, Sydney, 17 December 1992.
33   Graham Feakes, interviewed by Michael Wilson, 18 October – 24 November 1993, Canberra, NLA: Australian Diplomacy Oral History Project.
34   Hamish McDonald, 'A Testing Time for India—and Australia', *The Sydney Morning Herald*, 3 September 2011.

in a hostile, intractable and vicious conflict. Angry Indian Government officials summoned Feakes to the Ministry of External Affairs. He was castigated for this 'unfortunate and regrettable decision' and 'dismay and unhappiness' was expressed over the timing. They said they had 'least expected that a friendly Australia would take action which has the effect of further disturbing the stability of the region'.[35]

Foreign Minister Gareth Evans acknowledged that India froze all official dealings with Australia. They postponed high-level trade and investment talks, including an Indian delegation's travel to Australia to discuss Canberra's A$35 million aid allocation.[36] *The Times of India* put the angry Indian response on its front pages, reporting that High Commissioner Feakes had been 'summoned to the foreign office for the second time in three days and conveyed India's strong feelings'.[37]

Feakes was equally angry with Canberra. According to former diplomats, a dispatch from the high commissioner to the department is worth reading. It may explain whether the two departments of foreign affairs and defence were simply not coordinating on a government policy, unaware of its sensitivities. Or perhaps Pakistan was still seen in the Department of Defence as more central to Australia's security than India? Or maybe there were other forces at play. Until the files are opened, and Feakes's dispatch read, why this decision was taken remains an open question.

Graham Feakes — the Person[38]

Feakes was a true believer in the Australia–India connection, not unlike most of his predecessors, but also ahead of his time. He saw its future as a 50-year—not a five-year—challenge. India would one day be a great economic power, he believed, and Australia needed to be there when it happened. He despaired that Australia's leaders could not see that.[39] Ahead of his time also was his attitude to India's refusal to sign the

---

35   Ministry of External Affairs, 'Statement on Australia's Decision to Ship Mirage 111 Aircraft to Pakistan', press release, 19 October 1990, New Delhi.

36   'India Froze Diplomatic Ties: Evans', *The Age*, 2 August 1990.

37   *The Times of India* (Bombay), 25, 27 April 1990, 1.

38   For this section, I spoke to Bill Tweddell, Doug Woodhouse, Nicky Feakes, Richard Woolcott, Mack Williams and Richard Feakes. I am grateful to them for their time and thoughts. My description of the events outlined in this section are largely based on these discussions, plus news reporting. Most of the archives have not been released.

39   Graham Feakes's former colleagues, interview with author, August 2017.

Nuclear Non-Proliferation Treaty. He took the provocative step of urging the government to stop lecturing India about its stance. It was 'counter-productive to our interests', he argued in 1987: Australia was not listened to in India on other regional issues, because 'we continue to press them on something they will not change'. The Indians will 'not accept a status that is less than China's', and Australia overestimated what it 'can do about the problem'. Two months later, Canberra rejected his advice: 'it would be a considerable loss if we were to give up and do nothing'.[40]

Feakes was remembered for his integrity and decency. Former Australian diplomat Mack Williams, who enjoyed a long career in Asia and worked closely with Feakes when he was high commissioner to Malaysia, observed that he was 'not one of the boys … He was much liked around the office [and was] most respected as a guy with his feet on the ground'. Similarly, many liked his manner of 'calling a spade a spade'. Former ambassador to the Philippines and Vietnam, high commissioner to Sri Lanka and the Maldives, and deputy high commissioner to Feakes in New Delhi, Bill Tweddell served in India from December 1986 to June 1991. He described Feakes as the 'most wonderful, inspiring, courageous person for whom I ever worked—only daylight is second'. Doug Woodhouse, first secretary and consul in New Delhi during the Feakes era, praised him as 'the most impressive public official I knew: considered, honest, courageous, clever and smart. He was the best briefed person to take anywhere—he always knew what to do'. What was most admired was Feakes's moral courage.

My research for this paper unearthed a fascinating story to provide the evidence for these claims. There are few archives accessible, but I have found enough to provide some details. It involved the high commissioner, the foreign minister and a Russian defector.

On 17 December 1987, early in the afternoon, a 24-year-old Russian tourist walked up to the front desk of the consular section of the Australian High Commission in New Delhi and requested political asylum. His name was Alexandr Babiy and he was a postgraduate science student from Moscow University. He was in India as part of a tightly managed Soviet tour group of 35 junior scientists. They had been escorted by

---

40 Feakes to Secretary, 15 September 1987, 'India and the NPT'; Correspondence Feakes to Walker, 5 October 1987; Walker to Feakes, 10 December 1987, all NAA: A1838, 169/10/1 PART 59.

their minders to do some shopping in Old Delhi. Babiy managed to slip away in its tiny and crowded lanes, and make his way to the Australian mission in Chanakyapuri.

Babiy's request was rare. It stimulated a chain of events that reveal a great deal about High Commissioner Feakes. Babiy was to spend 33 days at the high commission compound, provided with safe refuge in the house of First Secretary Doug Woodhouse, while arguments went back and forth between various offices and departments in Canberra, New Delhi and Moscow over what to do with him.

Australia's response, it appears, was driven out of Hayden's office. Hayden and his chief of staff, Michael Costello, had been pursuing a more 'normalised' bilateral relationship with the Soviet Union all year. Hayden was pleased with the good contact established with Soviet Foreign Minister Edouard Shevardnadze, and in March had welcomed him to Canberra. The meeting was widely acclaimed as the highest-level talks between the two countries ever held in Australia, and described as 'quite a coup for Australia to get the visit'.[41] Just three weeks before Babiy appeared, Bob Hawke had been in Moscow, smiling for photos with Mikhail Gorbachev, praising perestroika, and negotiating the release of a group of Soviet Jewish emigres who had been trying to leave Russia for decades.

It appears that Hayden was not prepared to compromise Australian–Soviet relations for this young man. Instructions were clear. Feakes was told to hand him over to the Indians. It was emphasised that Babiy was not to be granted asylum. His application had been refused and Feakes was instructed not to upset the Russians.

But Hayden had misread the high commissioner. Feakes knew that Babiy would be deported back to the Soviet Union. He had a good sense of what might happen then. For nearly five weeks the deliberations continued. Soviet officials visited Babiy at the high commission and promised him a safe return. The Soviets sent his mother to New Delhi. She saw her son several times, in the garden and in the home of the first secretary, pleading for his return. The Americans offered asylum. But Babiy stubbornly refused, and held out for entry to Australia.

---

41 Andrew Fraser, 'Shevardnadze Visit Indicates Change in View of Region', *The Canberra Times*, 3 March 1987.

Canberra instructed Feakes to take Babiy to the office of the United Nations High Commission for Refugees (UNHCR) and leave him with them—at that point he would no longer be an Australian responsibility. Babiy was taken there by diplomatic car, accompanied by Deputy High Commissioner Bill Tweddell and First Secretary Woodhouse. While Babiy stayed in the car, the first secretary was told by the UNHCR staff that they could offer Babiy no diplomatic protection—the moment he left the car he would be arrested by Indian security.

The first secretary rang the high commissioner, who said to bring him straight back.

It seemed a stalemate: High Commissioner Feakes was refusing to budge. The minister's office wanted this problem to go away. The office was saying nothing publicly, but in off-the-record press briefings they were adamant that his application had been refused. Their public position was that they were in negotiations with the UNHCR who were trying to find a third country for him. This was untrue. Other than the one visit just mentioned, there were never any negotiations with UNHCR.

But on 20 January 1988, a day or so after their latest briefing that there would be no asylum for Babiy, the government changed its mind. Babiy was granted entry to Australia under its Special Humanitarian program. On 21 January, he was quietly taken to New Delhi airport and flown to Sydney, where he was met by a Department of Foreign Affairs and Trade official who took him to the Villawood Migrant centre. Babiy was now a free man. All this was announced five hours after his arrival in Australia.

The Indians had agreed to his passage out. It has been claimed that under Indian law, the immunity of diplomatic premises applies only to the land and diplomatic staff, so technically the Indian police were entitled to enter the high commission grounds and arrest him at any time. But this had never been put to the test, and it was not clear that this was possible. In fact, senior officials there at the time have stated that Indian authorities handled this episode very professionally. This was in part, they believe, because Feakes dealt 'upfront and inclusively' with the Indian senior bureaucracy at the official level, and kept politics out of it. He asked politely for their cooperation while making it very clear that Babiy would not be given up. 'Graham wasn't a man to be pushed around', according to (then) First Secretary Woodhouse.

It remains unclear why the foreign minister changed his mind.[42] There was one article that is said to have been influential. It was written by a journalist from *The Sydney Morning Herald*, Warren Osmond, who seemed to have the inside story.[43] It apparently unnerved Hayden and his office. It spoke highly of Feakes's 'noble' stance, was critical of what he saw as Hayden's egregious behaviour, and argued that this young man's life was being 'sacrificed' so as not to disturb the new Australian–Soviet détente established by Hayden and Shevardnadze.

Could one article have been a game-changer? Or did the foreign minister decide the issue was gaining press traction, and he wanted to kill the story before it grew bigger? Where did the pressure come from for his change of mind? Until the files are released, we cannot know. There was other press coverage, more sympathetic to Hayden, with one journalist claiming that Hayden was 'so angered' with a Soviet claim that Babiy was 'mentally ill' and must be sent back to Moscow, that he decided no longer to pursue the UNHCR option, which in turn paved the way for the offer of asylum.[44] But this story has been refuted, suggesting Hayden's 'rage' was a story fabricated by his office for the press and was not the reason for his change of mind.

Many of the key players in this story have spoken of Feakes's 'enormous moral and intellectual courage'. Bill Tweddell put it this way: 'he didn't trim his sails to any prevailing winds—it is said diplomats should give frank and fearless advice. Graham did it'.

Feakes, it has been noted, 'received considerable unfriendly incoming fire for his decision not to throw Alexandr to the bears'. But Feakes, his former colleagues said, 'understood the power of his own seniority and on this occasion was prepared to use it'. Doug Woodhouse believes that it was 'Graham's persistence and courage with Canberra that probably saved [Babiy's] life'.

---

42   The 1988 Australia–India files have recently been released. But certain sections have been withheld, and it appears they may be the files associated with Babiy's defection. There are no correspondence documents between New Delhi and Canberra to be found on this issue (nor in the 1987 files released last year). Doug Woodhouse officially interviewed Babiy several times during his time at the high commission but there are no records of these conversations.

43   Warren Osmond, 'A Defector Lost between Two Worlds', *The Sydney Morning Herald*, 11 January 1988.

44   John O'Neill, 'Hayden's Rage Paved Way to Refuge', *The Sydney Morning Herald*, 20 February 1988.

Nicky Feakes remembers the time well and still keeps in touch with Mr Babiy, who was eventually joined by his parents in Australia. Many close to him remember that Feakes had been prepared to resign if Hayden had not granted him asylum. Now *that* is frank and fearless.

Conclusion

When High Commissioner Feakes ended his time in India in 1990, he also retired from the diplomatic service. He felt there was no place for him back in the department and after a double posting in New Delhi, he was ready to retire.

Did he arrest the drift? He certainly worked very hard to do so. In terms of outcomes, it is difficult to measure his success. New institutional arrangements *were* put in place that established some new bilateral pathways. He *was* ahead of his time, describing India as a major economic power of the future, and he seemed permanently frustrated—indeed often disillusioned—that he couldn't convince more people of this. But he faced an uphill battle. Even in 1989, senior Australian Cabinet ministers were visiting India—partly in response to the urging of the high commissioner— and coming away 'with a sense of hopelessness and frustration'. Minister for Industry, Technology and Commerce John Button reported he found little interest in Australia from senior Indian politicians and bureaucrats: 'Australia [seemed] too far away, too small, and quite irrelevant to their daily preoccupations'.[45]

At the end of 1988, the department was noting that there was still a bilateral 'sense of drift' between Australia and India, and the government decided to investigate. The Senate Standing Committee on Foreign Affairs and Trade was asked to report on Australia–India relations with particular reference to prospects for increasing trade and the implications for the regional strategic outlook of India's enhanced defence capability. The committee submitted its report in July 1990, a few months before Feakes left India. It was not a positive picture and the report did not mince words: it considered India to be an important Asian power of the same order as China, but concluded that relations with India were underdeveloped, with an inadequate knowledge of India in Australian government and business. In short, it said all the things Feakes had been repeating for

---

45   John Button, *Flying the Kite* (Sydney: Random House, 1994), 149, 143.

a decade. (One of its recommendations was to create an Australia–India Council and a National Centre for South Asian studies, both of which were established by 1993. Feakes was the council's first chair.)[46]

High Commissioner Feakes's ideas for a more substantial bilateral relationship, with more government investment and commitment, were never realised to the extent he wished. His vision fell victim to timing and context. By the late 1980s, Hawke and Foreign Minister Gareth Evans were focused almost exclusively on APEC[47] and the Asia Pacific, an organisation and a region that did not include India. Also important to an understanding of this time is the fact that India did not deregulate its economy until 1992. It was to take another 15 years, following the departure of Graham and Nicky Feakes from New Delhi, for India and the newly conceptualised Indo-Pacific region to assume the importance in Australian foreign policy that they have today.

46 Senate Standing Committee on Foreign Affairs, Defence and Trade, *Australia–India Relations: Trade and Security* (Canberra: Australian Government Publishing Service, July 1990).
47 The Asia Pacific Economic Co-operation grouping, created in 1989. It was a key—perhaps *the* key—foreign policy initiative of the Hawke Government.

9

Trade and Education: Australia–India, 1998–2008

Michael Moignard and
Quentin Stevenson-Perks

The decade covered by this chapter covers a period of rapid change in the bilateral relationship between Australia and India, starting with the Indian Government's nuclear test at Pokhran in May 1998 and concluding just before the global financial crisis in 2008, with the election of the Rudd Labor Government.[1]

Throughout this period the trade relationship was dominated by two major developments: all things nuclear, including nuclear testing, the Nuclear Non-Proliferation Treaty and uranium sales; and the growth in the export of education services to Indian students. These two developments had a long-term impact on our bilateral foreign relations, people-to-people connections and cultural interactions.

This decade saw the historically biggest increase in trade between the two countries, with Australian exports of goods and services to India rising from around A$2.6 billion in 1998 to A$17.1 billion in 2008.[2] However, this did not translate into major investments in each other's markets.

1   The authors would like to thank Professor John Webb OAM and Michael Carter for their insights.
2   ABS Data, Cat. 5368.0, 'International Trade in Goods and Services, Australia'. The services export numbers for 1998 are estimates.

The tendency was to focus on transactional business; on Australia's part this meant concentrating on industrial, energy and resource inputs, and on India's, on small manufactures. This was also the case with the education relationship, which remained focused on the large-scale movement of Indian students to Australia (since Australian investment in India was restricted by opposition to foreign education institutions establishing a physical presence in India).

As such, despite significant improvements in this long-established relationship, many trade opportunities were frustrated and foregone both during the decade under discussion, and into the future. For example, in April 2008 both countries agreed to undertake a feasibility study for a possible bilateral free trade agreement (FTA) that explored the scope for building an even stronger economic and trade relationship. Ten years later, an FTA between the countries was still in negotiation.

Further, the 14th session of the Australia–India Joint Ministerial Commission in January 2013, co-chaired by Craig Emerson, then Australian minister for trade, and Anand Sharma, then commerce and industry minister of India, is an example of the overzealous optimism that is often seen at the official level. With two-way trade at A$21.9 billion, the meeting suggested this should double to A$40 billion by 2015.[3]

Yet, by 2015–16, the two-way trade in goods and services had shrunk to only A$19.4 billion.[4]

However, despite important figures pledging to meet unrealistic targets in recent times, the 1998–2008 period nevertheless resulted in a significant shift in the economic relationship between Australia and India. This was made possible by the opening of the Indian market in 1991 under then finance minister Manmohan Singh (later the prime minister of India from 2004 to 2014). Prior to this time, Australian exports to India were very small, even in the mining sector, where considerable work had been done with India's companies to support Australian expertise. One major project in the late 1980s was the Piparwar mine, an open-cut coal mine

---

3   'India–Australia FTA at Exchange-of-Offers Stage', India Link, 31 January 2013, webarchive. nla.gov.au/awa/20150618010822/http://pandora.nla.gov.au/pan/100144/20150618-0032/www. indianlink.com.au/aus-asia-award-takes-writer-to-india-2/index8d25.html, accessed 20 September 2018.

4   Department of Foreign Affairs and Trade, 'Australia's Trade with India', Business Envoy, Department of Foreign Affairs and Trade, webarchive.nla.gov.au/awa/20170424184022/http://dfat. gov.au/about-us/publications/trade-investment/business-envoy/Pages/april-2017/australias-trade-with-india.aspx, accessed 20 September 2018.

developed using Australian technology and equipment. Funded through Australia's aid program, it exposed Indian coal miners to Australian expertise, but, as mentioned in Chapter Eight, ultimately it yielded few new export opportunities.

By 1996, with the economic conditions now more favourable, Australia was confident enough in the relationship to deliver a whole-of-government market promotion program to India, entitled 'New Horizons',[5] designed to showcase the potential opportunities for collaboration between the two countries. The atmosphere between the two governments was very positive following the New Horizons program, but two years later, the relationship was to be severely tested, when the Indian Government exploded a nuclear device in May 1998.

1998: The Pokhran Incident

In May 1998, India conducted an underground nuclear test at Pokhran in central Rajasthan. Several days later, Pakistan conducted its own underground nuclear test in retaliation. These tests were widely condemned by the international community, including the United States, Canada and Australia. The timing was unfortunate for the growth of the Australia–India relationship that had been gaining some momentum, especially in trade and investment.

The upshot of the Pokhran crisis was the redeployment of Australia's Defence Attaché in New Delhi back to Canberra, and the cutback of official visits to India by Australian Government ministers. It also became very difficult to meet with Indian officials in New Delhi, reducing the effectiveness of the high commission in maintaining the bilateral relationship with the Indian Government.

This had repercussions for the trade office, Austrade, at the high commission. Austrade's role was to support Australian companies in their pursuit of business opportunities in India. As well as organising trade missions, exhibitions and market reports, Austrade was also responsible for liaising with Indian government departments such as Customs, Health, Agriculture, Mining, Manufacturing and Commerce and Food

5   Department of Foreign Affairs and Trade (ed.), *Australia India New Horizons: A Festival of Trade, Science, Technology, Sport and the Arts in India October to December 1996* (Melbourne: BRW Media for the Australian Department of Foreign Affairs and Trade, 1996).

Processing, as each of these had a role in trade and investment outcomes. However, meetings with these departments, particularly at senior levels, became difficult to organise during this period.

The only Australian minister to officially visit India in 1999 was the minister for trade, Tim Fischer, who attended a bilateral trade meeting in New Delhi. He stayed for less than 24 hours. This drought was broken in 2000 with a number of Australian ministers visiting India, including the prime minister in July 2000.[6] By then the differences of opinion between the two governments relating to Pokhran were no longer as acute.

Australian Representation in India

In addition to its staff at the High Commission in New Delhi, Austrade also had an office in Mumbai where its senior staff member was the consul general. Following the success of the New Horizons program, this representation was expanded with individual representatives being placed in Kolkata, Bengaluru and Chennai; these arrangements remained in place for the next 10 years.

A major change occurred in March 2006 with the second visit to India by Prime Minister Howard, who was accompanied by a significant business delegation. During his visit to New Delhi, Mumbai and Chennai, the prime minister announced the establishment of a full consulate in Chennai and the provision of extra funds to Austrade to expand its presence in India.[7] As a result, Austrade opened new offices in Jaipur, Pune, Kochi and Hyderabad, and also increased its staff in the High Commission in New Delhi and the consulates in Mumbai and Chennai.

The growth in Australia's bilateral relationship with India in the decade under review was reflected by the decision in 2003 to rebuild the high commission's chancery building, which had been opened by Sir Paul Hasluck in 1966, but was now too small to meet the staff needs of the growing relationship between Australia and India.

---

6   John Howard, 'Official Visit to India', PM Transcripts: Transcripts from the Prime Minister of Australia, 6 June 2000, transcript 11578, pmtranscripts.pmc.gov.au/release/transcript-11578, accessed 20 September 2018.

7   John Howard and Manmohan Singh, 'Joint Press Conference with Dr. Manmohan Singh, Prime Minister of India: Hyderabad House, New Delhi', PM Transcripts: Transcripts from the Prime Minister of Australia, 6 March 2006, transcript 22161, pmtranscripts.pmc.gov.au/release/transcript-22161, accessed 14 March 2018.

A formal report into the decision to rebuild the chancery was provided to parliament in 2003, outlining the need for a new and improved building, which would provide greater provision of space as well as enhanced security.[8] In 2004, the old chancery was subsequently demolished, and a new building was officially opened in 2008.[9]

During the construction phase, the high commission staff were housed in other buildings on the high commission compound. The deputy high commissioner's official residence became the main building housing the high commissioner and Department of Foreign Affairs and Trade staff, while Austrade took over a repurposed recreation centre. While it was crowded, the alternate accommodation worked well, and did not disrupt the work of the trade staff. The Austrade office moved into the first floor of the new chancery at the end of 2017.

Trade Flows

From 1998 to 2004, trade between the two countries continued to grow, more than doubling in value. Increases in gold and coal volumes helped to increase Australia's export values to A$6.47 billion by 2004.[10] An increase in services exports of about A$1 billion was reflecting the increasing growth of education services to Indian students in Australia.[11] As a result, between 2004 and 2008, Australian exports to India increased from A$6.4 billion to A$17.12 billion, making India the fifth-largest export destination by value for Australia. The number of Australian companies engaged in trade with India grew significantly as well.[12]

This was growth associated with a new optimism in India. Its GDP was growing at rates unseen before in India, and its expanding middle class began to make its economic presence felt. A renewed focus on opening the economy in India helped to create a climate of expanded interaction between India and advanced economies.

---

8   Australian Parliament Standing Committee on Public Works and J Moylan, *Construction of a New Chancery, New Delhi, India* (Canberra: Australian Parliament Standing Committee on Public Works, 2003).
9   It was officially opened by Simon Crean, minister for trade, January 2008.
10   ABS Data, Cat. 5368.0.
11   Department of Foreign Affairs and Trade, *Australia's Trade in Services with India* (Canberra: Statistics Section, Office of Economic Analysis, Investment and Economic Division, Department of Foreign Affairs and Trade, n.d.), Chart 1.
12   ABS Data, Cat. 5368.0. The number of Australian companies operating in India is based on anecdotal evidence.

While Australian export values increased in value during this period, there was little expansion in the type of Australian exports. Gold, coal, copper, grains and pulses continued to be the major products, with little in the way of high technology or manufactured products being exported. The significant growth in India's manufacturing sector, especially in the production of automobiles and motorcycles, was not reflected in Australia's exports or investments into its manufacturing sector.[13]

At this time, the Indian IT sector began to focus on providing call centres for supporting companies in Europe, North America and Australia. As such, many Australian companies began taking advantage of India's growing expertise in back office support such as accounting, record keeping and specialist skills, as well as software generation. These opportunities were outlined in a report by Ernst and Young and Austrade in 2001.[14]

Although there was considerable interest in mining investment from Australian mining companies, few ventures had made it beyond initial exploration, as India's mining laws in the early 1990s were not conducive to new entrants and were convoluted to administer. Changes to India's mining laws were made in the mid-1990s, based on the laws of Western Australia, which were meant to make applications for exploration leases easier, but the administration of exploration permits was left to individual Indian states, each of which did things differently. Andhra Pradesh and Orissa, for example, appeared to provide opportunities for exploration permits for foreign companies, but in fact, very few were ever provided. A further push to ease restrictions on exploration and mining permits was made in the early 2000s with a report to the Indian Government recommending changes to legislation, yet these, too, never eventuated. So, one of the major competitive advantages of the Australian economy, its mining sector, was unable to invest into India. Consequently, that left exports of mineral and energy commodities, and mining equipment and services, as the only means by which Australia could engage with India's mining sector.

---

13   Australian Trade Commission, 'Exporting to India: Riding the Elephant', presentation to Australian exporters in various states of Australia, September 2004.
14   Australian Trade Commission and Ernst & Young, *Emerging Opportunities in Information Technology for Australia and India* (Canberra: Australian Trade Commission, 2000).

The Energy Sector

It was clear in the early 2000s that India would need new sources of energy to achieve its ambition to double its energy capacity by 2020 and expand its economy. To do this would require more coal, gas and uranium. Renewables, in the form of hydroelectricity, wind and solar, were seen as adjuncts to the major initiative to build large power plants. New 400 MW coal-fired plants were to be the primary engines of electricity growth, but some gas-fired power stations were also under consideration. Both of these sources of fuel presented significant infrastructure issues, such as expanded port facilities for both imported coal and gas, and pipelines for gas distribution.

The Indian Government was aware of Australia's strength in the production of energy commodities, as the high commission had made the case for Australia very strongly and Australia was already a major exporter to India of steaming coal for electricity production. There was clearly potential for export of liquefied natural gas (LNG), and potentially uranium, and long-term contracts of energy products into India were seen as the link needed to strengthen the economic relationship between the two countries.

But the Indian Government did not take up the potential for expanded trade with Australia. Despite its growing LNG production in Western Australia, it was not India's only option for gas imports. It had multiple other choices: it was close to the Middle East, with its major gas fields; Iran held out the prospect of gas being piped overland, as did countries in Central Asia; India had its own gas reserves; and next door, Bangladesh had the potential to be a major producer of gas in South Asia.

All of these options, however, presented issues for India. A major stumbling block for overland gas distribution was the political instability in Afghanistan, while India's relationships with both Pakistan and Bangladesh undermined any prospects for trade with them, and imports of gas from Qatar also had security risks. So, from the perspective of reliability of supply and security, Australia should have been seen as a strong contender. The major issue relating to Australian supply was contractual. Australian providers required long-term price and quantity commitments similar to those accepted at the time by North Asian customers, but this was not achieved in the case of India. Some cargos of gas did reach India, but the potential for the trade relationship in gas went unrealised.

The supply of uranium for peaceful nuclear purposes was also replete with major policy issues. India's rejection of the Nuclear Non-Proliferation Treaty (NPT) of 1968 and its testing of nuclear weapons clashed with Australia's longstanding policy that constrained the export of uranium—exports could only be provided to countries that were signatories to the NPT and that had a Nuclear Safeguards Agreement allowing inspections of nuclear material and facilities by the International Atomic Energy Agency. Thus, India was not a country to which Australia could export uranium. Other uranium suppliers, such as Canada and the United States, also adhered to similar policies. Australia's strong reaction to the Pokhran test in 1998 was a political hindrance as well.

The terrorist attacks on the World Trade Centre in New York on 11 September 2001 changed this very significantly. The United States needed the support of India in its 'War on Terror', and President Bush began to build a deeper connection with India, based on security, defence and trade ties. Discussions began about India's induction into the Nuclear Suppliers Group, the first step to normalising India's role as a country with nuclear weapons. Bush's visit to India in February 2006 brought India into the nuclear fold. Prior to Prime Minister Howard's visit to India in March 2006, he was asked if Australia would consider selling uranium to India. While his answer was that India was not an eligible country under the Australian Government's then policy, the changes announced by India and the United States would be carefully considered by his government.[15] This was the beginning of the reconsideration of Australia's stance on supplying India with uranium, but it was to take several more years before the government committed itself to the sale.

Food Exports

Between 1998 and 2008, opportunities for expansion in the trade relationship presented themselves. Trade and investment in the food sector, for example, held much promise. In 2005, under a program supported by the Australian Government's policy initiative 'Supermarket to Asia', exports of Australian processed foods were trialled in South India. The program involved consolidating Australian processed food into one

---

15   John Howard, 'Doorstop Interview Taj Mahal Hotel, Delhi', PM Transcripts: Transcripts from the Prime Minister of Australia, 5 March 2006, transcript 22157, pmtranscripts.pmc.gov.au/release/transcript-22157, accessed 16 March 2018.

cargo and sending it to select supermarket outlets in southern India, especially Bengaluru, the fast expanding IT-based economy formerly known as Bangalore. This opened the market for products such as fruit juice, biscuits and other dry goods.

At the same time, there were opportunities opening for Australian wine and beer. The major hotels were able to import selected wines for their own use and in their restaurants. This enabled some wine labels to gain a niche in the high end of the hospitality market. However, market expansion was hampered by high tariffs and labelling and marketing issues. The latter two problems were complicated by the differing regulations in each Indian state.

Education Services Exports

In its June 1998 report on Australia's trade relationship with India, the Australian Parliament's Joint Standing Committee on Foreign Affairs, Defence and Trade identified services exports as being one of the key drivers of Australia's future trade prospects with India—and education services were perhaps the brightest prospect in that sector.[16]

The committee's focus on education services followed the success of the New Horizons program, which had highlighted the very early growth in the flow of Indian students to Australia from only 14 in 1987 to 5,600 in 1997.[17] While much of the subsequent success of Australia's trade in education services is attributable to the work of Australia's education and research institutions in promoting their range of education services, three key policy developments by the Australian Government at the beginning of the twenty-first century laid the groundwork.

---

16 Australian Parliament Joint Committee on Foreign Affairs, Defence and Trade, David McGibbon and Ian McCahon Sinclair, *Australia's Trade Relationship with India: Commonwealth, Common Language, Cricket and Beyond* (Canberra: Australian Parliament Joint Committee on Foreign Affairs, Defence and Trade, 1998), para. 6.94, nla.gov.au/nla.obj-1459375536, accessed 9 December 2020.
17 Australian Parliament Joint Committee on Foreign Affairs, Defence and Trade, McGibbon and Sinclair, *Australia's Trade Relationship with India*, para. 6.94.

The first of these was the Australian Government's *Education Services for Overseas Students Act 2000* (the ESOS Act),[18] which was the first such legislation in the world, and had far reaching implications for Australia's emerging international education sector. The ESOS Act provided Australia's growing international education sector with a clear framework of governance and code of practice for handling international students, a register of institutions and courses that were eligible to be offered to international students and, finally, a guarantee to international students of a refund of their tuition fees in the event that an Australian education institution was unable to complete a student's education. This gave international students certainty in education services that were being offered by Australia, which distinguished it from its other competitors (primarily the United States and the United Kingdom).

The second policy development, and probably the most important, was the Australian Government's reforms to the student visa program, which provided a simpler, global approach to processing student visas. This resolved concerns that the previous system had been too subjective. As noted by the 1998 Joint Committee Report:

> The Committee received evidence, generally of an anecdotal nature, that Indians wishing to travel to Australia, either for business or on a personal visit, experienced difficulties in getting a visa. Although the evidence tended to be of an anecdotal nature, the Committee was surprised at the continuing expression of concern at the difficulties that were being encountered.[19]

While India was still categorised at 'high risk' under the new student visa system, the establishment of a relatively simple set of non-subjective rules provided certainty to students, their families and the education agents who represented Australian institutions in India. The ease of this process was further helped along through the creation of new education loans by India's financial institutions. As a result, one of the greatest barriers to gaining an Australian student visa in India—the student's means of financing—was eliminated.

---

18   Australian Department of Education, Skills and Employment, 'The ESOS Legislative Framework', International Education Group, internationaleducation.gov.au/Regulatory-Information/Education-Services-for-Overseas-Students-ESOS-Legislative-Framework/ESOS-Regulations/Pages/default.aspx, accessed 3 April 2018.
19   Australian Parliament Joint Committee on Foreign Affairs, Defence and Trade, McGibbon and Sinclair, *Australia's Trade Relationship with India*, para. 5.53.

Finally, there was the decision to develop an international brand position for Australia's international education sector—'Study in Australia'. International market research showed that while Australia could not compete with the United States or the United Kingdom in terms of 'tradition and prestige', it had a unique selling point in being 'innovative and good quality'. While individual Australian institutions naturally used their own distinctive brands in marketing themselves and their courses, the development of an umbrella brand for Australia's education sector was crucial in a country such as India where, at the time, knowledge of Australia was poor. Indeed, the 1998 Joint Committee Report noted that:

> A common theme underlying the diverse range of evidence given to the Committee was the general lack of awareness and appreciation that Indians had about the different aspects of Australia, its way of life, culture and business and technological capabilities.[20]

The Study in Australia brand launch in 2002 was supported by the launch of a dedicated Australian Government website for students.[21] Using the register of institutions and courses that were approved under the new ESOS Act, the website provided an authoritative source of information that international students could access. This was of immense value given it was launched at the advent of the revolution in India's telecommunications, at a time when there was a vast array of misleading and confusing claims for potential international students and their families to contend with.

While these policy developments established a framework for future success, the decision by Australia's education institutions to use the services of local agents to help their marketing and recruitment in India (as well as assisting the students in negotiating the student visa process) proved pivotal. Unlike institutions in the United States, the use of appointed agents to promote individual institutions was well established by Australia's international education sector. Indeed, the Australian company, IDP Education Australia Ltd, which was wholly owned at the time by the Australian Vice-Chancellors Committee, led the way in India with the establishment of a network of professional, well-resourced offices, which set a new standard of service delivery to Indian students and their families.

---

20   Ibid., para. 5.29
21   Australian Government, Study Australia, studyinaustralia.gov.au.

The ability of these agents to deliver high-level services to students was enhanced in 1998 by the establishment of an agents' association—the Association of Australian Education Representatives in India (AAERI). Supported by both the education and immigration arms of the Australian high commission, AAERI allowed the high commission to communicate effectively with the agents about student visa regulations and market trends and receive feedback from the agents. AAERI also adopted the National Code of Practice, established by the ESOS Act, as its service charter to students, providing another important point of difference between Australia and its competitors in India.

Through these policy developments and marketing strategies, Australia was able to create a high-quality system of governance for its international education sector, a non-subjective student visa system, a new international brand identity and a network of education agents throughout India. As a result, Australia made rapid progress in growing its trade in education services with India in the following decade, from less than 10,000 in 1998 to more than 97,000 student enrolments in 2008.[22]

It should also be mentioned that the success of Australia's education sector in India was also driven by the decision of the Australian Government in 2001 to link its migration program to international student graduates with an Australian education qualification. In essence:

> international graduates with key skills that were needed in the economy who successfully completed their course of study at an Australian institution, and met other general eligibility requirements, were able to make an onshore application for permanent residency through the Skilled-Independent (and related) visa categories of the General Skilled Migration program (previously they had to leave Australia and apply offshore) … Unlike skilled migrants who applied offshore, former overseas students who made applications onshore were exempted from the requirement of obtaining work experience in their nominated occupation.[23]

22   Department of Education, Skills and Employment, 'International Student Data 2020', International Education, 2020 pivot tables, internationaleducation.gov.au/research/international-student-data/Pages/InternationalStudentData2020.aspx#Pivot_Table, accessed 30 October 2021.
23   Elsa Koleth, 'Overseas Students: Immigration Policy Changes 1997–May 2010', Parliament of Australia, 18 June 2010, www.aph.gov.au/About_Parliament/Parliamentary_Departments/Parliamentary_Library/pubs/BN/0910/OverseasStudents, accessed 2 December 2020.

The drawing of a direct link between the overseas student program and skilled migration program attracted strong growth in international student numbers, especially from South Asia. Thus, Australia's success in recruiting Indian students was partly fuelled by this policy change. This became more apparent in the latter part of the decade under review, as largely private vocational education colleges in Australia specifically targeted Indian students with qualifications that gained them an advantage under the Australian Government's Migration Program.

This helped promote exponential growth in the number of Indian students in Australia, specifically in Victoria. This unfortunately strained the support services available to international students in that state and led to the breakdown of the essential compact between the wider Australian community and the international student cohort. The scope and nature of those challenges and the successful responses of Australian governments and education institutions are another chapter in the growing relationship between both countries.

One of the long-term concerns of Australia's education relationship with India was that it was one-dimensional, represented by the travel of Indian students to Australia. As noted by the Indian high commissioner to Australia in the 1998 Joint Committee Report:

> at the present moment the Australian thrust has been largely on getting students from India. There is very little in the way of collaborative arrangements between educational institutions. The net result has been that you find our universities, because of the common English language, excellently networked with American and British counterparts but there is very little by way of educational networking with Australia.[24]

This focus on marketing Australia continued to sideline the potential for stronger academic linkages between two countries that have many shared concerns, such as renewable energy, dry land agriculture and water management, just to name a few. In contrast to India's academic relations with its counterparts in the United States, the United Kingdom and China, links to Australian universities were almost non-existent apart from Deakin University, which had established an office in Delhi as early as in 1994 with the objective of fostering partnerships with educational, corporate and research institutions in India.

---

24 Australian Parliament Joint Committee on Foreign Affairs, Defence and Trade, McGibbon and Sinclair, *Australia's Trade Relationship with India*, para. 6.100.

It was only towards the end of the 1998–2008 period that major steps were undertaken by both the Australian Government and the institutions themselves. For example, the March 2006 visit to India by Prime Minister Howard brought the announcement of the Australia–India Strategic Research Fund. An investment of A$130 million, it remains Australia's largest fund dedicated to bilateral scientific cooperation, and one of India's largest sources of support for international science.

Along with new linkages between academics and institutions, the fund has been instrumental in developing a stronger appreciation in both countries of each other's capabilities, and helped to re-imagine the image of Australia in India. While the Research Fund provided the financial incentive for this development, it remained the work of the institutions in both countries to respond to the challenge of driving closer bilateral scientific relations. On its tenth anniversary, the fund had delivered joint funding supporting over 300 collaborative science projects.

Conclusion

It is clear that in the mid-2000s, the stage was being set for a major increase in trade between Australia and India. By 2008–09, exports had reached A$10 billion, and was set to grow to A$14 billion a year later.[25] Coal, gold and education services were making the difference. It looked like the Australia–India economic relationship was on the verge of a major shift in gear. The future looked bright, and the relationship should have continued to grow.

Having found a balance in the relationship, could the two countries grasp the opportunity to increase the people-to-people links and a growing mutual understanding? The history of bilateral trade and investment had always been buffeted by political issues from both sides. However, it seemed by this time that these impediments could be overcome, and the two economies could become more closely linked.

Yet, this was not to be. The global financial crisis in 2008, concerns about safety and racism affecting Indian students in Australia and the lack of real economic liberalisation in India led to a stagnation and then decline in trade and investment, which was not to pick up again until 2015.

---

25   ABS Data, Cat. 5368.0.

10

Building an Indo-Pacific Security Partnership

Ian Hall

Hosting visits from politicians and officials is one of the key functions of embassies. But some embassies are, of course, busier than others, and the traffic they see depends on the perceived importance of the relationship Australia has with the country in which they are located. During the 1980s and 1990s, the footfall in the high commission in New Delhi was relatively light. Malcolm Fraser's five-day long sojourn in India in January 1979, during which he was the guest of honour at the Republic Day parade, was followed only by intermittent visits by his successors. Bob Hawke attended a Commonwealth Heads of Government Meeting in New Delhi and Goa in November 1983, but did not return to the country until 1989. Paul Keating went to Japan four times while in the top job, but never to India. During the whole of the 1990s, indeed, the high commission was spared a prime ministerial visit—it took until July 2000 before John Howard made the journey to New Delhi.

All this changed in the decade that followed. By 2008, diplomatic and political interaction between Australia and India had intensified to the point that no fewer than 39 delegations travelled to New Delhi that year, and 26 in the other direction, on their way to Canberra.[1] That year was not exceptional, as such interactions multiplied during the late 2000s and

---

1   Ian Hall, 'Australia's Fitful Engagements of India', in Ian Hall (ed.), *The Engagement of India: Strategies and Responses* (Washington, DC: Georgetown University Press, 2014), 144, n. 63.

2010s. Between 2000 and 2018, there were six visits by Australian prime ministers to India, and many more by foreign and defence ministers, officials and delegations of business leaders and university vice-chancellors. An Indian president and prime minister also travelled to Australia, and the number of visits by Cabinet ministers and high-level diplomats grew too. The work of the high commission in New Delhi intensified as a result, and resourcing expanded, if perhaps not at the same rate as the traffic it had to manage. This was partly caused by Australian ministers, diplomats, businesses and universities seeking out economic opportunities, but also because Canberra took the initiative in trying to strengthen defence and security ties to India, to cope with shifting strategic dynamics across what soon became known as the Indo-Pacific.

Since the mid-2000s, indeed, Australia and India have built a robust and broad security partnership, involving regular high-level dialogues between politicians and officials, inter-agency cooperation, regular joint military exercises, the sharing of intelligence and defence technology, and nascent defence industrial collaboration. Getting these various initiatives started has not been easy, and nor has keeping them running and making them work. But on the whole, more has arguably been achieved in defence and security cooperation between the two countries than in any other area of the bilateral relationship, including trade and investment. Despite high hopes and significant diplomatic effort, the value of two-way trade in goods and services barely increased in the decade or so between the late 2000s to the late 2010s.[2] By contrast, a great deal of progress was made— albeit in fits and starts—in constructing a security partnership.

This chapter explores how and why this occurred. To set the scene and provide a rough gauge by which to measure how far and fast the partnership has developed, the first section looks back to perhaps the lowest point in Australia–India relations, the late 1990s. It explores the role played by the September 11 attacks and their aftermath in driving an initial rapprochement, and then turns to the first attempts to build better defence and security ties in the last years of John Howard's government. The second section examines the turbulence experienced during Kevin Rudd's time in office. Under Rudd, the foundations were eventually laid

---

2   In 2009, two-way trade was valued at A$20.9 billion; in 2016, it was valued at A$21 billion. It did increase to A$27.5 billion in 2017, but at the cost of widening the trade deficit in Australia's favour. See: Ian Hall, 'The Struggle to Maintain Momentum in the Australia–India Partnership', The ASAN Forum, 11 February 2019, www.theasanforum.org/the-struggle-to-maintain-momentum-in-the-australia-india-partnership/, accessed 7 December 2020.

for a strategic partnership and a possible free trade agreement. But there were also disagreements, notably about the longstanding ban on the sale of Australian uranium to India and about the Rudd Government's decision to pull out of the so-called 'Quad', which sowed seeds of doubt in New Delhi about Canberra's reliability as a partner. The third section investigates Australia's turn to the 'Indo-Pacific' under the Julia Gillard and Tony Abbott governments, and its rethinking of India's regional role. The last section explores the coalescence of the defence and security elements of the strategic partnership after Narendra Modi's rise to power in May 2014. It argues that what has driven Australia and India together and—paradoxically—what has kept them from cooperating more closely is the same thing: China.

From Pokhran to the Quad 1.0: 1998–2007

On 11 May 1998 India tested three nuclear weapons, and two days later, two more, at the Pokhran range in the Thar desert in the west of Rajasthan.[3] Pakistan soon followed with six tests of its own, on 28 and 30 May. Both countries then declared that they would now develop fully-fledged nuclear deterrents. In so doing, they shook the nuclear nonproliferation regime, of which Australia had become a prominent champion during the 1980s and 1990s.[4] India's breakout, in particular, deeply upset Canberra. Foreign Minister Alexander Downer called the tests 'outrageous acts' that he judged 'in flagrant defiance of the international community's strong support for nuclear non-proliferation'.[5] To demonstrate Australia's displeasure, the high commissioner was recalled for consultations, defence cooperation was broken off and official visits to India were suspended. Three Indian military officers studying at Australian defence colleges were immediately sent home.

---

3   These tests were labelled Pokhran II, to distinguish them from India's first test back in 1974. They are also commonly referred to by their codename, 'Operation Shakti'. The earlier test was codenamed 'Smiling Buddha'.

4   For a useful contemporary assessment, see: William Walker, 'International Nuclear Relations after the Indian and Pakistani Test Explosions', *International Affairs* 74, no. 3 (1998): 505–28, doi.org/10.1111/1468-2346.00031.

5   Alexander Downer, 'Australian Response to India Nuclear Tests', Minister for Foreign Affairs, Media Release FA59, 14 May 1998, foreignminister.gov.au/releases/1998/fa059_98.html (site discontinued), accessed 2 February 2020.

New Delhi was not impressed by this reaction, which it saw as disproportionate and disrespectful.[6] It suggested 'double standards' were at play, observing that despite its bluster at India, Canberra was apparently happy to turn a blind eye to alleged Chinese violations of the nuclear nonproliferation and missile technology regimes.[7] With lasting damage done on both sides, it took some time for bilateral ties to return to normal.

In March 2000, almost two years on from the tests, Australia eventually took the initiative. Foreign Minister Alexander Downer travelled to India to try to patch up the relationship and to lay the groundwork for John Howard to visit New Delhi. When he did in July that year, he became the first Australian prime minister to go to India since Bob Hawke, 11 years earlier.[8] The trip was more than symbolic, however. In New Delhi, Howard delivered a frank message: Canberra still did not approve of India's nuclear program, but was no longer 'going to allow' differences on that issue 'to contaminate the whole relationship'. It was time, Howard declared, for a proper 'strategic dialogue' between the two, focusing on the Indian Ocean and Asia-Pacific regions, to see if they could find some 'common ground' and work together.[9]

It took time—and the shock of the September 11 and Bali attacks, which catalysed the process—for this conversation to develop.[10] In June 2001, India's External Affairs Minister, Jaswant Singh, travelled to Australia, and with Downer, in Adelaide, held the first annual Foreign Minister's Framework Dialogue.[11] Together, they gave their approval for the first formal Australia–India Strategic Dialogue. This meeting brought together delegations led by Australia's Department of Foreign Affairs and Trade (DFAT) first assistant secretary and India's Ministry of External Affairs joint secretary, to discuss a broad agenda involving various security and economic issues. Twelve days before al-Qaeda struck in New York, the first

---

6   For a discussion, see: Rupakjyoti Borah, 'Australia–India Relations during the Howard Era', in Darvesh Gopal (ed.), *India–Australia Relations: Convergences and Divergences* (Delhi: Shipra, 2008), 177.

7   Darvesh Gopal and Dalbir Ahlawat, 'Australia–India Strategic Relations: From Estrangement to Engagement', *India Quarterly* 71, no. 3 (2015): 212, doi.org/10.1177/0974928415584022.

8   Meg Gurry, 'India, The New Centre of Gravity: Australia–India Relations under the Howard Government', *South Asia: Journal of South Asian Studies* 35, no. 2 (2012): 286–87, doi.org/10.1080/00856401.2011.633299.

9   PS Suryanarayana, 'Differences Must Not Affect New Dialogue: John Howard', *The Hindu*, 26 June 2000.

10   Hall, 'Australia's Fitful Engagements of India', 136.

11   'Successful Visit to Australia by Jaswant Singh', Minister for Foreign Affairs, Media Release FA89, 25 June 2001, foreignminister.gov.au/releases/2001/fa089_01.html (site discontinued), accessed 2 February 2020.

of these strategic dialogues took place in New Delhi.[12] The deployment of Australian troops to Afghanistan soon after, and the heightened threat from terrorism, then put a premium on better intelligence on militant Islamism in Central, South and South-East Asia. This elevated India's importance to Australia, and thus Canberra sought—and in August 2003 concluded—a Memorandum of Understanding (MoU) with India that would facilitate better interagency cooperation and intelligence sharing between the two, to address that challenge.[13]

It took another three years before the next element of the security partnership was put in place. In the meantime, India's economy boomed, with GDP growth at or around 8 per cent between 2003 and 2007, and bilateral trade burgeoned too.[14] As a result, the Howard Government began to perceive India as a significant opportunity for Australian businesses and universities. When the prime minister returned to New Delhi in March 2006, he took with him a large delegation, praised India's 'spectacular' growth, and began to shift towards support for the country's membership of the Asia-Pacific Economic Cooperation (APEC) forum, which Canberra had hitherto opposed.[15] More substantively, Howard also signed an MoU on defence cooperation that moved the partnership beyond strategic dialogues and cooperation on counterterrorism. The new deal envisaged more dialogues, to be sure, and more professional exchanges of military officers, but also joint naval exercises and ship visits, as well as collaboration on the acquisition, development and management of military materiel.

The declared intentions of this enhanced defence cooperation were to better comprehend New Delhi's 'strategic outlook' and to 'encourage a positive contribution to global security from India'.[16] It was clear,

---

12   'India–Australia Strategic Dialogue', Australian High Commission New Delhi, Media Release PA/12/2001, 30 August 2001, india.embassy.gov.au/ndli/PA_12_01.html, accessed 7 December 2020.
13   'Australia and India Sign Counter-Terrorism MOU', Minister for Foreign Affairs, Media Release FA107, 28 August 2003, webarchive.nla.gov.au/awa/20031001172702/http://www.foreignminister. gov.au/releases/2003/fa107_03.html, accessed 2 February 2020.
14   For the GDP data, see: The World Bank, 'GDP Growth (Annual %)', The World Bank, data. worldbank.org/indicator/NY.GDP.MKTP.KD.ZG, accessed 2 February 2020. Between 2000 and 2009, the value of bilateral trade climbed from A$3.3 billion to A$20.9 billion. See: Sally Percival Wood and Michael Leach, '"Rediscovery", "Reinvigoration" and "Redefinition" in Perpetuity: Australian Engagement with India 1983–2011', *Australian Journal of Politics and History* 57, no. 4 (2011): 539, doi.org/10.1111/j.1467-8497.2011.01612.x.
15   Gurry, 'India, the New Centre of Gravity', 293.
16   Department of Defence, 'Inquiry into Australia's Relationship with India as an Emerging World Power: Department of Defence Submission to the Joint Standing Committee on Foreign Affairs, Defence and Trade', 8 June 2006, Executive Summary, 3, www.aph.gov.au/parliamentary_ business/committees/house_of_representatives_committees?url=jfadt/india2006/subs/sub20.pdf, accessed 7 December 2020.

however, that the Howard government was already convinced that India's outlook was substantially commensurate with Australia's, and that New Delhi was willing and able to make a positive contribution to regional and global security. Its controversial decision to involve Australia—along with India, Japan and the United States—in the so-called Quadrilateral Security Dialogue (QSD or Quad), a little over a year later in May 2007, reflected that view. Essentially a 'minilateral' officials' meeting, the Quad was first proposed by Japanese Prime Minister Abe Shinzo as one element of a broader political and military construct.[17] It extended a series of existing bilateral and trilateral strategic dialogues at various levels, and served as a kind of signalling exercise, principally to China, but also to the wider region about the intentions of all four states concerning regional security.[18] It also showed how far some in Canberra had come, in a relatively short period of time, in their perceptions of India as a putative security partner.

Some significant obstacles still lay in the way, however, of realising that objective. The biggest was Australia's longstanding ban on selling uranium to India, on the grounds that it was not a signatory to the Nuclear Non-Proliferation Treaty (NPT). As late as May 2007, the Howard Government was still insisting that the ban should stay in place, with Industry Minister Ian Macfarlane categorically ruling out the idea.[19] But some time earlier, Howard had decided to back the deal that the United States had struck with India in July 2005, effectively to allow civilian nuclear cooperation despite New Delhi's refusal to sign the NPT. This had given rise to an 'unresolved tension' in Canberra, lasting for more than a year, as Downer and DFAT held out against uranium sales in defence of the department's longstanding nonproliferation agenda. The issue was only settled in the dying days of the government.[20] In the end, Downer and DFAT lost the argument. In August 2007, three months out from the election, Howard

---

17   For useful contemporary discussions, see: Purnendra Jain, 'Westward Ho! Japan Eyes India Strategically', *Japanese Studies* 28, no. 1 (2008): 22–25, doi.org/10.1080/10371390801939070; and Aurelia George Mulgan, 'Breaking the Mould: Japan's Subtle Shift from Exclusive Bilateralism to Modest Minilateralism', *Contemporary Southeast Asia: A Journal of International and Strategic Affairs* 30, no. 1 (2008): 52–72.

18   On minilateralism more broadly, see: William T Tow and Brendan Taylor (eds), *Bilateralism, Multilateralism and Asia-Pacific Security: Contending Cooperation* (London: Routledge, 2013), doi.org/10.4324/9780203367087.

19   Katherine Murphy, 'No Uranium for India: Macfarlane', *The Age*, 23 May 2007.

20   Paul Kelly, *Howard's Decade: An Australian Foreign Policy Reappraisal*, Lowy Institute Paper 15 (Sydney: Lowy Institute for International Policy, 2006), 66.

told his Indian counterpart, Manmohan Singh, that Australia was now willing, in principle, to lift the ban, subject to the guarantee that any uranium sold would only be used for civilian purposes.[21]

Turbulence: 2007–13

From 2003 to 2007, the Howard Government worked with two different counterparts in New Delhi, the Hindu nationalist administration of Atal Bihari Vajpayee and the Congress Party–led coalition of Manmohan Singh, to construct practically from scratch a security partnership with a state that only a few years earlier Canberra had condemned as a destabilising force. It took barely four months for Kevin Rudd's Australian Labor Party (ALP) Government, however, to put what had been built in doubt. Rudd made it clear from the outset that he did not approve of lifting the uranium ban unless India signed the NPT, effectively endorsing DFAT's position and rescinding Howard's offer.[22] Prior to the election and after it, Rudd and his colleagues also expressed reservations about the Quad. In February 2008, these concerns coalesced into a decision to withdraw from the minilateral dialogue. Apparently without informing New Delhi or even Washington, and with his Chinese counterpart, Yang Jiechi, at his side, Stephen Smith, Rudd's foreign minister, abruptly announced this decision at a press conference.[23]

In New Delhi, these various moves, made by a Mandarin-speaking prime minister who repeatedly expressed his desire to see Canberra bolster ties with Beijing, generated concerns about the reliability of Rudd and of Australia as putative partners.[24] The Rudd Government did send out more positive signals to New Delhi in other areas, notably in its support for India

---

21   Australian Associated Press, 'Uranium Sales to India gets OK', *The Sydney Morning Herald*, 17 August 2007, www.smh.com.au/national/uranium-sales-to-india-gets-ok-20070817-gdqvov.html, accessed 7 December 2020.

22   Peter Mayer and Purnendra Jain, 'Beyond Cricket: Australia–India Evolving Relations', *Australian Journal of Political Science* 45, no. 1 (2010): 140, doi.org/10.1080/10361140903517759.

23   Rory Medcalf, 'Mysterious Quad More Phantom than Menace', *ABC News*, 9 April 2008, www.abc.net.au/news/2008-04-09/mysterious-quad-more-phantom-than-menace/2397936, accessed 7 December 2020.

24   Rory Medcalf, 'Australia–India Relations: Hesitating on the Brink of Partnership', *Asia Pacific Bulletin: East West Centre*, no. 13, 3 April 2008, www.eastwestcenter.org/system/tdf/private/apb013.pdf?file=1&type=node&id=32261, accessed 7 December 2020. See also: B Raman, 'Kevin Rudd: All the Way with China', *Raman's Strategic Analysis*, 23 April 2008, paper 2680, ramanstrategicanalysis.blogspot.com/2008/04/kevin-rudd-all-way-with-china.html, accessed 9 December 2020.

to become a member of the APEC Forum, and for it to be included in the 'Asia Pacific Community' the prime minister recommended for the region. It also made reassuring noises about improving bilateral ties and engaging more closely with key states. But after those early rocky months had passed, it took time for trust and momentum to be restored. Significantly, it also took a shift in the Rudd Government's perception of China and its intentions. This movement towards a more concerned view of China was demonstrated most clearly in the 2009 Defence White Paper. To the consternation of some analysts, that document pointed to China's military modernisation and observed that Beijing might be aiming to challenge the regional pre-eminence of the United States.[25] Importantly, the White Paper also foreshadowed a push to strengthen Australia's defence and security ties with other regional powers, including India.[26]

Soon after the White Paper appeared, Rudd moved to improve ties with New Delhi. He first signalled his government's seriousness by sending Peter Varghese, then the head of the Office of National Assessments and later secretary of DFAT, to New Delhi as high commissioner. Varghese's appointment was announced in February 2009. Rudd then travelled to New Delhi for an official visit in November 2009, and made two important steps. He signed a Joint Declaration on Security Cooperation and, together with Manmohan Singh, announced that Australia and India had decided to upgrade their relationship to a fully-fledged 'strategic partnership'. Both commitments were, to a degree, aspirational and signalled the desire to broaden defence and security ties beyond what was envisaged in the 2003 and 2006 agreements. However, they fell short of what Australia and India seemed willing to do with other partners, notably the United States and Japan.[27] And whatever progress was made continued to be overshadowed by the issue of uranium sales. But all this said, the Joint Declaration and the unveiling of the strategic partnership reflected a very different view of the bilateral relationship than the one that prevailed in Canberra at the beginning of Rudd's tenure.

---

25   Department of Defence, *Defending Australia in the Asia-Pacific Century: Force 2030* (Canberra: Commonwealth of Australia, 2009), 16, 34. For a critical view of the White Paper's assessment of China's intentions, see: Czeslaw Tubilewicz, 'The 2009 Defence White Paper and the Rudd Government's Response to China's Rise', *Australian Journal of Political Science* 45, no. 1 (2010): 149–57, doi.org/10.1080/10361140903517767.

26   Department of Defence, *Defending Australia in the Asia-Pacific Century*, 3, 95 and 96.

27   David Brewster, 'Australia and India: The Indian Ocean and the Limits of Strategic Convergence', *Australian Journal of International Affairs* 64, no. 5 (2020): 549–65, doi.org/10.1080/10357718.201 0.513369.

Rudd's replacement by Julia Gillard just over six months later, in June 2010, opened the way to more progress. In May 2011, the two countries opened negotiations for a free trade agreement, the Comprehensive Economic Cooperation Agreement (CECA). The change in leadership also allowed for a reconsideration of the uranium ban, both within the ALP and the bureaucracy. In November 2011, Gillard secured approval from the ALP caucus to lift the ban on uranium sales. When she went to New Delhi almost a year later, in October 2012, the two countries commenced discussions about a civil nuclear agreement and agreed to hold annual prime ministerial meetings, alongside the various ongoing strategic dialogues, either in each other's capitals or on the sidelines of regional summits. It was clear that India loomed ever larger in Canberra's thinking. In October 2012, DFAT also published its Asian Century White Paper, intended as a basis for a broad national strategy for regional engagement. India was cast as a key partner, mentioned more than a hundred times in the text.[28] This view was similarly reflected in the 2013 Defence White Paper, which muted some of the more robust language about China found in its predecessors, but which also introduced the concept of the 'Indo-Pacific' into Australian official discourse, with India a core element in this new geostrategic concept. The 2013 paper explicitly welcomed India's emergence as a 'global power', though it was vague on the manner in which Canberra wished to see the strategic partnership develop.[29]

Rudd's brief return to the prime ministership in 2013 did not disrupt this perception or the work being done to strengthen the relationship. Tony Abbott's election in September of that year did, however, add some impetus. He and his government introduced a markedly more ideological dimension to foreign policy, with a clear preference for aligning with democratic and English-speaking states, and a more critical tone on China's behaviour in the region.[30] That played—however awkwardly, given Australia and India's very different colonial pasts—in the relationship's favour. So too did the enhanced regional engagement promised by the Abbott Government, under the slogan 'more Jakarta, less Geneva', and

28   Department of Foreign Affairs and Trade, *Asian Century White Paper* (Canberra: Commonwealth of Australia, 2011).

29   Department of Defence, *2016 Defence White Paper* (Canberra: Commonwealth of Australia, 2016), 2.

30   Rory Medcalf, 'The Balancing Kangaroo: Australia and Chinese Power', *Issues and Studies* 50, no. 3 (2014): 103–35. See also: Priya Chacko and Alexander E Davis, 'The Natural/Neglected Relationship: Liberalism, Identity and India–Australia Relations', *The Pacific Review* 30, no. 1 (2017): 26–50, doi.org/10.1080/09512748.2015.1100665.

its shift away from high-minded multilateralism towards more pragmatic cooperation with like-minded states.[31] This drew the Abbott Government to India, which was perceived as having congruent interests and useful capabilities. But it did take time to secure any further agreements with New Delhi, because in late 2013 and early 2014, India's focus turned inward, as its general election loomed.

Modi and the Quad: 2014–19

Narendra Modi's rise to power in May 2014 was met with a mixture of optimism and concern in Australia. Influential analysts predicted that his government's trade and investment agenda could be advantageous.[32] Others expressed worries about the influence of hardline Hindu nationalists on Modi and his administration.[33] In Canberra, however, the Liberal–National Coalition Government welcomed Modi's win, and moves were made to arrange for Abbott to visit New Delhi and meet the new Indian leader as soon as practicably possible. Abbott made a phone call to congratulate Modi on his success, and to extend a personal invitation to the G20 meeting to be held in Brisbane later in the year.[34] Four months later, Abbott honoured his commitment to travel to New Delhi, travelling to India for a two-day state visit in early September 2014—the first such visit by a foreign leader since Modi's election. He took with him a landmark civil nuclear agreement, with provisions permitting uranium exports, which he and Modi duly signed during the trip. He was also accompanied by a business delegation, and both sides expressed the desire

---

31 Mark Beeson, 'Issues in Australian Foreign Policy: July to December 2013', *Australian Journal of Politics and History* 60, no. 2 (2014): 267, doi.org/10.1111/ajph.12059.

32 Rory Medcalf and Danielle Rajendram, 'India's Narendra Modi is Good News for Australia', *The Sydney Morning Herald,* 19 May 2014, www.smh.com.au/opinion/indias-narendra-modi-is-good-news-for-australia-20140519-zrhdd.html, accessed 7 December 2020.

33 See, for example: Amanda Hodge, 'Room for All who Accept India is Hindu Nation', *The Australian*, 3 May 2014, www.theaustralian.com.au/news/world/room-for-all-who-accept-india-is-hindu-nation/news-story/e22a46af3502e8f2de091b18f6bd062d, accessed 7 December 2020; and Kanishka Jayasuriya, 'Nationalism Marries Neoliberalism to Fuel Rise of Asia's New Right', *The Conversation*, 21 March 2014, theconversation.com/nationalism-marries-neoliberalism-to-fuel-rise-of-asias-new-right-24395, accessed 7 December 2020.

34 Narendra Modi, 'World Leaders Greet Narendra Modi on Record Win', Narendra Modi, 17 May 2014, www.narendramodi.in/world-leaders-greet-narendra-modi-on-record-win-6215, accessed 7 December 2020.

to conclude the CECA when practicable. Finally, the two prime ministers signalled that the first Australia–India joint naval exercise would soon be held, sometime in 2015.[35]

Abbott's solicitous engagement of Modi paid off a couple of months later, when he came to Brisbane for the G20 and stayed for a state visit, becoming the first Indian prime minister to travel to Australia since Rajiv Gandhi in 1986. The trip gave Modi the opportunity both to show how seriously India now took Australia as a partner, and to thank those in the Indian diaspora now living in Australia for their support for his election campaign earlier in the year.[36] Further, Modi was given an opportunity to address the Australian parliament, during which he remarked on the new closeness in the relationship, and displayed much bonhomie with his Australian counterpart. 'There was a time', he observed, 'when, for many of us, Australia was a distant land on the southern edge of the world'. But now, he went on, New Delhi welcomes Australia's 'growing role in driving this region's prosperity and shaping its security' and sees 'Australia as a vital partner in India's quest for progress and prosperity'. Modi said that he looked forward to Australia playing a bigger role in India in areas such as education and training, the provision of better housing and electricity, agriculture and food processing, healthcare, finance, manufacturing and building infrastructure in ways that are sustainable and environmentally sensitive. He foreshadowed deeper and broader security cooperation, 'to create [an] environment and culture that promotes the currency of co-existence and cooperation; in which all nations, small and big, abide by international law and norms, even when they have bitter disputes'. And he made particular reference to the need to work together on counterterrorism and fighting extremism.[37]

---

35   'Joint Statement by Prime Minister Abbott and Prime Minister Modi, visit to India September 2014', Department of Foreign Affairs and Trade, 5 September 2014, dfat.gov.au/geo/india/Pages/joint-statement-by-prime-minister-abbott-and-prime-minister-modi-visit-to-india-september-2014.aspx, accessed 7 December 2020.

36   On Modi's diaspora diplomacy in general, see: Ian Hall, *Modi and the Reinvention of Indian Foreign Policy* (Bristol: Bristol University Press, 2019), 98–102, doi.org/10.1332/policypress/9781529204605.001.0001.

37   'Prime Minister's Address to the Joint Session of the Australian Parliament', Ministry of External Affairs, Government of India, 18 November 2014, www.mea.gov.in/Speeches-Statements.htm?dtl/24269/Prime_Ministers_Address_to_the_Joint_Session_of_the_Australian_Parliament_18_November_2014, accessed 7 December 2020.

Modi's visit produced two results. First, the Indian prime minister made a pledge to have his government speed up negotiations on the CECA, with a view to signing a deal by the end of 2015.[38] Second, Australia and India signed a Framework for Security Cooperation. The agreement envisaged more cooperation on counterterrorism and border protection, committed both sides to greater cooperation on defence technology and export control regimes, and promised more collaboration between their respective navies on search and rescue, humanitarian assistance and disaster relief.[39] In its wake, there was a marked step-up in bilateral engagement on defence and security, despite the foundering of the CECA talks during the course of 2015, and their eventual suspension. In June 2015, Australia, India and Japan held a trilateral strategic dialogue in New Delhi, led by the respective heads of their foreign ministries, and promised to make the meeting an annual event.[40] In September, Australia and India completed their first bilateral naval exercise (AUSINDEX), involving frigates and tankers, as well as a Royal Australian Navy Collins-class submarine, in the Bay of Bengal.[41] In November, the two held a dialogue on maritime security, again in the Indian capital. Finally, Australia and India agreed to hold a so-called 2+2 meeting between foreign and defence ministers at some convenient time in the near future.

The changes here were both of tempo and substance, and they carried on after Malcolm Turnbull replaced Abbott as prime minister in mid-September 2015. It was obvious by the end of that year, if not before, that Modi's Government had adopted the language of the 'rules-based order' being deployed by like-minded states such as Australia, Japan and the United States, and was working to try to strengthen its strategic partnerships with each, and indeed with others.[42] New Delhi continued

---

38   'Joint Statement by Prime Minister Abbott and Prime Minister Modi'.

39   David Brewster, 'The Australia–India Framework for Security Cooperation: Another Step towards an Indo-Pacific Security Partnership', *Security Challenges* 11, no. 1 (2015): 39–48.

40   David Lang, 'The Not-Quite-Quadrilateral: Australia, Japan and India', *The Strategist*, 9 July 2015, www.aspistrategist.org.au/the-not-quite-quadrilateral-australia-japan-and-india/, accessed 7 December 2020.

41   Department of Defence, 'Australia and India in First Maritime Exercise', *Navy Daily*, 15 September 2015, news.navy.gov.au/en/Sep2015/Fleet/2298/Australia-and-India-in-first-maritime-exercise.htm#.XRg_7y1L1TY (site discontinued), accessed 7 December 2020.

42   This language was first adopted, in a major statement released the day prior to President Barack Obama's attendance as guest of honour at India's Republic Day parade: 'India–US Delhi Declaration of Friendship', Ministry of External Affairs, 25 January 2015, www.mea.gov.in/bilateral-documents. htm?dtl/24727/indiaus+delhi+declaration+of+friendship, accessed 7 December 2020. See also: Kanti Bajpai, 'Narendra Modi's Pakistan and China Policy: Assertive Bilateral Diplomacy, Active Coalition Diplomacy', *International Affairs* 93, no. 1 (2017): 69–91, doi.org/10.1093/ia/iiw003.

to keep its options open, preferring 'multialignment' to both alignment and non-alignment—but its preferred security partners and regional order were increasingly clearly defined.[43] It was also readily apparent from Australia's 2016 Defence White Paper, published in February, that Canberra had come to regard India as a significant partner, and one with which it would like to do more. The paper observed overlapping interests in 'maritime security, regional stability and countering terrorism' and shared values as bases for greater engagement.[44] A second maritime security dialogue followed in Canberra in October 2016, and a joint exercise for contingents from the two countries' special forces took place in the same month.

In April 2017, Turnbull made a five-day visit to India—the sixth by an Australian prime minister since Howard's first trip back in 2000. Despite the length of Turnbull's stay, however, only incremental steps were taken. He and Modi agreed to ensure the promised inaugural 2+2 meeting would soon be scheduled, and they announced that an army-to-army exercise would also be arranged. They also unveiled another MoU on counterterrorism.[45] The most dramatic initiative came about six months later. In Manila on 12 November 2017, on the sidelines of the ASEAN (Association of South-East Asian Nations) Summit, an Australian official met with their Indian, Japanese and American counterparts in a new set of quadrilateral 'consultations', as they were termed, at least in the beginning.[46] The new Quad was intended to serve most of the purposes of the old, but was packaged differently, given a more opaque name and dissociated from more ambitious notions, like Abe's Democratic Security Diamond.[47] Its reconstitution was meant as a signal to Beijing that its behaviour in the

---

43   Ian Hall, 'Multialignment and Indian Foreign Policy Under Narendra Modi', *The Round Table: The Commonwealth Journal of International Affairs* 105, no. 3 (2016): 271–86, doi.org/10.1080/003 58533.2016.1180760.

44   Ian Hall, 'India in Australia's 2016 Defence White Paper', *Security Challenges* 12, no. 1 (2016): 181–85. See also: Department of Defence, *2016 White Paper* (Canberra: Commonwealth of Australia, 2016).

45   'Joint Statement by Prime Minister Turnbull and Prime Minister Modi, visit to India 2017', Department of Foreign Affairs and Trade, 10 April 2017, dfat.gov.au/geo/india/Pages/joint-statement-by-prime-minister-turnbull-and-prime-minister-modi-visit-to-india-2017.aspx, accessed 7 December 2020.

46   'Australia–India–Japan–United States consultations on the Indo-Pacific', Department of Foreign Affairs and Trade, 12 November 2017, dfat.gov.au/news/media/Pages/aus-india-japan-us-consultations-on-the-indo-pacific.aspx, accessed 7 December 2020.

47   For a useful take on this idea, see: Lavina Lee and John Lee, 'Japan–India Cooperation and Abe's Democratic Security Diamond: Possibilities, Limitations and the View from Southeast Asia', *Contemporary Southeast Asia* 38, no. 2 (2016): 284–308.

Indo-Pacific region was a matter of concern to its four members, which demanded regular dialogues about its intentions, capabilities and policies. It also met a felt need for better policy coordination and a forum in which areas for deeper cooperation might be identified.[48]

During 2018 and 2019, the Quad and the other minilaterals continued to meet, and Australia and India continued to work on defence and security ties. New Delhi sought also to demonstrate how seriously it now took Australia, sending President Ram Nath Kovind for a visit in November 2018—the first ever by an Indian head of state.[49] Bilateral traffic went on apace. One analyst has calculated that in 2018 alone, there were 38 defence and security-focused dialogues and military exercises between the two, up from 11 in 2014.[50] In July and August 2018, the Indian Air Force participated for the first time in the regular 'Pitch Black' exercise in northern Australia. In April 2019, the two countries' navies held another iteration of AUSINDEX, this time focusing on anti-submarine warfare, with the Australian side—significantly—permitted to practice tracking an Indian submarine.[51] In parallel, to try to better facilitate these activities, future humanitarian and disaster relief operations, or other contingencies, Canberra proposed that Australia and India sign a logistics support agreement akin to those New Delhi has recently concluded with the United States and France.[52]

That deal was finally signed in early June 2020 during a virtual summit held between Modi and Scott Morrison that also elevated the bilateral relationship to the level of a 'Comprehensive Strategic Partnership' and signalled a willingness on both sides to restart negotiations for some kind

---

48   Ian Hall, 'Meeting the Challenge: The Case for the Quad', in Andrew Carr (ed.), 'Debating the Quad', *Centre of Gravity*, Series 39 (Canberra: Strategic and Defence Studies Centre, The Australian National University, 2018), 12–15.

49   'Visit to Australia by His Excellency Ram Nath Kovind, President of India', Department of Foreign Affairs and Trade, 24 November 2018, dfat.gov.au/news/media/Pages/visit-to-australia-by-his-excellency-ram-nath-kovind-president-of-india.aspx, accessed 7 December 2020.

50   Aakriti Bachhawat, 'No Longer in a Cleft Stick: India and Australia in the Indo-Pacific', *The Strategist*, 25 June 2019, www.aspistrategist.org.au/no-longer-in-a-cleft-stick-india-and-australia-in-the-indo-pacific/, accessed 7 December 2020.

51   Christopher Pyne, 'AUSINDEX 2019 Commences in India', Department of Defence, 9 April 2019, www.minister.defence.gov.au/minister/cpyne/media-releases/ausindex-2019-commences-india, accessed 7 December 2020.

52   Dipanjan Roy Chaudhury, 'Australia Moots Logistics Support Agreement with India to Widen Defence Partnership in Indo-Pacific Region', *The Economic Times*, 12 June 2019, economictimes. indiatimes.com/news/defence/australia-moots-logistics-support-agreement-with-india-to-widen-defence-partnership-in-indo-pacific-region/articleshow/69758255.cms, accessed 7 December 2020.

of economic cooperation agreement.[53] The meeting had originally been scheduled for January in New Delhi, but the bushfires that engulfed eastern Australia that month prompted a postponement by Morrison, and then the COVID-19 pandemic intervened to prevent an in-person discussion.[54] In the shadow of tensions with China involving both countries, the virtual summit involved another stepping up of political and defence security engagement, with the release of a 'Shared Vision' for maritime cooperation and the announcement of greater cooperation in cyber security. And it was followed in October 2020 by a widely anticipated invitation from India to Australia to participate once again in the Malabar naval exercises, along with the other two Quad partners, United States and Japan.[55]

In parallel, Quad interactions intensified too, driven in part by the need for coordinated responses to the various challenges posed by COVID-19, including vaccine manufacture and distribution, but also pandemic-driven and China-driven disruptions to economies and global supply chains. There were three high-level Quad meetings during the course of 2020, including one of foreign ministers. A virtual Quad leaders' discussion was convened in March 2021, followed by an in-person summit in Washington DC in September. Each of these interactions broadened the scope of cooperation and coordination between the four, encompassing not just maritime security, counterterrorism, intelligence sharing and infrastructure financing, but also vaccines, cyber security, supply chains, telecommunications and critical minerals. Working groups of officials from the partners were also created.[56]

---

53   'India, Australia Sign Logistics Pact to Access Each Other's Military Bases', *The Wire*, 4 June 2020, thewire.in/diplomacy/india-australia-meet-military-bases-pact.

54   Latika Bourke, 'Narendra Modi confirms Scott Morrison's India trip is cancelled', *The Sydney Morning Herald*, 4 January 2020, www.smh.com.au/politics/federal/narendra-modi-confirms-scott-morrisons-india-trip-is-cancelled-20200104-p53oqa.html, accessed 9 November 2021.

55   Andrew Greene, Stephen Dziedzic and James Oaten, 'Australia to Rejoin "Quad" Naval Exercises in Move Certain to Infuriate Beijing', *ABC News*, 20 October 2020, www.abc.net.au/news/2020-10-20/australia-rejoins-naval-exercise-in-move-certain-to-anger-china/12784186, accessed 7 December 2020.

56   Prime Minister's Office, 'Quad Summit Fact Sheet', 12 March 2021, www.pm.gov.au/sites/default/files/files/quad-summit-fact%20Sheet.pdf, accessed 9 November 2021.

Conclusion: The China Paradox

There is no doubt that Beijing's escalating assertiveness has been the primary cause of the strengthening of the defence and security partnership between Australia and India since the mid-2000s. Concern about terrorism—and, for that matter, about New Delhi's own intentions for the region—might have prompted Canberra to re-engage with India, but once the conversations began, they soon turned to China, especially as it grew more demanding and difficult to manage in the aftermath of the global financial crisis of 2007–08.[57] The dialogues and cooperation have continued, despite the lack of progress on bilateral trade and investment— and indeed despite issues like the uranium ban, which in the past, given India's well-attested and acute sensitivity about status, might have derailed the relationship.[58]

Yet while China has helped drive Australia and India into a closer security partnership, it has also generated tensions in bilateral ties, partly due to misperceptions of the others' relationships with Beijing.[59] The debate over the reconstitution of the Quad in late 2017 demonstrated this well. Inevitably, it generated controversy, but it was clear that, 10 years on, there was a firmer bipartisan consensus in Canberra that the initiative was useful and desirable, and there was a stronger commitment to it in New Delhi. At the same time, however, it did not prevent suggestions by Australian and Indian commentators that aspects of the others' ties to China made them unreliable as a security partner. Analyses arguing that one or other country was the Quad's 'weakest link' became once more something of a cottage industry.[60]

---

57   C Raja Mohan, *Modi's World: Expanding India's Sphere of Influence* (New Delhi: HarperCollins, 2015), 143–44. On China's changing behaviour after 2009, see: Aaron L Friedberg, 'The Sources of Chinese Conduct: Explaining Beijing's Assertiveness', *The Washington Quarterly* 37, no. 4 (2014): 133–50, doi.org/10.1080/0163660X.2014.1002160.

58   On status and Indian diplomatic behaviour, see: Baldev Raj Nayar and TV Paul, *India in the World Order: Searching for Major-Power Status* (Cambridge: Cambridge University Press, 2003), doi.org/10.1017/CBO9780511808593.

59   For a very helpful discussion, see: Frédéric Grare, *India Turns East: International Engagement and US–China Rivalry* (London: Hurst, 2017), 115–35, doi.org/10.1093/oso/9780190859336.001.0001.

60   See, for example: Hugh White, 'Why the US is No Match for China in Asia, and Trump Should Have Stayed at Home and Played Golf', *South China Morning Post*, 15 November 2015, www.scmp.com/comment/insight-opinion/article/2120010/why-us-no-match-china-asia-and-trump-should-have-stayed-home, accessed 7 December 2020; and Harsh V Pant and Kartik Bommakanti, 'Can the Quad Deal with China?', *Observer Research Foundation*, 26 November 2018, www.orfonline.org/research/can-the-quad-deal-with-china-45750/, accessed 7 December 2020.

While eminently contestable, these doubts reflected broader worries within both Canberra and New Delhi about the interests and intentions of the other, especially as pressure generated by China—intentionally and inadvertently—has grown. On the Australian side, the persistent belief that, in a crisis, India will stick to its old policy of non-alignment undermines confidence in New Delhi's repeated public commitments to the rules-based order and to its security partners.[61] On the Indian side, there is substantial concern about Australia's trading relationship with China, which some think generates an unhealthy dependence.[62] The worry is that Canberra might chose economic security over the interests of its friends and allies, and even over its continued political independence. So far, leaders and officials in both capitals, including respective high commissioners, have done a good job in managing these concerns, as have more intensive interactions within the context of the Quad, but they may remain obstacles to deeper and more substantive defence and security cooperation.

---

61   See, for example: Michael Wesley, 'The Elephant in the Room', *The Monthly*, February 2012, www.themonthly.com.au/issue/2012/february/1328594251/michael-wesley/elephant-room, accessed 7 December 2020.
62   Grare, *India Turns East*, 132–33.

11

High Commissioners as Scholarly Observers: Crocker on Nehru, and Grant on Indira Gandhi

David Lowe

This chapter focuses on two Australian high commissioners in other than their official roles. Such a task is made possible by two incumbents leaving a legacy of writing about their respective times in situ, and writing about Indian leaders in particular. The two high commissioners who left strong written records, the kind of records that enable us to say that their legacies endured well beyond their times in New Delhi, were Walter Crocker (1952–55 and 1958–62) and Bruce Grant (1973–76). What follows is an analysis of Crocker's and Grant's sketches of Indian leaders, Nehru and Indira Gandhi, respectively, with a view to addressing the more general questions around authority and diplomatic impact in the authorial voice of a former head of mission.

As Eric Meadows has outlined in Chapter Three, Crocker attached high priority during his two terms in India to improving relations between Nehru and the Australian Government, and to improving relations between the two nations in other ways. While in 1962, when he departed India, it would have been hard to conclude that he was successful to any marked degree, the potential for him to make immediate impact was severely limited. It is of more than historical interest now to investigate the longer-term, slower-burn impact that Crocker had and still has (in the manner of public diplomacy) for Australian–Indian relations through his writing. The same applies to the published work of Bruce Grant, whose profile and authority as a commentator on Australia in world affairs continued to grow during the 1980s and 1990s.

The first part of this chapter has at its centre Crocker's admirable pen-portrait of Nehru, *Nehru: A Contemporary's Estimate*, published in 1966;[1] but it also involves noting the different fates of Crocker and Nehru in the hands of their respective country's commentators; and it invites appreciation of a certain historical romanticism shared between the two— through participant observations of the momentous twentieth century— that emerges from Crocker's fine-grained observations of Nehru in both the published *Nehru* and in Crocker's diary entries. The second part of the chapter moves to the 1970s and early 1980s and focuses on Bruce Grant's observations of Indira Gandhi. These emerged primarily in an account of his time in India, *Gods and Politicians*,[2] published in 1982, but were supplemented by other writings as a journalist and in a recent memoir, *Subtle Moments*,[3] published in 2017. Grant's sketching was more the broad brush than the fine grain of Crocker's. It was notable for his positioning of Indira in overlapping political and culturally exotic landscapes. It accentuated the tension created for Indira by the formidable legacies of her father; and also featured Grant's attempt to connect India and Australia by reflecting on the crises in democracy both nations experienced in 1975.

Walter Crocker

'How empty Delhi seems when Nehru is away. It is a most curious fact— his personality or vitality seems to permeate the place when he is here.'[4] So began Walter Crocker's diary entry for 26 September 1953, nearly a year and a half into his first term as Australian high commissioner in Delhi. In this reflection is not only Crocker's preparedness for grand extrapolation, but also his belief in Nehru's extraordinary agency, his role

---

1   Walter Crocker, *Nehru: A Contemporary's Estimate* (London: George Allen & Unwin, 1966).
2   Bruce Grant, *Gods and Politicians: Politics as Culture—an Australian View of India* (Sydney: Allen Lane, 1982).
3   Bruce Grant, *Subtle Moments: Scenes on a Life's Journey* (Clayton: Monash University Publishing, 2017).
4   Crocker diary, 26 September 1953, copy held at Deakin University Library (DUL): 327.94 Crocke Cro/Dos.

as a carrier of national character and destiny. It was an observation that marked a deepening attraction to Nehru for Crocker, who would have, over the next decade, a privileged vantage point from which to write about the Indian leader.

We might note first the respective fates of Crocker and Nehru in the hands of their nation's commentators. Crocker's reputation as the scholar diplomat is well noted if not often expanded on at length. In addition to making prominent appearances in accounts of Australian–Indian relations, he has recently (in 2013) been incorporated in what James Cotton calls the 'Australian School of International Relations'. Such was Crocker's deep engagement with, and many published and unpublished reflections on, international affairs. As an international diplomat, Australian diplomat and scholar of international relations, he stands alongside the likes of William Macmahon Ball, W.K. Hancock and Frederic Eggleston in Cotton's account of eight early thinkers on Australia in world affairs.[5] Although hardly a household name, Crocker's acknowledgement in Australia and among those interested in the history of international affairs enjoys recurring moments of 'rediscovery'. He sits, courtesy of Cotton, among other thinkers who simultaneously embraced imperialism and British race patriotism on the one hand, and internationalism on the other, as a distinctively Australian way of thinking. This was the Australian School of International Relations. The two strands of thought were in constant tension, and Crocker was one among others who hoped for and, where possible, worked towards, a reconciliation of these two outlooks in international society. He, in particular, became convinced of Australia's need to respond constructively to the emergence of 'Afro-Asia' on to the world stage, and, according to Cotton, as he observed the great struggle of Australians to respond, Crocker concluded that 'Australia's imperial inheritance was more a liability than an asset'.[6] Some would want to qualify this conclusion, given Crocker's recurring pessimism and obsession with civilisational 'decline',[7] but his thoughtful grappling with the implications of decolonisation for Australia is widely acknowledged.

---

5   James Cotton, *The Australian School of International Relations* (New York: Palgrave Macmillan, 2013), 209–35.
6   Ibid., 210.
7   For example, see his essay, Walter Crocker, *The Racial Factor in International Relations* (Canberra: Australian National University, 1956).

Nehru, of course, enjoys far greater recognition, but in India his name and his achievements have been clouded by the legacy of his descendants. As the Nehru dynasty established a stranglehold on the Congress Party, the reputation of India's first prime minister became entangled in the fate of the family. Over the last 40 years in particular, since the time of Indira Gandhi's ill-fated declaration of a state of emergency, the family's standing has suffered repeated blows through its dominance of party politics and through the actions of those it has propelled into politics. It may sound callous, but from the perspective of Jawaharlal's reputation in India, not even one accidental death and two assassinations could end this, and today Sonia and Rahul Gandhi maintain that reverse legacy. As some have commented, including Ramachandra Guha recently:

> the posthumous career of Jawaharlal Nehru has come increasingly to reverse a famous biblical injunction. In the Bible, it is said that the sins of the father will visit seven successive generations. In Nehru's case, the sins of daughter, grandsons, granddaughter-in-law, and great-grandson have been retrospectively visited on him.[8]

The publicly known point of connection between Crocker and Nehru is, as mentioned, Crocker's published account of the latter's life. So highly regarded is this work that it was republished in 2008,[9] with some excisions of contextual nature and a new introductory essay by Guha, who admires Crocker's achievement. Guha's comments, which were also published as an essay in the Australian *Monthly* magazine in 2006,[10] highlight some of the strengths of Crocker's work. In particular, Guha notes the fascination Crocker quickly developed for Nehru and the affection that flows through his writing. Guha spent some time with the extraordinary Crocker diaries, notable for their detail and constant inquiring of human character, and Guha saw how rocked Crocker was in May 1964 upon learning of Nehru's death. At the time Crocker was Australia's ambassador to the Netherlands. It was in the wake of this that Crocker resolved to write his book, which he penned quickly over the next year. He sent a draft to his old conversational companion, British Indian expert Penderel Moon, for comments, and then the final manuscript on to Stanley Unwin in

---

8   Guha cites sociologist, André Béteille, in his 'Jawaharlal Nehru: A Romantic in Politics', in Ramachandra Guha (ed.), *Makers of Modern Asia* (Cambridge, MA: Harvard University Press, 2014), 145–46.
9   Random House India, New Delhi, 2008.
10   Ramachandra Guha, 'An Uncommon Diplomacy', *The Monthly*, November 2006, www.the monthly.com.au/issue/2006/november/1229991194/ramachandra-guha/uncommon-diplomacy, accessed 20 September 2015.

London, for publication. With some excisions of Crocker's sharpest criticisms, especially with regard to China and Kashmir (he was a serving Australian diplomat, after all), the book was published in January 1966.[11] Guha revisited some of the earliest reviews that, in India, were occasionally sharp, but this was also an India in the wake of humiliation at the hands of China, and an India of famine, and caste and communal conflicts. And, while noting that Crocker was indeed critical of Nehru on China, Kashmir and lack of succession planning, Guha admired the diplomat scholar's achievement:

> He was able to place his subject in context, to view him against the longue durée of Indian history, the better to understand how modern democracy departed from the traditions and accretions imposed by that history.[12]

Linking these admiring remarks to Guha's other analysis—his implied suggestion that Nehru's reputation will re-emerge more fully with the passing of his descendants' hold on the Congress Party—there may even be a 'Crocker on Nehru' third moment in the waiting. Alongside this somewhat playful suggestion I need to insert quickly my own conviction, agreeing with Guha and others, that contemporary biographical sketching that rises to artistry will endure as a powerful and popular mode of historical reading. In the periodic debates about relationships between biography and history, Virginia's Woolf's remarks still command respect. She stressed the artistry involved in a biographer's ability to use evidence to paint vivid pictures. 'The biographer', she wrote, 'does more to stimulate the imagination than any poet or novelist save the very greatest'.[13] Crocker's portrait of Nehru paints vividly and invites imaginative journeys via literary allusions and a sense of hero-tragedy. Take for example a few passages from his published biography by way of illustration:

> Nehru was that rare man who is both clever and good. It is hard to be clever. But it is harder still to be good. He was that very rare person, the clever man wielding power who remained good. No wonder Nehru wrote somewhere of the tempests raging around him being nothing to 'the storms within' him.[14]

---

11   Ibid.
12   Ibid.
13   As quoted in Ben Pimlott, 'Is Contemporary Biography History?', *Political Quarterly* 70, no. 1 (1999): 39–40, doi.org/10.1111/1467-923X.00202.
14   Crocker, *Nehru*, 144.

And: 'As 1963 opened Nehru looked on a prospect littered with ruins—the ruins of his hopes, and the ruins of a prestige seemingly so impregnable for a dozen years or more'.[15] Crocker lists Kashmir, Goa, the China border, communalism, five-year plans failing to live up to their promises, and so on. Then, he continues:

> Nehru probably took little comfort from the fact that whatever the truth about his failures the biggest truth of all was the immense scale of the problems the first Prime Minister of India had had to wrestle with, and how successful he had been with some of the problems and how near to succeeding with others. By 1962 and 1963 anyone knowing him over the preceding ten years was struck with the marks of sadness. His voice had lost some of its timbre; his silences had become longer and more enigmatic.[16]

And, towards the end of the book, having suggested that Nehru set himself the tasks of Sisyphus, and remarkably did not collapse under the weight, Crocker concludes:

> whatever his success or failure, the story of Nehru as a ruler will remain of great interest—how a man governed and shaped, or tried to shape, so big and so special a part of the human race in its first two decades of independence. But the man himself is still more interesting than his political history. Nehru might have made misjudgements; he might have been insufficiently in control; he might have destroyed much. But nothing can destroy his distinction. His supreme achievement was to have been Nehru, the fine spirit exercising power, the ruler who remained disinterested and compassionate.[17]

Crocker's diaries, on which the published portrait is very closely based, are absorbing. As anyone who has used them knows, their reading brings frustrations but the rewards outweigh these. Crocker wrote at the end of long days and he jotted down thoughts almost in shorthand style. His writing was tired and tiny. If he was nearing the end of a page and also the end of a day's reflections, he would simply go more miniscule in script rather than start a new page. His judgements of others could be severe—

---

15   Ibid., 130–31.
16   Ibid.
17   Ibid., 170.

like Nehru, he could be impatient with others, but he was also quick to soften some of the blows he landed with additional comments about the general decency, earnestness and manners of some of those he skewered.

Manners mattered to Crocker, and his observations of Nehru at work in hosting endless receptions with simple grace, cutting fruit for others, politely enduring tiresome guests and so on, undoubtedly fed into Crocker's high opinion of him. The newly arrived high commissioner's first impressions, when introduced to a preoccupied Nehru in 1952, were favourable: 'I like his voice, his English and his sensitive interesting face & personality. Whatever else he lacks or has, he is no vulgarian'.[18]

In the manner of an elite cosmopolitan, this was one of Crocker's chief sorting categories for people he met. A number of people he subsequently commented on in diary entries suffered the fate of being labelled 'vulgar' or 'vulgarian'. The same standard was applied by Nehru who laboured the word 'vulgar' in his earlier *Autobiography*.[19] Late-Victorian and Edwardian-born intellectuals also commonly dwelt on physical features of their contemporaries, and there are many Crocker entries bearing on Nehru's apparent fitness, large brown eyes, handsomeness and the smoothness of his skin.[20]

Australians often fared badly in these ventures into physiognomy. Consider, for example, Crocker's notes on taking Douglas Copland, esteemed economist and then vice-chancellor of The Australian National University, to visit Nehru:

> N[ehru] looked pure spirit and mind; I have never seen him look so striking. Douglas, in comparison, looked like a heap of meat, impregnated with alcohol and emitting spluttering coquette coughs. I had taken great pains to drill him for the occasion: N[ehru] is too sensitive, too important & too shy to take undue risks with, least of all, provincial egoists. Douglas did well & his 22 minutes went off without a hitch. Nehru wasn't impressed but he wasn't obviously bored.[21]

---

18   Crocker diary, 10 May 1952, DUL.
19   Jawaharlal Nehru, *An Autobiography* (London: The Bodley Head, 1936).
20   Crocker diary, 3 August 1953, 18 August 1953, DUL.
21   Crocker diary, 18 February 1953, DUL.

Also noteworthy for Crocker was Nehru's attraction to the beauty of nature, especially in Kashmir, which Nehru claimed marked him as different from many other Indians.[22] Nehru's aesthetic attractiveness was a constant refrain in Crocker's diary notes of meeting him at various dinners and other events. 'I have never met a man who is so much alive', wrote Crocker after lunch with Nehru in November 1958.[23] As well as being struck by the vitality of Nehru's eyes and skin, Crocker marvelled at Nehru's 'intellectual athleticism and range, the fine manners, the moral stature, the "interestingness" of the man, and moving timbre of his voice'.[24] Invoking the scholar who established the so-called 'Great Man' approach to history, on another occasion Crocker simply wrote that Nehru 'showed up again as one of Carlyle's heroes'.[25]

Nehru was renowned for readily seeing guests. Several of his closest advisers lamented the time and energy taken up with his hosting visitors and giving speeches. By serving in Delhi first in the early 1950s, when the number of foreign embassies was in the low 30s, Crocker was also able to see Nehru more than would become possible later in the decade, when more visitors and more crises ate into the prime minister's time. It would be wrong to suggest a closeness of special rapport between the two men but there are dotted throughout the diaries signs of Nehru's respect for Crocker, his appreciation of his intellect, and his ease in talking with him. When, for example, Crocker returned for his second posting in 1958, he called on Nehru on 15 November, the day after Nehru's 69th birthday. Nehru asked after Crocker's wife Claire and their two boys, and insisted that Crocker have some tea and birthday cake with him. It was half an hour before Crocker left.[26] Two years later over lunch the two ranged easily from water salinity and the mysteries of subterranean water supplies to the Delhi Botanical Gardens, Tolstoy, the literary struggle over George Orwell's political alignment, Nehru's love of flying and the 'the pace of progress and change in the last 50 years and how much greater it will be in the rest of this century—if we're not blown up'.[27]

---

22 Crocker diary, 7 July 1952, DUL.
23 Crocker diary, 23 November 1958, 3 June 1961, DUL.
24 Crocker diary, 24 February 1959, DUL.
25 Crocker diary, 3 March 1961, DUL.
26 Crocker diary, 15 November 1958, DUL.
27 Crocker diary, 7 December 1960, DUL.

Crocker was sensitive to the legacy of Nehru's English education, Harrow and Cambridge, where he studied science. In one early observation later to be expanded for the biography, he remarked that 'Nehru's mental stuffing … was derived from Western rationalism—G[eorge] B[ernard] S[haw], B. Russell, Fabian Socialists etc.'.[28] He also read Nehru's autobiography written from prison in the mid-1930s, and wrote copious notes on it as diary entries. One of his observations was that Nehru was driven by a desire to lift Indians to a newer, brighter future than had been their recent past: 'The more he admired the British, the more he hated Indian subjugation to the British'. Alongside this, Nehru wanted to rid India of communalism, create a socialist commonwealth in India and provide a new outlook that Crocker called 'an educational orientalism which would rest on science'.[29]

Crocker also witnessed what he called 'the formidable side' of Nehru's personality occasionally, including in December 1952 upon delivering a well-meaning but perhaps not carefully crafted message from Casey congratulating Nehru on his successful resolution on Korea in the United Nations General Assembly. Nehru read the message with barely concealed contempt, then sat in silence staring at the ground for some time before telling Crocker that all he could say by way of response was to thank Casey.[30] Neither did Prime Minister Menzies emerge favourably in Crocker's account of his visit to Delhi in the middle of 1959. The Australian prime minister talked too much, and talked over Nehru who, noted Crocker, 'could hardly conceal his boredom and impatience'. During his two-and-a-half day stay in Delhi, Menzies showed no interest in any of the sights and didn't ask Crocker a single question about India.[31]

Courtesy of Crocker's good standing and connections, he hosted a steady stream of senior Indian ministers and commentators willing to point out Nehru's weaknesses. Secretary of Cabinet N.R. Pillai was an especially regular source of information early on, on subjects ranging from Nehru's addiction to publicity, especially that involving children, to his apparent uncaring attitude towards his junior colleagues;[32] Foreign Secretary Subimal Dutt spoke of Nehru's fewer temper outbursts, and greater willingness to listen to criticism, and also of his loneliness, in

---

28 Crocker diary, 2 June 1952, DUL.
29 Crocker diary, 17 February 1959, DUL.
30 Crocker diary, 4 December 1952, DUL.
31 Crocker diary, 5 July 1959, DUL.
32 Crocker diary, 2 December 1959, 20 February 1961, DUL.

the late 1950s;[33] the remarkable Penderal Moon ventured on Nehru's susceptibility to flattery, poor judgement of some close to him and his reluctance to have showdowns with rogues;[34] journalist and politician Shiva Rao situated Nehru in the history of Indian nationalism, theosophy and current power dynamics;[35] and Nehru's sister and diplomat, Mrs Pandit, enjoyed expanding, over a drink or two, on diplomacy, Delhi political gossip and her brother's relentless work hours and health.[36]

Nehru constituted intellectual relief for Crocker who worked in settings not always intellectual. Such was his attraction that not only did Delhi seem empty without the Indian prime minister, but the whole country sometimes seemed divisible between a Nehru-influenced realm of enlightenment and a hinterland of darkness. Once when recounting another's story about meeting Morarji Desai, then chief minister of Bombay, Crocker recalled that Morarji had said he could not travel outside of India because that would require him to be vaccinated, and that his principles would not allow this on account of its entailing suffering to animals. 'This is the kind of India', noted Crocker, 'that one forgets in Delhi, especially when thinking of Nehru'.[37] An Australian intellectual with acute colonial Enlightenment values, Crocker found both stimulation and refuge in Nehru's leadership.

Bruce Grant

The other Indian prime minister who has been featured in a high commissioner's published work is Nehru's daughter, Indira Gandhi, prime minister, 1966–77 and 1980–84. While she was not the main subject of High Commissioner Bruce Grant's attention, she featured significantly in his *Gods and Politicians,* an account described on its dust jacket as 'a private odyssey' of his posting to New Delhi, 1973–76.[38] One of Grant's first pen portraits of Indira Gandhi drew on his observations of her on the campaign hustings:

33 Crocker diary, 17 December 1958, DUL.
34 Crocker diary, 13 January 1959, 29 March 1959, DUL.
35 Crocker diary, 22 September 1960, DUL.
36 Crocker diary, 21 September 1960, 7 February 1961, DUL.
37 Crocker diary, 24 July 1954, DUL.
38 Grant, *Gods and Politicians*, dust jacket.

> Like her father, she had physical charm. She could be skittish or somber, according to mood and circumstances. At times, when laughing, she could look like a girl. At other times, with her face shrouded by a shawl, she could look like Kali, the Hindu goddess of destruction.[39]

These arresting images convey the confidence of Grant, an accomplished journalist and writer, in locating a political leader within a part-known and part-exotic context.

Such confidence undoubtedly grew from Grant's experiences in Asia, including India: his first appointment as a news correspondent covering Asia in 1957; his visits to India during this time, including in 1959 and 1961; and his having met and interviewed Nehru. His strong style also reflected Grant's written accomplishments as journalist, published commentator on Indonesia, and novelist, prior to his arrival as high commissioner in New Delhi in September 1973. Grant was a multi-genre writer as much as, if not more, than he was diplomat. Indeed, while in India, he used spare evenings to extend his writing of fiction, short stories and essays.[40]

Significant too, was the transformational change in Australian politics that resulted in Grant's appointment to New Delhi, for this context shaped both his approach to his role and his subsequent written reflections. After 23 years of Liberal–Country Party coalition rule, the Australian Labor Party under Gough Whitlam finally won power at the end of 1972. With Whitlam came a determination to signal to the world a shift towards greater independence and embrace of region in Australia's international identity, including by swift recognition of communist China, removing the last vestiges of the restrictive (white) immigration policy, changing the national anthem from *God Save the Queen* to *Advance Australia Fair* and voting in the United Nations against apartheid in South Africa and Rhodesia. Grant arrived in New Delhi as Gough Whitlam's appointee rather than from the ranks of professional diplomats, with a mission to translate the new independence in Australian foreign policy into 'relations of substance' with India.[41] He helped convey a new era of potential in Australia's overseas relations more than a set of carefully thought-out policy initiatives relating to India. Grant benefited in India from the strong

---

39   Ibid., 75.
40   Grant, *Subtle Moments,* 214.
41   Ibid., 209.

signals in Canberra that Australia was striding out in new international directions. With Indira Gandhi especially, he benefited from being Australian rather than American: 'Like her father, she did not trust the Americans. So she regarded a friendly face from a fellow Commonwealth country like Australia as an unexpected pleasure'.[42]

In his own words, Grant became familiar with Mrs Gandhi's thinking through official contacts that became increasingly personal. Part of the reason was the elaborate 'and even intimate' negotiations needed to ensure that Australian and Indian governments paid each other due respect on their respective national days, Australia Day and Republic Day, both on 26 January. He recalled, in a separate memoir published in 2017, two occasions on which he and his wife Joan dined only with Indira and her family members. He suggested that the Indian prime minister welcomed both the new Australia he represented and the familiarity of the Commonwealth connection.[43] Grant felt that, far from being an authoritarian, as suggested by some commentators,[44] Indira was insecure as leader. This was, he felt, partly due to her consciousness of the nation-making heroism of her father and Mahatma Gandhi before her, and partly due to the internal political unrest she faced.[45]

Grant's analysis of Indira Gandhi was understandably shaped by the Emergency that lasted for 21 months, thus enduring beyond Grant's return to Australia in 1976. As is told elsewhere, the Emergency was triggered by the Allahabad High Court's finding, on 12 June 1975 that Indira had been guilty of corrupt electoral practice in the election of 1971. In the background, her attempts to control the judiciary had been leading to a confrontation of some sort, she faced rising unrest in the state of Bihar from mobilised students, industrial action by railway workers and the open challenge of enigmatic socialist politician Jayaprakesh Narayanan (known as JP), around whom a coalition of opposition to Indira was gathering.[46] At the time, Grant and his colleagues in the high commission reported on Indira's dramatic suspension of democratic government, including

---

42   Ibid., 229.

43   Ibid., 228–29.

44   Katherine Frank, *The Life of Indira Nehru Gandhi* (London: Harper Collins, 2001). For a psychological study see, Blema S Steinberg, 'Indira Gandhi: The Relationship between Personality Profile and Leadership Style', *Political Psychology* 26, no. 5 (2005): 755–89, doi.org/10.1111/j.1467-9221.2005.00443.x.

45   Grant, *Subtle Moments*, 229; Grant, *Gods and Politicians*, 135–54.

46   See Ramachandra Guha, *India after Gandhi: The History of the World's Largest Democracy* (London: Picador, 2008), 467–522.

the imprisonment of JP and other opponents, and her censorship of the press. In his later writing, Grant was relatively forgiving of her drastic actions. He reflected that, for a time at least, the Emergency emboldened Indira into reforms that she had hitherto been too easily deterred from undertaking. Trains ran on time (even if the echo of Mussolini was unwanted), tax evaders and black marketeers were pursued and prices of essential items were fixed. He recalled Indira's assurances that the Emergency would not endure for long and that democratic government would return, adding that he believed her sincerity.[47]

Unlike Crocker, Grant's sketches of Indira Gandhi were not based on detailed diary entries, the recurrence of which, with Crocker's pen, could cumulatively build a complex personal portrait. In Grant's *Gods and Politicians*, the dramatis personae were quickly sketched and set against a rich political–cultural landscape that hovers between hope and crisis for democracy. The two constitutional crises of 1975, India's Emergency declared by Indira Gandhi on 25 June and in Australia the dismissal of the Whitlam Government on 11 November, became, according to Grant, 'linked in my own mind and influenced subsequent decisions and actions'.[48] Thus, another major difference from Crocker was the task of joining Australia and India that Grant set himself when writing. Unlike the detachment from Australia that Crocker achieved in his admired portrait of Nehru, Grant's *Gods and Politicians* was an effort to entwine India's and Australia's evolving national stories in a volatile contemporary history.

As mentioned above, Grant's style reflected his earlier life as a successful journalist. He was one of a handful of Australian journalists whose rise to prominence as overseas correspondent was via Asia—in Grant's case, in Singapore from 1959 to 1962. It was in Asia, he recalled, that his perception of Australia changed profoundly:

> I saw Australia for the first time, not as an outpost of European colonialism nor as a strategic adjunct of the United States, but as a large landmass between the Indian and Pacific oceans, looking out at a neighbourhood of largely unknown nations and cultures.[49]

---

47   Grant, *Gods and Politicians*, 151–54.
48   Ibid., vii.
49   Grant, *Subtle Moments*, 114.

His pioneering standing among other Australians as an early 'Asianist' provided Grant with a strong sense of licence. Both the large Australian landmass and the unknowns of nations and cultures to its north provided canvas on which broad literary brushstrokes could sweep. In the process, his sketches of humans would gesture towards common strengths and failings of the human condition but could also be somewhat two-dimensional and fleeting.

In Grant's writing, Indira was perhaps destined to suffer from comparisons with her father, whom Grant had met twice and interviewed. When he travelled to India for this purpose in February 1961, Grant was first briefed by Crocker, then in his second term as high commissioner, and Grant returned to the high commission the following day to recount his experience. Crocker recorded that, instead of the scheduled 20 minutes, Nehru spoke to Grant for one hour and 10 minutes, listening with close attention to Grant's recent visit to Indochina. What struck Grant the most, according to Crocker, was Nehru's 'playfulness, ... and wit. He seemed to have not a care in the world'.[50]

Uncharacteristically, Crocker did not jot down any first impressions of his fellow countryman journalist, but there was, in noting the length of interview and Nehru's willingness to listen, an implicit tone of approval. Grant's memory of meeting Nehru in *Subtle Moments* was something of anticlimax. He recalled Nehru's commenting that, when asked by others to agitate on behalf of colonial Papua New Guinea, he told them that it was Australia's business, just as he expected Australians would understand that Kashmir was India's business.[51]

But Nehru, and his omnipotent legacy, was very present in Grant's assessments of his daughter. This is evident in two sketches, both published in 1982, the first of which appeared in *Gods and Politicians*, and related to his mid-1970s observations as high commissioner, and the second constituting a later update following an extended interview after Indira had returned to power. In the first, Grant concluded that:

> despite her reputation and the crises she has weathered, the impression remains of a difficult personality, without the intellectual command that her father had of the issues of his

---

50   Crocker diary, 7 February 1961, DUL.
51   Grant, *Subtle Moments*, 116–17.

time, and with little sense of history. Nor did she appear to have a grasp of the policy issues confronting her government, or a gift for organization.[52]

But in his extended interview with the banished-and-returned-to-power Indira, published in *The Canberra Times* on 15 January 1982, Grant found that electoral defeat had been good for her soul. This was his first interview with Indira since 1976, conducted during her visit to Australia, and he remarked on her new capacity to admit mistakes, her greater confidence and her determination to achieve results in India's economy and defence. She did not mention new policies but appeared less encumbered:

> Now aged 64, Indira Gandhi has at last come into her own. The shadow of her father and of his and her accumulated political enemies has lifted, and she can now do what she has always wanted to do, which is to offer creative leadership to her country.[53]

Indira thus became a central character and her strengths and weaknesses were laid bare in Grant's compelling accounts. She also had to fit in to his particular style of writing. In reviewing Grant's whole-of-life memoir, *Subtle Moments*, published in 2017, Brian McFarlane recalled Grant as 'the best film critic in Australia' of the 1950s.[54] Upon completing his arts/journalism degree at the University of Melbourne, Grant had become a successful theatre and film critic with *The Age* newspaper in the 1950s. The cinematic sensibility carried into his writing about India, in which persons are sketched against exciting, dynamic backdrops, rather than causing the narrative to pause while their characters are fleshed out in greater depth. India offered new modes of directing a script. It was, he later wrote, 'the perfect venue, as anyone who has read the Bhagavad-Gita can attest, to consider the relationship between thought and action, reconciled in Hindu philosophy by disinterest, action without attachment to the result'.[55] One of the most lasting images is at the start of *Gods and Politicians*, of Grant, having just arrived at the high commission, luxuriating in the scene he found himself in:

---

52   Grant, *Gods and Politicians*, 139.
53   *The Canberra Times*, 15 January 1982, 2
54   Brian McFarlane, '*Subtle Moments* Review: Bruce Grant's Memoir of a Full and Productive Life', *The Sydney Morning Herald*, 30 April 2017, www.smh.com.au/entertainment/books/subtle-moments-review-bruce-grants-memoir-of-a-full-and-productive-life-20170428-gvuu0s.html, accessed 30 January 2018.
55   Grant, *Subtle Moments*, 213.

> what I remember now especially about that evening is the quality
> of the air, the most extraordinary air I had ever encountered.
> It was warm, yet mysteriously topped up with a freshness that was
> almost a chill, as if mountain air were drifting over a heated valley
> in which I stood waist deep …

> I sat in a white cane chair in the middle of the lawn and drew deep
> breaths, taking the air into myself, forcing its unmixed elements
> into my body. A servant placed a small table at my side and stood
> back expectantly, one arm clasping a silver tray against his chest.[56]

India also retained its mystery, fascination and frustration. Grant's love of
the sensuous qualities of Asian life, and his desire to find paths by which
Australia could better connect with Asia, are features of his several other
written works. One of these, the novel *Cherry Bloom*, was published in
1980, two years before *Gods and Politicians*. Although set in Singapore
rather than India, *Cherry Bloom* ties Australia to Asia through the main
character, Australian woman Cherry Bloom, returning home from
Singapore pregnant with the child of a man of mixed Chinese–American
heritage. The novel blends conventional romance and political messages,
and its sketching of Asian characters has attracted criticism on grounds of
orientalist 'Othering',[57] but it earnestly reaches for a future Australian–
Asian embrace. Much earlier, in 1964, Grant's first book, *Indonesia*, was
a mixture of personal encounter and political–historical observations
of that country. It began with an air of beguiling attraction that runs
through his later works:

> Indonesia did not beckon with a mysterious past, as China, India
> and Japan do, but writing urgently of what was taking place I was
> always aware of the country itself, untouched by cabled dispatches,
> breathing softly in the available distance.[58]

While very different, *Gods and Politicians* also bears signs of yearning
for connections, for common measures by which to assess Australia
and India, while finding these elusive and relying instead on the self-
reflectivity of an (occasionally orientalist) essayist to carry the story. Some

---

56   Grant, *Gods and Politicians*, 11.
57   Ouyang Yu, 'How Post Are They Colonial: An Enquiry into Christopher Koch, Blanche
d'Alpuget and Bruce Grant's Representation of Chinese in Recent "Asian Writing"', in Charles Ferrall,
Paul Millar and Keren Smith (eds), *East by South: China in the Australasian Imagination* (Wellington:
Victoria University Press, 2005), 254–56.
58   Bruce Grant, *Indonesia*, 3rd ed. (Melbourne: Melbourne University Press, 1996), preface to first
edition, x.

of Grant's recorded frustrations were understandable, and also led towards overly sweeping conclusions for one based in India for less than three years. 'We used statistics at the mission in our reporting to Canberra', he wrote, 'but the more you saw of the way things worked, the more you distrusted the statistical picture'.[59] India's fourth Five-Year Plan, concluded in 1973–74, offered no help, as the targets were not met, it meant little to those Grant spoke to and stimulated only radicals with its enduring intellectual appeal. More implacable forces governed India's progress:

> The climate and the people, not the Plan, ruled India. Each year, as we waited for the monsoon, this was burned on our brains, and the Plan, with its elegant facts about kilowatts and tonnes and infrastructures, became a mirage in the desert.[60]

Perhaps not surprisingly, Indira Gandhi dismissed with impatience Grant's suggestion to her that India's system, including its religious culture and poverty, worked in spite of, rather than because of, efforts to modernise. For Indira, the need to continue the project of modernisation was crucial.[61]

The Enduring Voices of Diplomats

Can we suggest that Crocker's pictures of Nehru and Grant's of Indira Gandhi reveal more than the evocative workings of literary-minded diplomats? In the case of both Crocker and Grant, there is a case for answering 'yes'. This chapter has not tried to measure their effectiveness as high commissioners but their significance as observer-participants, and their enduring diplomatic significance, given that both have enjoyed a public visibility beyond a single publishing splash. In the case of Crocker, the above-mentioned reprint of his portrait of Nehru in 2008, with Guha's admiring essay, ensured renewed attention—and given the inglorious fate of the Congress Party since then, invites revisiting for those asking: 'what went so wrong?' In studying 'Crocker on Nehru' we are considering a very distinctive Australian high commissioner, whose significance among Australian international relations thinkers has been noted. He will most likely continue to attract scholarly interest. His biography awaits, and his copious diaries continue to tantalise historians.[62] His reputation as

59 Grant, *Gods and Politicians*, 59.
60 Ibid., 61.
61 Ibid., 62–63.
62 Crocker diary, 31 March to 8 April 1954, DUL.

an Australian with a highly developed affinity for Indian affairs adds to his standing in studies of the bilateral relationship. During his time in New Delhi, Crocker knew that he was regarded as something of an oddity within the Australian Department of External Affairs (something not helped by Casey's circulation of some of Crocker's longer scholarly dispatches); and when Departmental Secretary Arthur Tange visited early in 1961 he let slip the general view that Crocker was too pro-Indian and not forceful enough in Australia's corner.[63]

In the case of Grant, his many publications, especially long-form journalism, novels and his two memoirs, ensure him high standing as a pioneering Australian journalist whose reputation was forged in reporting Asia, and for whom Asian–Australian relations, past, present and potential, provided the drive in much of his work. In Grant's writing, Indira Gandhi might not have emerged with the same acuity and nuance as her father did in Crocker's, but she took on Shakespearean dimensions of colour, strengths, flaws, struggling with parental legacies, determined to shape destinies—in ways that Australian readers who had wrestled with high school literature could find familiar. Grant's skill was in joining Australia and India in ways that others had found too hard. He brought both familiarity and the exotic into a highly readable and dynamic form.

Both Australian high commissioners were gifted in sketching life stories, a form of connecting minds that has endured. Indeed, this is well recognised in the modern Australian Department of Foreign Affairs and Trade (DFAT) where public diplomacy strategies take shape. Taking, for example, the legacies of international students sponsored to study in Australia, it is clear that among all the quantitative measures capturing numbers of people, the entwining of student life stories between Asian counties and Australia remains one the most effective ways of engaging a broader interest in connections between countries.[64]

Drawing these ideas together is Virginia Woolf's artistry in a biographer's power to inspire the imagination of others. One of the first declarations in DFAT's comprehensive public diplomacy strategy is that they will engage audiences and facilitate connections between people and institutions 'to build understanding, trust and influence in advancing

63   Crocker diary, 24 March 1961, DUL.
64   See David Lowe, 'Australia's Colombo Plans Old and New: International Students as Foreign Relations', *International Journal of Cultural Policy* 21, no. 4 (2015): 448–62, doi.org/10.1080/10286 632.2015.1042468.

our national interests'.[65] In his literary power and romanticism, Crocker on Nehru, in published and unpublished forms, constitutes an ongoing means of Australians engaging Indian audiences; and may be especially valuable when the climate in India becomes more welcoming of Nehru appreciation. And, while very different, Grant's writing on Indira Gandhi, for its drawing on universal themes of human ambition and frailty and its reaching towards Australian–Indian connectedness, will most likely reward revisiting in the longer story of Australian–Indian relations.

---

65   'DFAT Public Diplomacy Strategy 2014–16', Department of Foreign Affairs and Trade, dfat.gov. au/people-to-people/public-diplomacy/Pages/public-diplomacy-strategy.aspx, accessed 15 Oct 2016.

Reflections on Australia–India Relations since the 1990s, by Peter Varghese AO, October 2016

As reported by David Lowe

Peter Varghese is arguably the most qualified to offer reflections on the Australia–India relationship from the 1990s towards 2020. His early overseas postings with the Department of Foreign Affairs and Trade (DFAT), during the 1980s, were to Austria and the United States. Subsequent overseas postings were to Tokyo, and later to Kuala Lumpur as high commissioner, 2000–02. Of special note for this volume, Peter was high commissioner to India from August 2009 to December 2012. By the time he went to New Delhi, his seniority in the Australian policymaking community flagged the importance that the Australian Government attached to the post. He had served as first assistant secretary of the Public Diplomacy and International Security Divisions of DFAT, and deputy secretary of the department from 2002 to 2003. He had also been former prime minister Hawke's senior international adviser in 2003; and seconded first assistant secretary of the International Division of Prime Minister and Cabinet, and was director-general of the Office of National Assessment, 2004–09.

Upon returning to Canberra from New Delhi in 2012, Peter became secretary of DFAT from December that year until his retirement from the department in July 2016. In July 2018 he presented his 500-page report, *An India Economic Strategy to 2035*,[1] commissioned by then prime minister Malcolm Turnbull. The report's 90 recommendations were broadly welcomed by business, political and trade leaders, and the report's implementation is being supervised by a group of Cabinet ministers. The double impact of Prime Minister Modi's economic nationalism and, most recently, the COVID-19 pandemic, has set back near-term reforms in the relationship. But it was fitting that a special, concentrated focus on India preceded both Peter's rise to leadership of DFAT, and also his major post-departmental contribution to policy formulation.

In addressing the group of academics and former diplomats gathered to commence the work that has resulted in this book, Peter's key observation was that the story of the Australia–India bilateral relationship from the mid-1990s is the evolution towards a more multidimensional relationship. This change was driven by a sharper economic agenda, more congruent strategic perspectives, Australian governments more focused on the Asia growth story, Indian governments more prepared to vary the settings of foreign and economic policies and the rapid growth of a substantial Indian diaspora in Australia.

In deriving the maximum benefit from these changes, Peter said that a key element here was making the economic relationship the central, but by no means the only, axis in our dealings with India.

Reflecting on the origins of the changes, Peter reminded the group that the main driver was, of course, the economic reforms of the early nineties under Prime Minister Narashima Rao and Finance Minister Manmohan Singh, who later, as prime minister, continued the liberalisation of India's economy. Rao's legacy was of particular importance to Australia–India relations.

At the same time, the 1990s saw a sharper focus on trade and economic issues within the relatively newly amalgamated DFAT. Peter does not subscribe to the view that the old Department of Foreign Affairs did not bother itself with economics. He reminded listeners that it had a very

---

1   Available on the DFAT website. Peter Varghese, *An India Economic Strategy to 2035: A Report to the Australian Government by Peter N. Varghese AO* (Canberra: DFAT, 27 April 2018), Executive Summary and Overview, www.dfat.gov.au/publications/trade-and-investment/india-economic-strategy/ies/overview.html, accessed 2 January 2020.

clear political economy perspective, although the separate existence of the trade commissioner service did limit its role in the narrower area of trade promotion.

But the opening of the Indian economy in the early nineties was, according to Peter, a seminal moment. Even if the subsequent path has been more zigzag than linear, it will in time be seen as a historic shift, not unlike what Deng Xiaoping did in China in the late seventies. For the bilateral relationship it gave us a point of traction in what had been until then a relationship that had struggled to find common ground around our respective hard security and economic interests.

In fact, much of Ross Garnaut's analysis of the structural complementarities between Australia and an industrialising and urbanising North-East Asia can also be applied to India; notwithstanding that India's growth model is quite different to the East Asia experience, is based more on consumption and is more similar to an industrialising United States.

In terms of the bilateral relationship, the period from the early 1990s until the signing of the US–India nuclear deal in 2005 was dominated by the economic agenda. During this time, Peter suggests that it is fair to say that it was Australia that did most of the heavy lifting in building the agenda. Most of the Australian work went towards addressing the distance between our strategic interests, reinforced by the strong Australian response to India's nuclear tests in 1998; some Indian perceptions of Australia as a client of the United States, on account of these responses to the tests; and India's reluctance in finding common ground between Australia's institutional agenda in East Asia and its own 'Look East' policy.

In the last decade, Peter said, we have seen a relationship that has broadened out considerably. The key factors driving this include:

- Expanded economic relations including negotiations on a free trade agreement (still under negotiation) and more dialogue machinery such as a CEOs forum.
- Strategic cooperation that, under the Modi Government, has gone more quickly than expected.
- The shared embrace the 'Indo-Pacific' construct as a means of regional orientation.

- A shared concern to find ways to balance the rise of China in the region, as evident in the subsequent revival of the 'Quad'—Australia, India, Japan and the United States.
- The continued growth of the Indian diaspora in Australia.
- The deepening and expanding relationships in education.
- Mutual interests in a broader regional agenda including the East Asia Summit, the Indian Ocean Rim Association, and the unfinished business of the Asia-Pacific Economic Cooperation group (APEC), of which India is not yet a member but might secure membership with the assistance of Australia.

What has all this meant for Australia's diplomatic representation?

First, the size and scope of Australia's high commission has grown significantly with many more attached agencies, such that there is now Immigration, Education, Resources, Industry, Police and Intelligence, Defence, Agriculture and the Australian Centre for International Agricultural Research, and Austrade. At the same time, Australia's regional footprint has grown, with nine to 10 Austrade offices, and consuls general in Chennai and Mumbai (and now also Kolkata), and with it a more regional economic strategy.

Second, our corresponding engagement with the Indian system has also broadened. For example, Peter recalled that he spent quite a bit of time on water issues and the Australian experience of public sector reforms. Third, state governments in both countries loom much larger in our work than previously.

Fourth, Australia's public diplomacy has expanded enormously in recent times. This can be seen most clearly in the 'New Horizons' promotion in 1997. It was also evident in the intense media activity following the student safety issues of 2009–10, and the success of Oz Fest in 2012–14 and various cultural exchanges. These examples are part of a broader shift recognising the importance of public advocacy in Australian–Indian relations.

Fifth, the size of the diaspora has created a network of connections outside government that the high commission inevitably engages with, noting that India is our largest source of skilled migrants.

By way of perspective, Peter compared his time as Australia's high commissioner in India with how he imagined that of say, Tange and Plimsoll, or even Feakes, concluding that the differences were many. His own tenure from August 2009 to December 2012 was:

- much more demanding in terms of time pressures
- included a business agenda that was barely there beforehand
- shaped by a much larger and more complicated high commission to run
- characterised by a much broader engagement with other agencies in Canberra and Delhi
- inclusive of an Indian state agenda that is much more detailed than anything beforehand
- encompassing a reach back to Australian states, which would have been non-existent in the time of those he was referencing
- marked by a work profile outside of government.

Peter added that some of these trends apply to the evolution of Australian diplomacy generally, in all parts of the world; but most of them flow from the changes in the content and scope of the bilateral Australia–India relationship.

Finally, Peter emphasised the point that he very consciously sought to have the high commission drive the relationship. Again, this might not have been a totally novel feature, but he felt that the resource pressures on Canberra was making this a more established pattern in Australian diplomacy. In a phrase that is sometimes used, the 'bandwidth in Canberra' is limited. A post is therefore best placed to see how the various moving parts of a relationship come together, and have the strongest sense of what works and does not work.

How does the relationship look today? The economic complementarities between Australia and India are strong but will also take time to play out fully. A congruence of strategic interests is moving fast. Peter suggested that the history of thickening relations between Australia and Japan might be instructive, for its starting with a relatively narrow economic basis and broadening in more recent decades. In India's case, the diaspora element and the key role of education are added factors. He looked forward to what he hoped would be next stage developments in the field of education, something that would also, from an Australian perspective, spread the risk of reliance on students from China. And he added that it was important not to hold the development of the relationship hostage to a free trade agreement. In the end, however, Peter, said the headroom for growth in the bilateral relationship will be determined by India's economic performance more than any other single factor.

Australian High Commissioners to India

Iven Mackay	Nov. 1943–1948
Charles Kevin (acting)	1948
Roy Gollan	1948
Walter Crocker	1952–1955
Peter Heydon	1955–1958
Walter Crocker	1958–1962
Bill Pritchett (acting)	1962–1963
James Plimsoll	1963–1965
Arthur Tange	1965–1969
Patrick Shaw	1970–1973
Bruce Grant	1973–1976
Peter Curtis	1976–1979
Gordon Upton	1979–1984
Graham Feakes	1984–1990
David Evans	1990–1993
Darren Gribble	1994–1997

Rob Laurie   1997–2001

Penny Wensley   2001–2004

John McCarthy   2004–2009

Peter Varghese   2009–2012

Patrick Suckling   2012–2016

Harinder Sidhu   2016–2020

Barry O'Farrell   2020–

Note: First years listed indicate the year of appointment.

Select Bibliography

Australian Department of Defence. *2016 Defence White Paper*. Canberra: Commonwealth of Australia, 2016.

Australian Department of Defence. *Defending Australia in the Asia-Pacific Century: Force 2030*. Canberra: Commonwealth of Australia, 2009.

Australian Department of Defence. 'Inquiry into Australia's Relationship with India as an Emerging World Power: Department of Defence Submission to the Joint Standing Committee on Foreign Affairs, Defence and Trade'. 8 June 2006.

Australian Department of Foreign Affairs and Trade, eds. *Australia India New Horizons: A Festival of Trade, Science, Technology, Sport and the Arts in India October to December 1996*. Melbourne: BRW Media for the Australian Department of Foreign Affairs and Trade, 1996.

Australian Department of Foreign Affairs and Trade. *Asian Century White Paper.* Canberra: Commonwealth of Australia, 2011.

Australian Department of Foreign Affairs and Trade. 'Australia's Trade with India'. Business Envoy, Department of Foreign Affairs and Trade. www.dfat.gov.au/about-us/publications/trade-investment/business-envoy/Pages/april-2017/australias-trade-with-india. Accessed 20 September 2018.

Australian Department of Foreign Affairs and Trade. 'Public Diplomacy Strategy 2014–16'. Department of Foreign Affairs and Trade, dfat.gov.au/people-to-people/public-diplomacy/Pages/public-diplomacy-strategy.aspx. Accessed 15 October 2016.

Australian High Commission New Delhi. 'India–Australia Strategic Dialogue'. Media Release PA/12/2001, 30 August 2001, india.embassy.gov.au/ndli/PA_12_01.html. Accessed 7 December 2020.

Australian Joint Standing Committee on Foreign Affairs, Australian Departments of Defence and Trade. *Australia's Relationship with India as an Emerging World Power*. Canberra: The Committee, 2009.

Australian Parliament Joint Committee on Foreign Affairs, Defence and Trade, David McGibbon and Ian McCahon Sinclair. *Australia's Trade Relationship with India: Commonwealth, Common Language, Cricket and Beyond.* Canberra: The Committee, 1998, nla.gov.au/nla.obj-1459375536. Accessed 9 December 2020.

Australian Parliament Standing Committee on Public Works and J Moylan. *Construction of a New Chancery, New Delhi, India.* Canberra: The Committee, 2003.

Australian Senate Standing Committee on Foreign Affairs, Defence and Trade. *Australia–India Relations: Trade and Security.* Canberra: Australian Government Publishing Service, July 1990.

Australian Trade Commission and Ernst & Young. *Emerging Opportunities in Information Technology for Australia and India.* Canberra: Australian Trade Commission, 2000.

Australian Trade Commission. 'Exporting to India: Riding the Elephant'. Presentation to Australian exporters in various states of Australia. September 2004.

Bachhawat, Aakriti. 'No Longer in a Cleft Stick: India and Australia in the Indo-Pacific'. *The Strategist*, 25 June 2019. www.aspistrategist.org.au/no-longer-in-a-cleft-stick-india-and-australia-in-the-indo-pacific/. Accessed 7 December 2020.

Bajpai, Kanti. 'Narendra Modi's Pakistan and China Policy: Assertive Bilateral Diplomacy, Active Coalition Diplomacy'. *International Affairs* 93, no. 1 (2017): 69–91. doi.org/10.1093/ia/iiw003.

Beaumont, Joan, Christopher Waters, David Lowe, with Garry Woodard. *Ministers, Mandarins and Diplomats: Australian Foreign Policy Making, 1941–1969.* Melbourne: Melbourne University Press, 2003.

Bongiorno, Frank. 'British to the Bootstraps? H.V. Evatt, J.B. Chifley and Australian Policy on Indian Membership of the Commonwealth, 1947–49'. *Australian Historical Studies* 36, no. 125 (2005): 18–39. doi.org/10.1080/10314610508682909.

Bongiorno, Frank. 'Commonwealthmen and Republicans: Dr. H. V. Evatt, the Monarchy and India'. *Australian Journal of Politics and History* 46, no. 1 (2000): 33–50. doi.org/10.1111/1467-8497.00084.

Borah, Rupakjyoti. 'Australia–India Relations during the Howard Era'. In *India–Australia Relations: Convergences and Divergences*, edited by Darvesh Gopal. Delhi: Shipra, 2008.

Brands, HW. 'India and Pakistan in American Strategic Planning, 1947–54: The Commonwealth as Collaborator'. *The Journal of Commonwealth and Imperial History* 15, no. 1 (1986): 41–54. doi.org/10.1080/03086538608582728.

Brewster, David. 'The Australia–India Framework for Security Cooperation: Another Step Towards an Indo-Pacific Security Partnership'. *Security Challenges* 11, no. 1 (2015): 39–48.

Brewster, David. 'Australia and India: The Indian Ocean and the Limits of Strategic Convergence'. *Australian Journal of International Affairs* 64, no. 5 (2020): 549–65. doi.org/10.1080/10357718.2010.513369.

Button, John. *Flying the Kite*. Sydney: Random House, 1994.

Casey, Lord. *An Australian in India.* London: Hollis and Carter, 1947.

Chacko, Priya and Alexander E Davis. 'The Natural/Neglected Relationship: Liberalism, Identity and India–Australia Relations'. *The Pacific Review* 30, no. 1 (2017): 26–50. doi.org/10.1080/09512748.2015.1100665.

Chapman, Ivan. *Iven G. Mackay: Citizen and Soldier.* Melbourne: Melway Publishing, 1975.

Chusid, Jeffrey M. 'Joseph Allen Stein's Experiments in Concrete in the U.S. and India'. *The Journal of Preservation Technology* 48, no. 1 (2017): 23–31.

Crisp, LF. *Ben Chifley: A Biography.* London: Longmans, 1963.

Critchley, TK. 'View from the Good Offices Committee'. In *New Directions in Australian Foreign Policy: Australia and Indonesia 1945–50*, edited by John Legge. Clayton: Monash Asia Institute, 1997.

Crocker, Walter. *Nehru: A Contemporary's Estimate*. London: G. Allen and Unwin, 1966.

Crocker, Walter. *The Racial Factor in International Relations*. Canberra: Australian National University, 1956.

Crocker, Walter. *Travelling Back: The Memoirs of Sir Walter Crocker.* South Melbourne: Macmillan 1981.

Dhar, PN. *Indira Gandhi, the 'Emergency', and Indian Democracy*. New Delhi: Oxford University Press, 2001.

Downer, Alexander. 'Australian Response to India Nuclear Tests'. Minister for Foreign Affairs, Media Release FA59. 14 May 1998. foreignminister.gov.au/releases/1998/fa059_98.html (site discontinued). Accessed 2 February 2020.

Edwards, Peter. *Arthur Tange: Last of the Mandarins*. Sydney: Allen & Unwin, 2006.

Edwards, Peter, with Gregory Pemberton. *Crises and Commitments: The Politics and Diplomacy of Australia's Involvement in Southeast Asian Conflicts, 1946–1965*. North Sydney: Allen and Unwin, 1992.

Efstathopoulos, Charalapos. 'Reinterpreting India's Rise through the Middle Power Prism'. *Asian Journal of Political Science* 19, no. 1 (2011): 74–95. doi.org/10.1080/02185377.2011.568246.

Frank, Katherine. *The Life of Indira Nehru Gandhi*. London: Harper Collins, 2001.

George, Margaret. *Australia and the Indonesian Revolution*. Carlton: Melbourne University Press, 1980.

Goad, Philip. 'Designed Diplomacy: Furniture, Furnishing and Art in Australian Embassies for Washington DC and Paris'. *The Politics of Furniture: Identity, Diplomacy and Persuasion in Post-War Interiors*, edited by Fredie Floré and Cammie McAtee. Abingdon: Routledge, 2017. doi.org/10.4324/9781315554389-11.

Gopal, Darvesh and Dalbir Ahlawat. 'Australia–India Strategic Relations: From Estrangement to Engagement'. *India Quarterly* 71, no. 3 (2015): 206–20. doi.org/10.1177/0974928415584022.

Gopal, Sarvepalli. *Jawaharlal Nehru*. Vol. 2, *1947–56*. London: Johnathan Cape, 1980.

Gordon, Sandy and Henningham, Stephen (eds). *India Looks East: An Emerging Power and its Asia-Pacific Neighbours*. Canberra: Strategic and Defence Studies Centre, Research School of Pacific and Asian Studies, The Australian National University, 1995.

Grant, Bruce. *Gods and Politicians: Politics as Culture—An Australian View of India*. Sydney: Allen Lane Australia, 1982.

Grant, Bruce. *Subtle Moments: Scenes on a Life's Journey*. Clayton: Monash University Publishing, 2017.

Grare, Frédéric. *India Turns East: International Engagement and US–China Rivalry*. London: Hurst, 2017. doi.org/10.1093/oso/9780190859336.001.0001.

Guha, Ramachandra. 'An Uncommon Diplomacy'. *The Monthly*, November 2006. www.themonthly.com.au/issue/2006/november/1229991194/ramachandra-guha/uncommon-diplomacy. Accessed 20 September 2015.

Guha, Ramachandra. *India after Gandhi: The History of the World's Largest Democracy*. London: Picador, 2008.

Gurry, Meg. *Australia and India: Mapping the Journey 1944–2014*. Carlton: Melbourne University Press, 2015.

Gurry, Meg. 'A Delicate Balance: Australia's "Tilt" to Pakistan and its Impact on Australia–India Relations'. *Australian Journal of International Affairs* 67, no. 2 (2013): 141–56. doi.org/10.1080/10357718.2012.750641.

Gurry, Meg. 'India, The New Centre of Gravity: Australia–India Relations Under the Howard Government'. *South Asia: Journal of South Asian Studies* 35, no. 2 (2012): 282–305. doi.org/10.1080/00856401.2011.633299.

Gurry, Meg. 'Leadership and Bilateral Relations: Menzies and Nehru, Australia and India, 1949–1964'. *Pacific Affairs* 65, no. 4 (1992–93): 510–26. doi.org/10.2307/2760317.

Hall, Ian. 'Australia's Fitful Engagements of India'. In *The Engagement of India: Strategies and Responses*, edited by Ian Hall. Washington DC: Georgetown University Press, 2014.

Hall, Ian. *Modi and the Reinvention of Indian Foreign Policy*. Bristol: Bristol University Press, 2019. doi.org/10.1080/14662043.2021.2018967.

Hall, Ian. 'Multialignment and Indian Foreign Policy under Narendra Modi'. *The Round Table: The Commonwealth Journal of International Affairs* 105, no. 3 (2016): 271–86. doi.org/10.1080/00358533.2016.1180760.

Hayden, Bill. 'Australian Government's Views on the Indian Ocean'. 20 June 1984. *Australian Foreign Affairs Record* 55, no. 6 (1984): 576–84.

Hearder, Jeremy. *Jim Plim: Ambassador Extraordinary: A Biography of Sir James Plimsoll*. Ballarat: Connor Court, 2015.

Hopper, W David. 'An Interlude with Indian Development'. In *Policy and Practice: Essays in Honour of Sir John Crawford*, edited by LT Evans and JDB Miller. Canberra: Australian National University Press, 1987.

Howard, John and Manmohan Singh. 'Joint Press Conference with Dr. Manmohan Singh, Prime Minister of India: Hyderabad House, New Delhi'. PM Transcripts: Transcripts from the Prime Minister of Australia. 6 March 2006. Transcript 22161, pmtranscripts.pmc.gov.au/release/transcript-22161. Accessed 14 March 2018.

Hudson, WJ. 'The Making of Australian Foreign Policy 1945–1992'. In *Former Secretaries Meeting. The Making of Australian Foreign Policy 1945–1992*. Griffith University: Centre for the Study of Australia-Asia Relations, Griffith University, 1992.

India International Centre. 'About IIC'. India International Centre. www.iicdelhi. nic.in/User_Panel/UserView.aspx?TypeID=1025. Accessed 20 May 2018.

India Link. 'India–Australia FTA at Exchange-of-Offers Stage'. India Link. 31 January 2013. webarchive.nla.gov.au/awa/20170424184022/http://dfat. gov.au/about-us/publications/trade-investment/business-envoy/Pages/april-2017/australias-trade-with-india.aspx. Accessed 20 September 2018.

Jayasuriya, Kanishka. 'Nationalism Marries Neoliberalism to Fuel Rise of Asia's New Right'. *The Conversation*. 21 March 2014. theconversation.com/ nationalism-marries-neoliberalism-to-fuel-rise-of-asias-new-right-24395. Accessed 7 December 2020.

Jeffrey, Robin. 'Australia-India: Reimagining the Relationship'. *Inside Story*, 15 February 2010.

Khare, NB. *My Political Memoirs of Autobiography.* Nagpur: J.R. Joshi, 1959.

Kobayashi, Ai. *W. Macmahon Ball: Politics for the People.* North Melbourne: Australian Scholarly Publishing, 2013.

Kux, Dennis. *India and the United States: Estranged Democracies.* Honolulu: University Press of the Pacific, 2002.

Lang, David. 'The Not-Quite-Quadrilateral: Australia, Japan and India'. *The Strategist.* 9 July 2015. www.aspistrategist.org.au/the-not-quite-quadrilateral-australia-japan-and-india/. Accessed 7 December 2020.

Lee, David. 'Australia, the British Commonwealth, and the United States, 1950–1953'. *The Journal of Imperial and Commonwealth History* 20, no. 3 (1992): 445–69. doi.org/10.1080/03086539208582880.

Lee, David. 'Australia and the Security Council'. In *Australia and the United Nations*, edited by James Cotton and David Lee. Canberra: Department of Foreign Affairs and Trade, 2012.

Lloyd, Lorna. *Diplomacy with a Difference: The Commonwealth Office of High Commissioner, 1880–2006.* Diplomatic Studies 1. Leiden: Martinus Nijhoff, 2007. doi.org/10.1163/ej.9789004154971.i-353.

Lowe, David. 'Australia's Colombo Plans Old and New: International Students as Foreign Relations'. *International Journal of Cultural Policy* 21, no. 4 (2015): 448–62. doi.org/10.1080/10286632.2015.1042468.

Lowe, David. 'Canberra's Colombo Plan: Public Images of Australia's Relations with Post-Colonial South and Southeast Asia in the 1950s'. *South Asia: Journal of South Asian Studies*, n.s., 25, no. 2 (2002): 183–204. doi.org/10.1080/00856400208723481.

Maclean, Kama. *British India, White Australia: Overseas Indians, Intercolonial Relations and the Empire.* Sydney: UNSW Press, 2020.

Malone, David M. 'The Modern Diplomatic Mission'. In *The Oxford Handbook of Modern Diplomacy,* edited by Andrew F Cooper, Jorge Heine and Ramesh Thakur. Oxford: Oxford University Press, 2013. doi.org/10.1093/oxfordhb/9780199588862.013.0007.

Mayer, Peter and Purnendra Jain. 'Beyond Cricket: Australia–India Evolving Relations'. *Australian Journal of Political Science* 45, no. 1 (2010): 133–48. doi.org/10.1080/10361140903517759.

McCallum, JA. 'The Asian Relations Conference'. *The Australian Quarterly* 19, no. 2 (1947): 16–17. doi.org/10.2307/20631455.

McCallum, JA. 'Personalities at the Asian Relations Conference'. *The Australian Quarterly* 19, no. 3 (1947): 39–44.

Meadows, Eric. '"He No Doubt Felt Insulted": The White Australia Policy and Australia's Relations with India, 1944–1964'. In *Australia and the World: A Festschrift for Neville Meaney,* edited by Joan Beaumont and Matthew Jordan. Sydney: Sydney University Press, 2013. doi.org/10.2307/j.ctv1rm259b.9.

Meadows, Eric. 'India: A Problematic Relationship'. In *Making a Difference: Australian International Education,* edited by Dorothy Davis and Bruce Mackintosh. Sydney: UNSW Press, 2011.

Medcalf, Rory. 'Australia–India Relations: Hesitating on the Brink of Partnership'. *Asia Pacific Bulletin: East West Centre,* no. 13, 3 April 2008. www.eastwestcenter.org/system/tdf/private/apb013.pdf?file=1&type=node&id=32261. Accessed 7 December 2020.

Medcalf, Rory. 'The Balancing Kangaroo: Australia and Chinese Power'. *Issues and Studies* 50, no. 3 (2014): 103–35.

Menon, KPS. *Many Worlds: An Autobiography.* London: Oxford University Press, 1965.

Mohan, C Raja. *Modi's World: Expanding India's Sphere of Influence.* New Delhi: Harper Collins, 2015.

Moredoundt, Wayne. 'Mr Casey Goes to Calcutta: The Controversial Australian Governor of Bengal, 1944–46'. In *Midnight to Millennium: Australia–India Interconnections*, edited by Auriol Weigold. Canberra: High Commission of India, Canberra, 1999.

Nayar, Baldev Raj and TV Paul. *India in the World Order: Searching for Major-Power Status*. Cambridge: Cambridge University Press, 2003. doi.org/10.1017/CBO9780511808593.

Nehru, Jawaharlal. *An Autobiography*. London: The Bodley Head, 1936.

Packer, Gerald. 'The Asian Relations Conference: The Group Discussions'. *Australian Outlook* 1, no. 2 (1947): 3–7. doi.org/10.1080/00049914708565300.

Percival Wood, Sally and Michael Leach. '"Rediscovery", "Reinvigoration" and "Redefinition" in Perpetuity: Australian Engagement with India 1983–2011'. *Australian Journal of Politics and History* 57, no. 4 (2011): 526–42. doi.org/10.1111/j.1467-8497.2011.01612.x.

Pothen, Nayantara. *Glittering Decades: New Delhi in Love and War*. New Delhi: Penguin, 2012.

Purnendra Jain. 'Westward Ho! Japan Eyes India Strategically'. *Japanese Studies* 28, no. 1 (2008): 15–30. doi.org/10.1080/10371390801939070.

Raghavan, Srinath. *1971: A Global History of the Creation of Bangladesh*. Cambridge MA: Harvard University Press, 2013.

Raghavan, Srinath. *India's War: The Making of Modern South Asia, 1939–1945*. Milton Keynes: Allen Lane, Penguin, 2016.

Raghavan, Srinath. *War and Peace in Modern India*. Basingstoke: Palgrave Macmillan, 2010. doi.org/10.1057/9780230277519.

Reid, William. 'Sir Owen Dixon's Mediation of the Kashmir Dispute, 1950'. BA (Hons.) thesis, Deakin University, 2000.

Spender, Percy. *Exercises in Diplomacy: The ANZUS Treaty and the Colombo Plan*. Sydney: Sydney University Press, 1969.

Stein, Joseph Allen, NH Ramachandran and Geeti Sen. 'The India International Centre: Concept and Design: Joseph Allen Stein in conversation with N. H. Ramachandran and Geeti Sen'. *India International Centre Quarterly* 22, no. 4 (1995): 128.

Stevens, Bertram. *New Horizons: A Study of Australian–Indian Relationships*. Sydney: Peter Huston, under the auspices of the Australian Institute of International Affairs, New South Wales Branch, 1946.

Stuart, Francis. *Towards Coming of Age: A Foreign Service Odyssey*. Nathan: Griffith University, Centre for the Study of Australian-Asian Relations, 1989.

Suares, Julie. 'Engaging with Asia: The Chifley Government and the New Delhi Conferences of 1947 and 1949'. *Australian Journal of Politics and History* 57, no. 4 (2011): 495–510. doi.org/10.1111/j.1467-8497.2011.01610.x.

Varghese, Peter. *An India Economic Strategy to 2035: A Report to the Australian Government by Peter N. Varghese AO*. Canberra: Department of Foreign Affairs and Trade, 27 April 2018. www.dfat.gov.au/publications/trade-and-investment/india-economic-strategy/ies/index.html. Accessed 30 March 2019.

Walker, David. 'General Cariappa Encounters "White Australia": Australia, India and the Commonwealth in the 1950s'. *Journal of Imperial and Commonwealth History* 34, no. 3 (2006): 389–406. doi.org/10.1080/03086530600826017.

Walker, William. 'International Nuclear Relations after the Indian and Pakistani Test Explosions'. *International Affairs* 74, no. 3 (1998): 505–28. doi.org/10.1111/1468-2346.00031.

Waller, Keith. *A Diplomatic Life: Some Memories*. Nathan: Centre for the Study of Australia-Asia Relations, Griffith University, 1990.

Waters, Christopher. 'A Failure of Imagination: R. G. Casey and Australian Plans for Counter-subversion in Asia, 1954–1956'. *Australian Journal of Politics and History* 45, no. 3 (1999): 347–61. doi.org/10.1111/1467-8497.00069.

Waters, Christopher. 'War, Decolonisation and Postwar Security'. In *Facing North, A Century of Australian Engagement with Asia*. Vol 1, *1901 to the 1970s,* edited by David Goldsworthy. Carlton South: Melbourne University Press, 2001.

Waters, Christopher. *The Empire Fractures: Anglo-Australian Conflict in the 1940s*. Melbourne: Australian Scholarly Publishing, 1995.

Watt, Alan. *The Evolution of Australian Foreign Policy, 1938–1965*. London: Cambridge University Press, 1967.

Wesley, Michael. 'The Elephant in the Room'. *The Monthly*, February 2012. www.themonthly.com.au/issue/2012/february/1328594251/michael-wesley/elephant-room. Accessed 7 December 2020.

Westrip, Joyce and Peggy Holroyde. *Colonial Cousins: A Surprising History of Connection between India and Australia*. Kent Town: Wakefield Press, 2010.

White, Stephen. *Building in the Garden: The Architecture of Joseph Allen Stein in India and California*. Delhi: Oxford University Press, 1993.

Notes on Contributors

Peter Edwards AM has published extensively on the history of Australian defence and foreign policies and policymaking, with special reference to the Australian–American alliance, the Vietnam War and other conflicts in South-East Asia, and the intelligence agencies. As the official historian of Australia's involvement in South-East Asian conflicts 1948–75, he was general editor of the nine-volume series and author of the volumes dealing with strategy and diplomacy, *Crises and Commitments* (Allen & Unwin, 1992) and *A Nation at War* (Allen & Unwin, 1997). His most recent books are *Australia and the Vietnam War* (NewSouth Books, 2014) and *Law, Politics and Intelligence: A Life of Robert Hope* (NewSouth Books, 2020).

Meg Gurry is an academic researcher who is a former lecturer in Australian foreign policy at La Trobe University, where she also taught Australian politics, international relations and the politics of South Asia. Her area of scholarship and publications focus on Australia's engagement with the states of Asia since 1945. She is the author of *Australia and India: Mapping the Journey, 1944–2014* (Melbourne University Press, 2015). She has a BA and DipEd from Monash University and a PhD in politics from La Trobe University. She is currently a fellow of the Australia India Institute in Melbourne.

Ian Hall is a professor of international relations and Deputy Director (Research) of the Griffith Asia Institute at Griffith University, Queensland, Australia. He is also an academic fellow of the Australia India Institute at the University of Melbourne and a co-editor (with Sara E. Davies) of the *Australian Journal of International Affairs*. He has published several books and over 70 articles and chapters on the history of international thought and India's international relations, including *Modi and the Reinvention of Indian Foreign Policy* (Bristol University Press, 2019). He is currently writing a book on how Hindu nationalists want to change the world.

David Lee is associate professor in the School of Humanities and Social Sciences, University of New South Wales, Canberra. He researches Australia's external relations with the countries of the Asia-Pacific. He has edited volumes of official documents on Australia's relations with Indonesia and the People's Republic of China. He has also authored or co-authored monographs on Australian foreign and international economic policy, Australia's relations with the United States and the resources trade with East Asian countries after 1960. He is collaborating on a biography of Sir John Crawford and researching the development of Australian economic relationships with Japan and China.

David Lowe is Chair in Contemporary History in the School of Humanities and Social Sciences. David is a co-founder of the Australian Policy and History network. His research centres on cultural aspects of the history of international relations, including Australia's role in the world, and on remembering the legacies of modern wars and empires in comparative contexts. His recent publications include (with Carola Lentz) *Remembering Independence* (Routledge, 2018) and (edited with David Lee and Carl Bridge), *Australia Goes to Washington: 75 Years of Australian Representation in the United States,* 1940–2015 (ANU Press, 2016). He is currently researching the history of postwar foreign aid, including the Colombo Plan and Australia's foreign aid program. He was visiting professor in Australian studies at the Centre for Pacific and American Studies, University of Tokyo, 2019–20.

Eric Meadows is an honorary fellow in the Contemporary Histories Research Group at Deakin University. He has published on the history of international education in Australia, on the impact of Australia's immigration policies on its relations with India and on public diplomacy and education. He was formerly pro vice-chancellor (international) at Deakin University, deputy principal (international programs) at the University of Melbourne and started his career as an Australian diplomat in New Delhi and then Tel Aviv.

Michael Moignard spent 35 years as an Australian public servant working in trade and resources policy, and trade promotion. He holds a Masters in science (chemistry) from the University of Melbourne, a BA (Hons) in history and economics from The Australian National University, and a Diploma of Education from La Trobe University. Michael spent close to seven years in India, as senior trade commissioner for South Asia with the Australian High Commission in New Delhi. He first served in New Delhi from 1998 to 2000, and again from 2004 to 2008, most recently in late 2012. He also served with the Australian Trade Commission (Austrade) in New York, Santiago de Chile, Manila and Singapore. Michael is an honorary academic fellow of the Australia India Institute. Michael was a member of the Australia India Business Council Victoria Committee from 2016 to 2018, and was president of the chapter from March to May 2017.

Ric Smith AO PSM is a visiting fellow at the Lowy Institute for International Affairs, an adjunct professor at Griffith University, and co-chair of AusCSCAP (the Australia Council for Security Cooperation in the Asia Pacific). He joined the Australian Department of External Affairs in 1969 and served in Australia's diplomatic missions in India, Israel, the Philippines and Hawaii. He was a deputy secretary of the Department of Foreign Affairs and Trade from 1992 to 1994, and deputy secretary of the Department of Defence in 1994–95. He served as ambassador to China and Mongolia from 1996 to 2000, and as ambassador to Indonesia in 2001–02. He was appointed as secretary of the Department of Defence in 2002, and retired from the public service in 2006.

Quentin Stevenson-Perks, after 22 years in the Australian Public Service, was appointed as the Department of Education's counsellor for education and training at the Australian High Commission in New Delhi, India. During the period of his appointment, from January 2001 to July 2005, he oversaw Australia's official engagement with Indian Government education and training agencies and worked with the committee representing Indian education recruitment agents for Australia's public and private education institutions to promote Australia as a study destination. Following the completion of his term in India, he subsequently served as Ccounsellor for education and training at the Australian Embassy in Beijing, China, from July 2007 to May 2010. Then he was appointed as Austrade's assistant general manager for international education from May 2010 until his retirement in September 2015.

Julie Suares completed her PhD at Deakin University in October 2015. Her book *JB Chifley: An Ardent Internationalist* was published by Melbourne University Press in 2019. In 2011, her article, 'Engaging with Asia: The Chifley Government and the New Delhi Conferences of 1947 and 1949' was published in the *Australian Journal of Politics and History*. From 2002 to 2014, she worked as an electorate officer for the former member for Ripon in the Bracks and Brumby governments. She has been a consultant for Primary Skills Victoria. She has also worked as a library technician, farmhand and shearers' cook.

Peter Varghese AO is Chancellor of the University of Queensland (since July 2016). Prior to this appointment, his extensive career in public service and diplomacy spanned 38 years and included senior positions in foreign affairs, trade policy and intelligence. Most recently, he served as secretary of the Department of Foreign Affairs and Trade (2012–16). Previous senior appointments included high commissioner to India (2009–12), high commissioner to Malaysia (2000–02), director-general of the Office of National Assessments (2004–09) and senior advisor (international) to the prime minister of Australia (2003–04). He was the author of a comprehensive India Economic Strategy to 2035 commissioned by the Australian prime minister and submitted in July 2018.

Index

Abbot, Tony, 16, 191–193
Abe Shinzo, 188
ADFA (Australian Defence Force
    Academy). *see* Australian Defence
    Force Academy (ADFA)
AIIA (Australian Institute
    of International Affairs).
    see Australian Institute of
    International Affairs (AIIA)
AIPS (Australian Institute of Political
    Science). *see* Australian Institute
    of Political Science (AIPS)
Allen, Jim, 111
*An India Economic Strategy to
    2035,* 1–2, 17–18, 222. *see also*
    Varghese, Peter
Anderson, David, 119, 125
Ansari, Hamid, 159
anti-communism, 5, 41, 77. *see also*
    communism
    Colombo Plan, 65–66
ANZUS (Australia, New Zealand and
    United States) Treaty, 5, 61, 82
apartheid. *see* South Africa
APEC (Asia-Pacific Economic
    Cooperation) forum. *see* Asia-
    Pacific Economic Cooperation
    (APEC) forum
architecture
    Australian High Commission in
        India, 8–9, 10–11, 21, 86,
        94–98, 103, 172–173
    influence on workplaces, 97

modernism, 87, 89–90, 94
nationalism, 89
role in diplomacy, 88–90, 96–97,
    102–103
ASEAN (Association of South-East
    Asian Nations). *see* Association
    of South-East Asian Nations
    (ASEAN)
Asia-Pacific Economic Cooperation
    (APEC) forum, 187, 190, 224
Asia-Pacific region. *see also* South-East
    Asia
    Australia's role in region, 29,
        66–68
    decolonisation, 46–47
    relationship with Australia, 19,
        31, 39, 55, 82, 140
    unity, 53
Asian Relations Conference, 26–28,
    42–45
    attendees, 42–43
    Australian participation, 41–42,
        43–44, 45–47
    significance, 45–50
Association of South-East Asian
    Nations (ASEAN), 195
Australia. *see also* White Australia
    policy
    aid, 5, 111–112, 121, 140, 145
    attitudes towards Asia, 84
    Bangladesh crisis, 110–116,
        120–122, 124–129
    colonial attitudes, 37

Education Services for Overseas Students Act 2000 (ESOS Act), 178, 179
as a middle power, 11, 55, 120, 137, 145–146
relationship with China (People's Republic of), 59, 189–190, 198–199
relationship with Pakistan, 12, 58, 129, 161–162
relationship with Soviet Union, 164
relationship with United States, 122–124, 132–133, 146, 223
shift in foreign policy approach, 39–40
Australia–India Business Council, 5, 158
Australia–India Council, 14, 168
Australia–India Strategic Dialogue, 186
Australia, New Zealand and United States treaty. *see* ANZUS (Australia, New Zealand and United States) Treaty
Australian Defence Force Academy (ADFA), 85
Australian diplomacy
alignment with United States, 5, 11, 37, 79, 82, 84–85, 122–129
ambassadors and high commissioners, 76
Australian School of International Relations, 203
changes to, 224–225
characteristics of, 6–7
to China (People's Republic of), 121
drift in Indian relationship, 12, 57, 62, 70–71, 73, 154–162
evacuation of diplomatic staff, 115
great and powerful friends, 79

Joint Ministerial Commission, 160
leaks, 149–150
oldest continuous relationship, 1, 19
participation in international conferences, 55
policy towards India, 58–63
presence in Asia, 9, 10
prime ministerial visits to India, 140, 195 (*see also under* individual prime ministers)
prioritising Indian relationship, 12
professionalisation of, 4
public diplomacy, 224
recognition of Bangladesh, 119–120, 121–123
recognition of China (People's Republic of), 139
role in Bangladesh crisis, 111–116, 132–134
role of treaties, 82
tension with White Australia policy, 10, 69–71
Australian High Commission in India
Australia-based staff, 99, 102–103
buildings, 8–9, 10–11, 21, 86, 94–98, 103, 172–173
changes to, 224–225
diplomatic staff, 6–9
high commissioners, 227–228
locally engaged staff, 8–9, 11, 88, 98–102
Australian Institute of International Affairs (AIIA), 9, 43
Australian Institute of Political Science (AIPS), 9, 43
Australian international reputation. *see also* White Australia policy
branding, 179
diplomatic approach, 54
immigration policy, 20, 26, 69–71, 82
Indian perceptions of, 50, 61, 65, 67–68, 223

political allegiance, 48
trade commitments, 23
Australian–Indian relationship,
121, 125–126, 134, 151. *see also*
Australian diplomacy
Australian delegations to India,
183–184
Australian neglect of, 23, 24, 72,
82, 142, 147
chronology, xi–xiv
Comprehensive Economic
Cooperation Agreement
(CECA), 191, 193
cultivation of, 14
establishment, 19–22
future directions, 225–226
improvement, 201, 223–224
ministerial consultations, 84,
186–187
New Horizons program, 171,
172, 177
nuclear non-proliferation,
162–163
obstacles, 17, 20–22, 37, 167–
168, 182
prioritisation of, 12
role of China (People's Republic
of), 198–199
Study in Australia branding, 179

Babiy, Alexandr, 163–167
Bajpai, Girja Shankar, 50, 54
Ball, William Macmahon, 40–41
Bandung Conference, 7, 66–68
Australian participation, 10,
67–68
Bangladesh, 134–135
Australian aid, 5, 111–112, 121
Awami League, 106, 110,
134–135
independence, 11, 12, 119–120
Mukti Bahini, 106, 114
war of independence, 105–107,
108–119, 134–135

Barwick, Garfield, 77, 82
Bhutan, 80
Bhutto, Zulfikar Ali, 106, 132
biography, 205, 218–219
Blood, Archer, 133
Bowen, Nigel, 115, 117, 121, 122,
126, 127
Britain, 1
in Bangladesh crisis, 120
presence in India, 20
relationship with India, 19
relationship with Netherlands,
40–41
role in Australian diplomacy, 9,
79, 203
trade in India, 23
British Commonwealth
Commonwealth Heads of
Government meetings
(CHOGM), 155, 183
Commonwealth Prime Ministers
meetings, 36, 41
conflict resolution, 52
disputes, 34
India, 25–26, 28, 37, 69, 141
role in world affairs, 1
Burton, John, 30–31, 33
New Delhi Conference on
Indonesia, 49, 51–52, 54
Bury, Leslie, 127
Bush, George W., 176

Canada, 83, 155–156, 171
aid to India, 145
immigration, 69, 70
relationship with India, 21, 65
relationship with Pakistan, 120
Casey, Richard, 10, 35, 67, 71, 82,
209, 218
anti-communism, 62–63
Colombo Plan review, 64–66
Central Treaty Organization
(CENTO), 118

Chifley Government, 4
    priorities in international
      relations, 39–40
    support for Indonesia, 47–48
Chifley, Ben, 30–31, 141
China (People's Republic of), 13, 17,
    107
    annexation of Tibet, 80
    India–China War, 5, 10, 77
    Kissinger visit, 107, 113
    recognition of, 59, 61, 139, 211
    relationship with Australia, 59,
      189–190, 198–199
    relationship with India, 198–199
    relationship with Pakistan, 83,
      130
    relationship with United States,
      113, 125
    Sino–Soviet Treaty of Friendship
      and Alliance, 58
    and South-East Asia, 47, 198–199
Cold War, 2, 90, 91, 149
    in Asia, 62, 79
    influence, 37, 53
Colombo Conference of
    Commonwealth Foreign
    Ministers, 32–33
Colombo Plan, 32, 64–66
Commonwealth of Nations
    Commonwealth Heads of
      Government meetings
      (CHOGM), 155, 183
    Commonwealth Prime Ministers
      meetings, 36, 41
    conflict resolution, 52
    disputes, 34
    India, 25–26, 28, 37, 69, 141
    role in world affairs, 1
communism, 32, 34, 41, 57. *see also*
    anti-communism
    in India, 61–62
    spread through Asia, 58–59
Cook, Michael, 143
COVID-19 pandemic, 17, 197, 222

Crawford, John, 60, 140–141
Crocker, Walter, 5, 67, 71–73
    appointment, 57, 60–61
    Australian High Commission in
      India design, 94
    immigration issues, 68–70
    land acquisition, 90–91
    legacy, 72–73, 201, 203, 217–218
    relationship with Nehru, 10, 204,
      206–210
    reputation, 7
    writings, 13, 202–210, 217–218
Curtin Government, 24
Curtis, Peter, 11
    appointment to Australian
      High Commission in India,
      146–147
    background, 146
    support of Fraser, 148

decolonisation, 26–27, 39, 41,
    46–47, 90, 203
defence forces
    AUSINDEX, 194, 196
    Australian–Indian alliance, 24–26,
      194
    Australian–Pakistan agreements,
      12
    Defence White Papers (Australia),
      190, 195
    intelligence sharing, 187
    security and strategic cooperation,
      13, 25, 184, 190, 193–199
    security concerns, 32–33
    terrorism, 186–187
    training agreements, 85
Deng Xiaoping, 223
Desai, Morarji, 146, 157, 210
DFAT (Department of Foreign
    Affairs and Trade) (Australia). *see*
    under trade
diplomacy
    changing dynamics, 19
    diplomatic protection, 165

intercultural exchange among staff, 100–103
locally engaged staff, 8–9, 11, 88, 98–102
obstacles, 1, 4
purpose of, 3, 22, 133
role of architecture, 88–90, 96–97, 102–103
status of high commissioner, 20–21, 86
studies of, 2, 6
Dixon, Owen, 5
role in India–Pakistan dispute, 34–36
Downer, Alexander, 185, 186, 188

East Pakistan. *see* Bangladesh
education. *see also* trade
Association of Australian Education Representatives in India (AAERI), 180
Australia–India Strategic Research Fund, 182
as diplomacy, 12, 16, 23–24, 173, 177–182, 270
Education Services for Overseas Students Act 2000 (ESOS Act) (Australia), 178, 179
student visas, 178
Study in Australia branding, 179
Evans, David, 14
Evans, Gareth, 131, 162
Evatt, Herbert Vere, 24–25
interest in Indian relationship, 29
priorities in international relations, 40

Feakes, Graham, 12
Alexandr Babiy episode, 163–167
frustrations, 157–158, 162
as high commissioner, first term, 154–159
as high commissioner, second term, 159–162
legacy, 153, 163–168

Fischer, Tim, 172
FitzGerald, Stephen, 121
Foreign Minister's Framework Dialogue, 186
Fraser Government, 11, 146, 150
Fraser, Malcolm, 146, 150, 157
visit to India, 147–148, 154, 183

Gandhi, Indira, 85, 130, 141, 149, 151, 204
Bangladesh crisis, 110, 114
comparisons with Nehru, 214–215
death, 132
Emergency, 212–213
Grant's study of, 13–14, 211, 212–213, 214–216
relationship with Fraser, 150
visit to Australia, 84
Gandhi, Rajiv, 5, 12, 155–156, 158
Garnaut, Ross, 223
Gillard Government, 5
Gillard, Julia, 16, 191
Gollan, Roy, 5, 10, 29–32, 37, 52, 54
Gorton, John, 84
Grant, Bruce, 11, 143–145
appointment to Australian High Commission in India, 143, 211–212
background, 143
impressions of Nehru, 214
legacy, 201, 218
relationship with Indira Gandhi, 212
writings, 13–14, 202, 210–217, 218
Greet, Ray, 157–158
Gribble, Darren, 15

Harris, Stuart, 129, 154, 159
Hasluck, Paul, 82, 84, 172
Hawke, Bob, 5, 12, 155–156, 158
visit to India, 160, 161, 183
visit to Russia, 164

Hayden, Bill, 154–155, 164–166
Henderson, Peter, 125, 149, 154
historiography, 2, 3–4
Hook, Don, 108, 111
Howard Government, 188–189
Howard, John, 13, 15
  visit to India, 183, 186

immigration, 6. *see also* White
    Australia policy
  within Asia, 45
  Indian diaspora, 14, 16
  political asylum, 163–167
  quotas, 26, 27, 69–70
  refugee migration, 11, 106–107
  skilled migration program,
    180–181
  students, 12, 16, 64–65, 170,
    177–182
India, 217
  anti-colonialism, 60
  Australian sale of uranium, 5, 13,
    15–16, 176, 188–189, 191,
    192
  Australian–Indian civil nuclear
    agreement, 192
  and Canada, 70
  communism, 61–62
  Department of Overseas Indians,
    20
  economic growth, 172–174, 187,
    226
  economic liberalisation, 5, 14,
    170, 222
  energy sector, 175–176
  independence, 3, 4, 28, 41
  invasion of Goa, 71
  involvement in Alexandr Babiy
    episode, 165–166
  Janata Dal administration, 14
  member of British
    Commonwealth, 25–26, 28,
    37, 69, 141
  as a middle power, 11, 137, 145

New Delhi, 90, 91–92
non-alignment, 5, 26, 27, 37, 59
nuclear testing, 5, 11, 145–146,
    171–172, 185–186, 223
  opposition to Southeast Asia
    Treaty Organization
    (SEATO), 63
  Partition, 9, 29, 105
  perception of Australia, 50, 61,
    65, 67–68, 223
  postcolonial development, 8, 11,
    87
  relationship with Canada, 21, 65
  relationship with China (People's
    Republic of), 198–199
  relationship with New Zealand,
    65
  relationship with Pakistan, 33–36,
    63, 83, 107, 161–162
  relationship with South-East Asia,
    14, 139–140, 142
  relationship with Soviet Union,
    83, 107, 113, 139, 149
  relationship with United States,
    107, 113, 116–119, 130, 176,
    223
  role in Bangladesh crisis, 106,
    107, 115–118
  role in world affairs, 42
  Treaty of Peace and Friendship
    (Indo–Soviet Treaty), 107,
    113, 130
  Vietnam War, 83
India–China War, 5, 10, 77
Indo–Soviet Treaty. *see* Treaty of Peace
    and Friendship (Indo–Soviet
    Treaty)
Indonesia, 140
  Australian support, 47
  Confrontation of Malaysia, 79, 83
  independence, 40, 41, 47–48, 53
  relationship with United States,
    53
  War of Independence, 30

International Convention on Intervention and State Sovereignty (ICISS), 131–132

Japan, 37, 138, 144, 188, 194, 225. *see also* Quadrilateral Security Dialogues

Kashmir dispute, 5, 33–36, 58, 161
Khan, Yahya, 106, 110, 115, 132
Kissinger, Henry, 118, 125, 134. *see also* Nixon, Richard
  Bangladesh crisis, 120, 122, 123
  visit to China, 107, 113
Korean War, 2, 37, 63
Kovind, Ram Nath, 196
Krishnamachari, TT, 78

Laurie, Rob, 15
liquefied natural gas (LNG), 175

Macfarlane, Ian, 188
Mackay, Iven, 1, 5, 9, 19
  appointment to Australian High Commission in India, 20–22
  Asian Relations Conference, 43
  legacy, 28–29
  opposition to White Australia policy, 26
McCallum, John, 44, 46
McCarthy, John, 15–16
McEwen, John, 71
McMahon, William, 110, 114–115, 119–120, 123, 127–129
Menon, Krishna, 25, 61, 62, 68, 84
Menzies Government
  anti-communism, 61, 73
  policy towards India, 58–59
  role of treaties, 82
Menzies, Robert, 5, 10, 35, 36, 67
  opinion of Crocker, 68–69
  visit to India, 209
middle power countries, 11, 137–151
mining, 174, 175

Piparwar coal-mining project, 159, 160–161, 170
Modi, Narendra, 16, 222
  election, 192
  relationship with Australia, 192–194
Moodie, Colin, 27, 30
  appointment, 21
  Asian Relations Conference, 43–44, 45–46
  New Delhi Conference on Indonesia, 49, 54
Morrison, Scott, 196–197
Mulroney, Brian, 155–156

Nehru, Jawaharlal, 4, 7, 24
  Asian Relations Conference, 42, 44
  Bandung Conference, 68
  and communism, 41
  Crocker's study of, 13, 201–210, 217
  descendants, 204, 205
  independence movement, 26–27
  Japanese Peace Treaty, 37
  in Kashmir dispute, 34–35, 36, 37
  legacy, 204, 205
  modernisation, 90–91
  New Delhi Conference on Indonesia, 50, 51–52
  non-alignment policy, 59–60
  personality, 202, 205, 208–210
Netherlands, 40–41, 48
New Delhi Conference on Indonesia, 30–31, 51–53
  Australian participation, 48–50
  resolution, 53
  significance, 53–54
New Zealand, 42–43
  Bandung Conference, 66, 67, 68
  New Delhi Conference on Indonesia, 50, 51
  recognition of Bangladesh, 120

relationship with India, 65
role in Asia-Pacific region, 50, 51,
    66, 67, 68
Nixon, Richard, 107, 116–117, 123,
    124, 125, 134. *see also* Kissinger,
    Henry
Nuclear Non-Proliferation Treaty, 5,
    162–163, 176, 185, 188–189
nuclear power
    Australian sale of uranium to
        India, 5, 13, 15–16, 176,
        188–189, 191, 192
    Australian–Indian agreement, 192
    Indian nuclear testing, 5, 11,
        145–146, 171–172, 185–186,
        223

O'Farrell, Barry, 17
Oakes, Laurie, 149

Packer, Gerald, 44
Pakistan, 12, 33–36
    Bangladesh war, 105–107,
        108–119, 134–135
    history, 105–107
    relationship with Australia, 12,
        58, 129, 161–162
    relationship with Canada, 120
    relationship with China (People's
        Republic of), 83, 130
    relationship with India, 33–36,
        63, 83, 107, 161–162
    relationship with United States,
        36, 107, 130
    Southeast Asia Treaty
        Organization (SEATO)
        membership, 83
Peacock, Andrew, 150
Piparwar coal-mining project, 159,
    160–161, 170
Plimsoll, James, 10, 114, 117, 119,
    122, 124, 143
    appointment to India, 77, 79–81
    background, 75–76

legacy, 81
reputation, 76

Quadrilateral Security Dialogues, 13,
    188, 195–196, 197

racism, 69–70. *see also* White
    Australia policy
    Indian students in Australia, 181,
        182
    Malcolm Government, 146
    Racial Discrimination Act 1975
        (Australia), 139
    Whitlam Government, 144
Rahman, Sheikh Mujibur, 106, 108,
    132
Rao, Narashima, 222
Ray, Robert, 161
Ray, Shankar, 110
refugees, 11, 106–107
religious division, 105–107
Renouf, Alan, 6–7
Rodgers, Peter, 109
Rogers, William, 122
Rudd Government, 189–190
Rudd, Kevin, 13, 16, 191
    perception of China, 189–190
    withdrawal from Quadrilateral
        Security Dialogues, 189
Russia. *see* Soviet Union

SEATO (Southeast Asia Treaty
    Organization). *see* Southeast Asia
    Treaty Organization (SEATO)
Second World War, 3–4, 22–23
security partnerships, 184, 193–199.
    see also defence forces
September 11 attacks, 176, 186
Shann, Keith, 68
Shaw, Patrick, 11, 111–112, 113–
    115, 119, 142, 143
    appointment to Australian High
        Commission in India, 138
    background, 138

Sidhu, Harinder, 17, 97–98
Singh, Jaswant, 186
Singh, Manmohan, 5, 170, 189, 190, 222
Singh, Swaran, 121
South Africa, 20, 79, 82, 155–156, 158, 211
South-East Asia, 32–33. *see also* Asia-Pacific region; Asian Relations Conference
    and China (People's Republic of), 195–196
    communism, 34
    decolonisation, 26–27, 39, 41, 46–47, 90, 203
    immigration, 45
    independence movements, 46–47
    political change, 39
    regional organisations, 141–143, 150, 187–188, 190
    role of India, 41, 47
    and Soviet Union, 47
    and United States, 47, 79
Southeast Asia Treaty Organization (SEATO), 63, 82, 83, 118
Soviet Union
    defection from, 163–167
    invasion of Afghanistan, 11, 130, 149, 151
    as potential threat, 25, 26, 34, 47
    relationship with Australia, 164
    relationship with India, 81, 130
    Sino–Soviet Treaty of Friendship and Alliance, 58
    spread of communism, 58–59
    Treaty of Peace and Friendship (Indo–Soviet Treaty), 107, 113, 130
Spender, Percy, 35, 58–59
    Colombo Plan, 32
Stein, Joseph, 8, 10–11, 87
    Australian High Commission in India design, 94–98
    design approach, 92–93

influence on New Delhi, 91–92, 98, 103
Stone, Edward, 89–90
Stuart, Francis, 11, 36, 111, 112–113, 114, 119
Sturkey, Doug, 111
Suckling, Patrick, 16

Tange, Arthur, 10, 60, 126–127, 218
    appointment to India, 82–86
    in Australian Department of External Affairs, 81–82
    background, 75–76
    legacy, 76–77
terrorism, 16
Thatcher, Margaret, 156
Tibet, 80
trade, 64. *see also* education
    Austrade, 171–173
    Australian Department of Foreign Affairs and Trade (DFAT), 15, 218–219, 222–223
    Australian relationship with India, 12, 156–157, 159–162, 169–171, 173–177
    Australian–Chinese relationship, 199
    Australian–Indian trade agreements, 31–32, 170
    coal mining, 159–162
    exports to India, 2, 22–23, 31–32, 85, 101, 169–170, 173–177
    Indian economic liberalisation, 4–5
    Indian exports, 22
    permit raj, 31–32
    research exchanges, 23–24, 181–182
Treaty of Peace and Friendship (Indo–Soviet Treaty), 107, 113, 130
Turnbull, Malcolm, 194–196

United Nations
    Asian Relations Conference attendance, 42

High Commission for Refugees
(UNHCR), 165
involvement in India–Pakistan
dispute, 33, 35–36
resolution on Bangladesh conflict,
116
Responsibility to Protect (R2P),
132
Security Council, 33, 47–49, 55
United States, 47, 79
diplomatic architecture, 89–90
relationship with Australia,
122–124, 132–133, 146, 223
relationship with China (People's
Republic of), 113, 125
relationship with India, 107, 113,
116–119, 130, 176, 223
relationship with Indonesia, 53
relationship with Pakistan, 36,
107, 130
role in Bangladesh crisis, 116–
119, 124–129
Upton, Gordon, 11
appointment to Australian High
Commission in India, 149
background, 149
uranium, 5, 13, 15–16, 176, 188–
189, 191, 192
USSR (Union of Soviet Socialist
Republics). *see* Soviet Union

Varghese, Peter, 1, 14, 16, 17, 221–
226. *see also An India Economic
Strategy to 2035*
appointment to Australian High
Commission in India, 190,
221
Vietnam War, 79, 83, 124, 140

Waller, Keith, 118, 119–120, 126,
142
Watt, Alan, 35, 67
Wensley, Penny, 15
wheat exports, 22–23, 85

White Australia policy. *see also*
Australian international
reputation; immigration
Crocker's opposition to, 10,
69–71
impact on Australian reputation,
5, 43, 45
Indian perceptions of, 4, 26–28,
82
repeal of, 139
Whitlam Government, 11, 150
demilitarisation, 146
Nuclear Non-Proliferation Treaty,
145–146
policies, 138–139, 144, 211
recognition of China (People's
Republic of), 139
Whitlam, Gough, 121, 128
dismissal, 213
visit to India, 140, 141–142

Yeend, Geoffrey, 156–157

Zhou Enlai, 121

www.ingramcontent.com/pod-product-compliance
Lightning Source LLC
Chambersburg PA
CBHW040151270326
41926CB00076B/4624